CAPITAL PUNISHMENT IN AMERICA

GARLAND REFERENCE LIBRARY
OF SOCIAL SCIENCE
(VOL. 466)

CAPITAL PUNISHMENT IN AMERICA
An Annotated Bibliography

Michael L. Radelet
Margaret Vandiver

GARLAND PUBLISHING, INC. • NEW YORK & LONDON
1988

Library of Congress Cataloging-in-Publication Data

Radelet, Michael L.
  Capital punishment in America : an annotated bibliography
Michael L. Radelet and Margaret Vandiver.
      p. cm. — (Garland reference library of social science; vol.
466)
  Includes index.
  ISBN 0–8240–1623–8 (alk. paper)
  1. Capital punishment—United States—Bibliography. I. Vandiver,
Margaret. II. Title. III. Series: Garland reference library of
social science ; v. 466
Z5703.4.C36R3 1988
[HV8699.U55]
016.3646'6'0973—dc19   88-23249
                                                                    CIP

Printed on acid-free, 250-year-life paper
Manufactured in the United States of America

For Marylee Mason Vandiver
1924–1987

CONTENTS

INTRODUCTION

In the 1972 decision _Furman_ v. _Georgia_, the U.S. Supreme Court effectively invalidated all existing death penalty statutes in the United States. While some believed that the _Furman_ decision would forever ban capital punishment in America, legislators in many states drafted new death penalty statutes in the hope of satisfying the concerns raised in _Furman_. Their hopes were realized. The Supreme Court approved several of these new statutes in 1976, and the next year Gary Gilmore broke a ten-year moratorium on the death penalty when he dropped his appeals and was executed in Utah.

By mid-1988, nearly 100 men and women in a dozen states had followed Gilmore's lead to the hands of American executioners, and some 2,000 more were living under a sentence of death. Even if the current pace of executions doubled to a national rate of one execution per week, all persons now on death row would not be executed until the year 2025. And an additional 300 people convicted of murder are being sentenced to death each year.

The importance of the issue of capital punishment is not simply a matter of numbers. Proponents and opponents of the penalty agree that it has moral, social, legal, and symbolic implications which extend far beyond its immediate effects. The proper role and limit of government power, the meaning of justice, the morality and efficacy of punishment, and the uses of retribution and mercy are only some of the issues brought into focus by the debate over capital punishment. This debate began during the Enlightenment, continues to the present, and, given the numbers of condemned prisoners and the strong feelings of persons on both sides of the issue, promises to be studied and debated in American legislatures, courtrooms, and

universities in the future as never before. We
offer this Bibliography to participants in this
debate who wish to base their position on fact and
systematic reasoning, rather than emotion and
dogma.

Several methodological decisions were
necessary in order to choose which articles and
books should be included in this Bibliography. The
first decision involved the span of time to be
covered. While the great bulk of the materials
included was first published after 1972, the reader
will see that roughly one-tenth of our choices
violate this policy. The year 1972 is a convenient
dividing point, because that was the year of the
Furman ruling. We included exceptions if they were
classics (e.g., Bye, 1919, cited as item 186
below), although we made no systematic attempt to
list all the classics (students of Beccaria,
Bentham, Kant, Marx, and Romilly will be quick to
note the absence of direct citations to the work of
these scholars). We also violated our pledge to
stick with more recent publications if the pre-1972
work remains the best available on a particular
issue (e.g., Albert Post's work on the anti-gallows
movement in Ohio, cited below as item 697). Other
important bibliographies were the only type of work
that we systematically attempted to include,
regardless of date.

A second limit of this Bibliography is region.
Almost all the work included centers on the United
States, and all the cited work is written in
English. Again, exceptions to the former rule are
made, notably with Canadian and British work, but
we made no attempt to catalogue the wealth of
Canadian, or especially British scholarship, that
is easily found on this subject.

A third inclusion criterion is accessibility.
If the work is not available at a leading
university or public library, we rarely included
it. All but a couple of dozen entries can be found
in the libraries at the University of Florida,
Florida State University, University of Texas, or
the Boston Public Library, which are the four
libraries that we used for our research. Again,
there is some work that is so outstanding we could
not resist the temptation to call it to the
readers' attention, even though the staff at Inter-
Library Loan Offices will have to be asked to order
it (e.g., Michael Kroll's piece on the executioners
of San Quentin, cited below as item 529). With

accessibility in mind, we excluded virtually all newspaper articles and all the materials available on the death penalty through the United Nations. Even among the post-1972 work found at large libraries, some choices had to be made. We eliminated several short or sloppy essays that contribute little that is not said better elsewhere, but we were quite conservative in applying this criterion. More importantly, we did not attempt to provide complete listings of "Case Notes" written by law students on important Supreme Court decisions. We included what we thought were the best Case Notes for some of the decisions, but realize that readers might find our selection of Case Notes insufficient and even arbitrary.

Our search for relevant articles and books led us to many sources. Those we examined are:

Abstracts in Anthropology
America: History and Life
British Humanities Index
Criminology and Penology Index
Current Law Index
Essay and General Literature Index
General Science Index
Historical Abstracts
Humanities Index
Index to Legal Periodicals
Index Medicus
Index of Periodical Articles Related to Law
Infotrac
International Political Science Abstracts
The Left Index
Legal Resource Index
Philosopher's Index
Psychological Abstracts
Public Affairs Information Service
Religious and Theological Abstracts
Social Science Citation Index
Social Sciences Index
Sociological Abstracts

We also relied a great deal upon references cited in recent important books and articles, and on friends who knew about this Bibliography and who sent us notes urging us to include certain items that had escaped our attention.

Using the above methodological procedures, we have assembled a list of slightly more than 1,000 items. Most are books and articles; Part II

includes Congressional Publications (often too
broad to succinctly annotate -- so we did not).
Part III lists and briefly describes the most
important death penalty decisions made by the U.S.
Supreme Court over the last 20 years.

Finally, we thank Hugo Adam Bedau for his
guidance and suggestions, Elizabeth Vandiver for
her help in checking items at the University of
Texas in Austin, and Terry Farley for her extensive
assistance in canvassing the Florida State
University libraries.

MLR and MV

Gainesville and Boston

June 1, 1988

CAPITAL PUNISHMENT IN AMERICA

I. BOOKS AND ARTICLES

1. Abel, Ernest L. HOMICIDE: A BIBLIOGRAPHY. Westport, Conn.: Greenwood Press, 1987.

   A comprehensive listing of references to homicide published in the scientific literature through 1984. The book includes statistics, demographics, theories, and legal implications.

2. Abramowitz, Elkan, and David Paget. "Executive Clemency in Capital Cases." NEW YORK UNIVERSITY LAW REVIEW 39 (1964): 136-92.

   A classic examination of executive clemency in 43 American jurisdictions with the death penalty. Includes an excellent discussion of the history of clemency, and state by state criteria for clemency for death row inmates. Procedures and criteria for clemency for convictions under federal jurisdictions are also discussed.

3. Acker, James R. "Mandatory Capital Punishment for the Life Term Inmate Who Commits Murder: Judgments of Fact and Value in Law and Social Science." NEW ENGLAND JOURNAL ON CRIMINAL AND CIVIL CONFINEMENT 11 (1985): 267-327.

   Questions whether mandatory capital punishment is constitutionally permissible for prisoners who murder while serving a life term. Examines the research on the deterrent effects of such punishment and discusses incapacitation and retribution. The author argues that courts' consideration of the issue should include social science research.

4. Acker, James R. "Capital Punishment by the Numbers: An Analysis of McCleskey v. Kemp." CRIMINAL LAW BULLETIN 23 (1987): 454-82.

   An overview of the McCleskey decision, the data presented to the Court in the case, and a discussion of the role of social science research in future capital punishment litigation.

5. Adelstein, Richard P. "Informational Paradox and the Pricing of Crime: Capital Sentencing Standards in Economic Perspective." JOURNAL OF CRIMINAL LAW AND CRIMINOLOGY 70 (1979): 281-98.

Reviews recent Supreme Court decisions on capital punishment, asking how much individualized sentencing is required under the Eighth Amendment. Proposes an economic analysis of sentencing procedures so that the consequences of committing a crime can be more accurately predicted.

6. Adkins, James C. "Eighteen Years in the Judicial Catbird Seat." NOVA LAW JOURNAL 11 (1986): 1-24.

An autobiographical account of the author's years on the Florida Supreme Court, in which he discusses his support for the death penalty as a "deterrent" (by which he means the person executed will never kill again).

7. Adler, Stephen J. "Florida's Zealous Prosecutors: Death Specialists." AMERICAN LAWYER (September, 1981): 35-7.

Interviews high-ranking attorneys in Florida's Attorney General's office about their work opposing death penalty appeals. One of the lawyers states that he was deterred from a homicide when an image of an electric chair appeared to him as he was choking one of his ex-wives.

8. Adler, Stephen J. "The Cure That Kills." AMERICAN LAWYER (September, 1986): 1, 29-33.

A review of the case of Florida death row inmate Gary Alvord. Alvord was judged to have become insane while on death row and was transferred to a mental hospital, where mental health professionals were asked to restore him to sanity so he could be put to death.

9. Alexander, Larry. "Retributivism and the Inadvertent Punishment of the Innocent." LAW AND PHILOSOPHY 2 (1983): 233-46.

Since capital punishment inevitably involves

executing the innocent, and retribution generally forbids punishing the innocent, can the death penalty be justified? The author answers affirmatively, saying there are several versions of retributivism, only one of which forbids punishing the innocent. This article argues principally with Lempert's "Desert and Deterrence," cited below as item 551.

10. Allison, Ralph B. "Difficulties Diagnosing the Multiple Personality Syndrome in a Death Penalty Case." INTERNATIONAL JOURNAL OF CLINICAL AND EXPERIMENTAL HYPNOSIS 32 (1984): 102-17.

An examination of the case of Kenneth Bianchi (a.k.a. the "Hillside Strangler"). Bianchi was originally diagnosed as a multiple personality, but the diagnosis was later changed to atypical dissociative disorder. Argues it may be impossible to determine the correct diagnosis of a dissociating defendant in a death penalty case.

11. American Psychological Association. "In the Supreme Court of the United States: Lockhart v. McCree: Amicus Curiae Brief for the American Psychological Association." AMERICAN PSYCHOLOGIST 42 (1987): 59-68.

Argues the evidence submitted in the McCree case shows conclusively that death qualified juries are conviction prone and are not representative of a fair cross-section of the community.

12. American Public Health Association. "Policy Statement 8521: Participation of Health Professionals in Capital Punishment." AMERICAN JOURNAL OF PUBLIC HEALTH 76 (1986): 339.

Resolves that "health personnel ... should not be required nor expected to assist in legally authorized executions."

13. American Public Health Association. "Policy Statement 8611: Abolition of the Death Penalty." AMERICAN JOURNAL OF PUBLIC HEALTH 77 (1987): 105-6.

Calls upon legislators, executive officials, and professional organizations of health workers to work for the abolition of capital punishment.

14. Amnesty International. THE DEATH PENALTY. London: Amnesty International Publications, 1979.

The most authoritative and useful source for international information on capital punishment. Advocates complete abolition of the death penalty. Outlines the statutory history and current status of the death penalty for each country in the world and discusses U.N. efforts to end its use.

15. Amnesty International. UNITED STATES OF AMERICA: THE DEATH PENALTY. London: Amnesty International Publications, 1987.

An outstanding overview of the death penalty in America. Included are discussions on recent historical background, laws and procedures, the role of the jury, prosecutorial discretion, race, appeals, clemency, death row conditions, and the execution of juveniles and the mentally ill.

16. Amsterdam, Anthony G. "The Case Against the Death Penalty." JURIS DOCTOR 2 (November 1971): 11-2.

An argument against capital punishment based on its violence and irrationality.

17. Amsterdam, Anthony G. "Capital Punishment." Pp. 346-58 in Bedau, 1982, cited below as item 100.

A short, concise, and extremely powerful statement of the abolitionists' position on the death penalty.

18. Amsterdam, Anthony G. "The Supreme Court and Capital Punishment." HUMAN RIGHTS 14 (Winter, 1987): 14-7+.

Criticizes the Supreme Court for giving death-sentenced inmates fewer, not more, chances than other litigants. Reviews typical post-conviction procedures in capital cases and Supreme Court decisions of the last dozen years (particularly Barefoot).

19. Andenaes, Johannes. "The Morality of Deterrence." UNIVERSITY OF CHICAGO LAW REVIEW 37 (1970): 649-64.

   Is punishment on the basis of deterrence justifiable? The author, using case examples from Norway, answers affirmatively, but reviews several issues that need to be considered.

20. Andenaes, Johannes. PUNISHMENT AND DETERRENCE. Ann Arbor: University of Michigan Press, 1974.

   A series of essays on the operation and efficacy of deterrent sanctions.

21. Andenaes, Johannes. "General Prevention Revisited: Research and Policy Implications." JOURNAL OF CRIMINAL LAW AND CRIMINOLOGY 66 (1975): 338-65.

   An overview of deterrence research by one of the pioneers in the field. Different ways of conceptualizing and measuring deterrence are discussed.

22. Anders, James. "Should Juvenile Murderers be Sentenced to Death? Punish the Guilty." AMERICAN BAR ASSOCIATION JOURNAL 72 (June 1, 1986): 32-3.

   In a debate with Richard Brody (see item 172 below), Anders argues that no minimum age restrictions on death sentences should be established.

23. Annas, George J. "Nurses and the Death Penalty." NURSING LAW AND ETHICS 1 (May, 1980): 3.

   A discussion of whether nurses and physicians should participate in executions by lethal injection. Argues that nurses should not only

refuse to participate, but should fight to
abolish the death penalty completely.

24. Annas, George J. "Killing with Kindness: Why
the FDA Need not Certify Drugs Used for
Execution Safe and Effective." AMERICAN
JOURNAL OF PUBLIC HEALTH 75 (1985): 1096-9.

Reviews the unanimous Supreme Court's refusal
to require the FDA to approve the drugs used
in lethal injections. While he argues that
this decision was correct, he points out that
the real issue in this debate is the death
penalty itself.

25. Annual Chief Justice Earl Warren Conference on
Advocacy in the United States. THE DEATH
PENALTY: FINAL REPORT. Washington, D.C.: The
Roscoe Pound-American Trial Lawyers
Foundation, 1980.

A report by the Roscoe Pound-American Trial
Lawyers Association calling for the abolition
of the death penalty. Three background papers
are included: "Caprice and Racism in the Death
Penalty," by Charles Black, Jr., "Retribution,
Morality and Capital Punishment," by Walter
Berns, and "Desert and Deterrence: An
Evaluation of the Moral Bases for Capital
Punishment," by Richard O. Lempert.

26. Appelbaum, Paul S. "Psychiatrists' Role in
the Death Penalty." HOSPITAL AND COMMUNITY
PSYCHIATRY 32 (1981): 761-2.

Discusses the role of psychiatrists in
predicting dangerousness, pointing out that
such predictions have dubious validity.

27. Appelbaum, Paul S. "Death, the Expert
Witness, and the Dangers of Going Barefoot."
HOSPITAL AND COMMUNITY PSYCHIATRY 34 (1983):
1003-4.

Describes the role of psychiatrists in
predicting dangerousness in Texas death
penalty cases. The author discusses the Texas
case of Thomas Barefoot (who was predicted to
be dangerous by a psychiatrist who never
examined him), and the unsuccessful work of

the American Psychiatric Association in supporting Barefoot's objection on appeal.

28. Appelbaum, Paul S. "Hypotheticals, Psychiatric Testimony, and the Death Sentence." BULLETIN OF AMERICAN ACADEMY OF PSYCHIATRY AND THE LAW 12 (1984): 169-77.

Criticizes the psychiatric prediction of dangerousness in capital cases, particularly by clinicians who have never examined the inmate. Argues that such hypothetical questions should be prohibited.

29. Appelbaum, Paul S. "Competence to be Executed: Another Conundrum for Mental Health Professionals." HOSPITAL AND COMMUNITY PSYCHIATRY 37 (1986): 682-4.

Discusses whether physicians should become involved in the determination of competency to be executed and whether they should treat inmates found incompetent.

30. Archer, Dane and Rosemary Gartner. VIOLENCE AND CRIME IN CROSS-NATIONAL PERSPECTIVE. New Haven: Yale University Press, 1984.

Presents data on major crimes for 100 countries, asking if the level of violence increases after wars (yes), whether homicide rates are always directly correlated with urbanity (yes--at least relative to the country's overall homicide rate), and, most importantly, whether homicide rates tend to increase after the abolition of the death penalty (no).

31. Archer, Dane, Rosemary Gartner, and Marc Beittel. "Homicide and the Death Penalty: A Cross-National Test of a Deterrence Hypothesis." JOURNAL OF CRIMINAL LAW AND CRIMINOLOGY 74 (1983): 991-1013.

Data from 14 countries are used to test for various types of deterrence. It is found that more often than not, abolition of the death penalty is followed by decreases in the homicide rate. Different approaches to the data find no support for deterrence theory.

32. Arendt, Hannah. EICHMANN IN JERUSALEM: A REPORT ON THE BANALITY OF EVIL. New York: Viking Press, 1963.

An account of the trial and execution of Adolph Eichmann in Israel for crimes against the Jewish people and against humanity, committed while Eichmann was a Nazi official. The author discusses wider issues of justice against the historical background of the Nazi's Final Solution.

33. Arkin, Steven D. "Discrimination and Arbitrariness in Capital Punishment: An Analysis of Post-Furman Murder Cases in Dade County, Florida, 1973-1976." STANFORD LAW REVIEW 33 (1980): 75-101.

Examines 350 Miami homicide cases, of which ten resulted in a death sentence. Although blacks with white victims received the most severe sentences, the author finds no conclusive evidence of racial discrimination.

34. Atholl, Justin. SHADOW OF THE GALLOWS. London: John Long, Ltd., 1954.

A general history of the death penalty in England, including a discussion of the use of gibbets, public executions, and the last days of the condemned.

35. Auerbach, Stephanie. "Common Myths About the Death Penalty." GEORGIA JOURNAL OF CORRECTIONS 3 (1974): 41-54.

An examination of the case histories of fifty Georgia criminals, 1943-65, whose original death sentences had been commuted and who eventually were released on parole. The author exposes various myths about capital punishment, such as the claim that those sentenced to death are habitual and incorrigible criminals.

36. Avrich, Paul. THE HAYMARKET TRAGEDY. Princeton: Princeton University Press, 1984.

The definitive history of the Haymarket Riot
in Chicago in 1886. Eight anarchists were
convicted of murder; four were hanged and a
fifth took his own life. The three survivors
were pardoned in 1891 because the governor
believed all eight were innocent.

37. Azarian, David P. "Barclay v. Florida: An
Examination of the Burger Court and Capital
Punishment." OHIO NORTHERN UNIVERSITY LAW
REVIEW 11 (1984): 813-25.

Discusses the Barclay case, in which the
Supreme Court refused to vacate a death
sentence even though it was based in part on a
nonstatutory aggravating circumstance.

38. Babcock, Barbara Allen. "Gary Gilmore's
Lawyers." STANFORD LAW REVIEW 32 (1980):
865-78.

A review of Norman Mailer's book on the
Gilmore case (see item 587 below), focusing on
what both Mailer and Babcock believe was
inadequate work by Gilmore's attorneys.

39. Bailey, William C. "Murder and the Death
Penalty." JOURNAL OF CRIMINAL LAW AND
CRIMINOLOGY 65 (1974): 416-23.

Rates of first- and second-degree murder for
40 states are compared. No support is found
for the deterrence hypothesis when comparing
death penalty and abolitionist jurisdictions.

40. Bailey, William C. "Murder and Capital
Punishment: Some Further Evidence." AMERICAN
JOURNAL OF ORTHOPSYCHIATRY 45 (1975): 669-88.
Reprinted in Bedau and Pierce, 1976, in item
110 below.

Critically reviews the literature on the
relation between murder rates and capital
punishment, and analyzes data on murder rates
(1967-68) in death penalty and abolition
states. No support is found for the
deterrence hypothesis.

41. Bailey, William C. "Use of the Death Penalty
v. Outrage at Murder: Some Additional

Evidence and Considerations." CRIME AND
DELINQUENCY 22 (1976): 31-9.

Comments on a paper by Glaser and Zeigler,
cited below as item 384. Argues they are
incorrect in their conclusions that 1)
homicide rates can be reduced by the abolition
of the death penalty, and 2) that both
frequent use of the death penalty and high
murder rates are consequences of a low
valuation of life. Glaser's response is cited
below as item 381.

42. Bailey, William C. "Rape and the Death
Penalty: A Neglected Area of Deterrence
Research." Pp. 336-58 in Bedau and Pierce,
1976, cited below as item 110.

One of the few papers to examine the deterrent
effect of the death penalty on rape. Rape and
execution rates were computed for all states,
1933-36 and 1944-67. It is found that the
rate of rape is actually higher in death
penalty states, and that the death penalty
exerts no deterrent effects on rape.

43. Bailey, William C. "Imprisonment v. the Death
Penalty as a Deterrent to Murder." LAW AND
HUMAN BEHAVIOR 1 (1977): 239-60.

Examines the simultaneous deterrent effect of
executions and imprisonment on homicide rates
in 1920 and 1960. Neither executions nor the
severity of prison sentences are found to
affect homicide rates.

44. Bailey, William C. "Deterrence and the
Violent Sex Offender: Imprisonment vs. the
Death Penalty." JOURNAL OF BEHAVIORAL
ECONOMICS 6 (1977): 107-44.

Examining the effect of executions on rape
with 1951 and 1961 data, the author finds a
very weak deterrent effect, although the
unemployment rate and the certainty and
severity of imprisonment exert stronger
predictive powers.

45. Bailey, William C. "Some Further Evidence on
Imprisonment vs. the Death Penalty as a

Deterrent to Murder." LAW AND HUMAN BEHAVIOR
2 (1978): 245-60.

An extension of an earlier paper by Bailey
(see item 40 above) reexamining the data with
alternative statistical procedures. The
reanalysis again fails to support the ideas
that certainty of execution or severity of
imprisonment deters homicide.

46. Bailey, William C. "Deterrence and the Death
Penalty for Murder in Utah: A Time Series
Analysis." JOURNAL OF CONTEMPORARY LAW 5
(1978): 1-20.

Examines homicide and execution rates in Utah,
1910-1962; no evidence of deterrence is found.
Finds that various sociodemographic variables
are better predictors of homicides than are
executions.

47. Bailey, William C. "The Deterrent Effect of
the Death Penalty for Murder in California."
SOUTHERN CALIFORNIA LAW REVIEW 52 (1979):
743-64.

Examines the deterrent effect of the death
penalty in California, 1910-62. No evidence
of a deterrent effect is found.
Sociodemographic variables are better
predictors of homicide than certainty of
executions.

48. Bailey, William C. "The Deterrent Effect of
the Death Penalty for Murder in Ohio: A Time
Series Analysis." CLEVELAND STATE LAW REVIEW
28 (1979): 51-81.

Examines the relationship between the
certainty of execution and the homicide rate
in Ohio, 1910-1962. No support for the
deterrence hypothesis is found; instead, the
proportion of the population male, aged 20-40,
nonwhite, urban, and unemployed is the best
predictor of the homicide rate.

49. Bailey, William C. "Deterrence and the Death
Penalty for Murder in Oregon." WILLAMETTE LAW
REVIEW 16 (1979): 67-85.

Examines homicides in Oregon, 1918-1962. The author finds that execution rates and homicide rates are positively associated, not negatively, as deterrence theory would predict.

50. Bailey, William C. "An Analysis of the Deterrent Effect of the Death Penalty in North Carolina." NORTH CAROLINA CENTRAL LAW JOURNAL 10 (1979): 29-52.

Examines the certainty of execution and homicide rates in North Carolina, 1910-62. Finds that changes in the certainty of execution are unrelated to homicide rates. Instead, homicide rates are associated with the percent of the population male, urban, unemployed, and aged 20-40 years old.

51. Bailey, William C. "Deterrent Effect of the Death Penalty: An Extended Time Series Analysis." OMEGA 10 (1979-80): 235-59.

Examines the effect of certainty of execution and homicide rates. Data on 37 states are examined. Income, education, unemployment, urban population, and race are found to be related to homicide rates, while the use of the death penalty is not.

52. Bailey, William C. "A Multivariate Cross-Sectional Analysis of the Deterrent Effect of the Death Penalty." SOCIOLOGY AND SOCIAL RESEARCH 64 (1980): 183-207.

Homicide and execution rates are examined for 28 years selected from the period between 1910-62. A small deterrent effect is found, although demographic factors are better predictors of homicide rates than are execution rates. Where severity of imprisonment measures are available, this factor has more deterrent effect than execution rates.

53. Bailey, William C. "Deterrence and the Celerity of the Death Penalty: A Neglected Question in Deterrence Research." SOCIAL FORCES 58 (1980): 1308-33.

While most deterrence studies examine the certainty of executions, this paper analyzes its celerity, testing the proposition that there will be more deterrence if offenders are executed swiftly after their condemnation. Cross-sectional analysis of state level data fails to show that either certainty or celerity affects homicide rates.

54. Bailey, William C. "Capital Punishment and Lethal Assaults Against Police." CRIMINOLOGY 19 (1982): 608-25.

Examining national state-level data from 1961-71, the author finds that the threat or use of the death penalty is unrelated to variation in the number of murders of police officers. These variations appear to be due to sociodemographic factors.

55. Bailey, William C. "Disaggregation in Deterrence and Death Penalty Research: The Case of Murder in Chicago." JOURNAL OF CRIMINAL LAW AND CRIMINOLOGY 74 (1983): 827-59.

Reviews recent deterrence research and problems of aggregation (i.e., the difficulty of measuring rates of first-degree murder, rather than the general homicide rate). Presents data from a study of monthly first-degree murder rates in Chicago, 1915-21. Results tend to support the existence of a brutalization effect.

56. Bailey, William C. "Murder and Capital Punishment in the Nation's Capital." JUSTICE QUARTERLY 1 (1984): 211-33.

The relationship between homicide rates and the certainty of executions is studied in Washington, D.C., 1890-1970. At odds with the deterrence argument, there is a slight tendency for the homicide rate to increase after executions.

57. Bailey, William C., and Ruth P. Lott. "An Empirical Examination of the Inutility of Mandatory Capital Punishment." JOURNAL OF BEHAVIORAL ECONOMICS 6 (1977): 153-88.

Examines the effects of mandatory death
penalty laws on the certainty of execution by
looking at 1) changes in execution rates for
states that have moved from a mandatory to
discretionary death penalty law, and 2) how
these changes compare to changes in the
execution rate for states that did not modify
their laws. Mandatory death penalty statutes
are found to neither reduce nor increase
execution rates.

58. Bailey, William C., and Ruth D. Peterson.
"Police Killings and Capital Punishment: The
Post-Furman period." CRIMINOLOGY 25 (1987):
1-25.

Examines the effects of the death penalty on
lethal assaults on police, 1973-84. No
evidence is found to support the contention
that the death penalty affects rates of police
killings.

59. Bailey, William C., and Ronald W. Smith.
"Punishment: Its Severity and Certainty."
JOURNAL OF CRIMINAL LAW, CRIMINOLOGY, AND
POLICE SCIENCE 63 (1972): 530-9.

A general discussion of deterrence theory and
application to six major felonies. It is
found that both the severity and certainty of
punishment affect crime rates, but with only a
small negative impact.

60. Baldus, David C., and James W.C. Cole. "A
Comparison of the Work of Thorsten Sellin and
Isaac Ehrlich on the Deterrent Effect of
Capital Punishment." YALE LAW JOURNAL 85
(1975): 170-86.

Compares two different methodologies used to
examine the deterrent effect of capital
punishment: Sellin's comparison of neighboring
states (see item 789 below) and Ehrlich's
econometric technique (see item 291 below).
Concludes that Sellin's approach, though not
without problems, is more reliable. Responded
to by Ehrlich in item 290 below.

61. Baldus, David C., Charles A. Pulaski, Jr., and

George Woodworth. "Comparative Review of
Death Sentences: An Empirical Study of the
Georgia Experience." JOURNAL OF CRIMINAL LAW
AND CRIMINOLOGY 74 (1983): 661-753.

Initial results are reported from the authors'
study of Georgia sentencing patterns, focusing
on the identification of comparatively
excessive sentences. The authors find that
the Georgia Supreme Court never vacates death
sentences because of excessiveness, though
some cases identified by the authors as
excessive were reversed on other grounds. A
main reason for the inaction of the Georgia
Supreme Court is that it usually examines only
death sentences--not similar cases that
resulted in a prison term.

62. Baldus, David C., Charles A. Pulaski, Jr., and
George Woodworth. "Arbitrariness and
Discrimination in the Administration of the
Death Penalty: A Challenge to State Supreme
Courts." STETSON LAW REVIEW 15 (1986):
133-261.

Reviews the basic structure of capital
sentencing in the U.S., and outlines two
methods through which excessiveness and
discrimination in sentencing can be
identified. Data are reported on death
sentencing in Colorado and Georgia, and
estimates of death sentencing rates are given
for every retentionist state in the U.S. The
authors conclude that almost one-third of the
death sentences imposed in Georgia may be the
result of race-of-victim discrimination.

63. Baldus, David C., George Woodworth, and
Charles A. Pulaski, Jr. "Monitoring and
Evaluating Contemporary Death Sentencing
Systems: Lessons from Georgia." UNIVERSITY OF
CALIFORNIA-DAVIS LAW REVIEW 18 (1985):
1375-1407.

The authors discuss Arnold Barnett's
classification of Georgia homicide cases (see
item 70 below), compare Barnett's methodology
with their own, and show how both approaches
lead to similar results.

64. Baldus, David C., Charles A. Pulaski, Jr.,
     George Woodworth, and Frederick D. Kyle.
     "Identifying Comparatively Excessive Sentences
     of Death: A Quantitative Approach." STANFORD
     LAW REVIEW 33 (1980): 1-74.

     The authors develop a quantitative approach to
     identify cases in which death sentences were
     given despite the existence of factually
     similar cases in which lesser sentences were
     imposed.

65. Balske, Dennis N. "New Strategies for the
     Defense of Capital Cases." AKRON LAW REVIEW
     13 (1979): 331-61.

     Attempts to provide some ideas to help improve
     the skills of defense attorneys working on
     capital cases. The author discusses involving
     the defendant, plea bargains, preparing
     numerous pretrial motions, _voir_ _dire_, etc.

66. Balske, Dennis N. "Prosecutorial Misconduct
     During Closing Argument: The Arts of Knowing
     When and How to Object and of Avoiding the
     'Invited Response' Doctrine." MERCER LAW
     REVIEW 37 (1986): 1033-66.

     Twenty-two examples of improper prosecutorial
     arguments are given, as are directions for how
     to preserve the error for appeal.

67. Barfield, Velma. WOMAN ON DEATH ROW.
     Nashville: Oliver-Nelson Books, 1985.

     The autobiography and account of the religious
     conversion of Velma Barfield, who was
     convicted of murdering four people and
     executed in North Carolina in 1984.

68. Barnett, Arnold. "Crime and Capital
     Punishment: Some Recent Studies." JOURNAL OF
     CRIMINAL JUSTICE 6 (1978): 291-303.

     A critical overview of the work of both Isaac
     Ehrlich and his critics. Outlines some
     directions that future researchers should take
     in assessing possible deterrent effects of the
     death penalty.

69. Barnett, Arnold. "The Deterrent Effect of Capital Punishment: A Test of Some Recent Studies." OPERATIONS RESEARCH 29 (1981): 346-70.

Three recent regression-based statistical studies on deterrence are examined, and found to include large systematic errors.

70. Barnett, Arnold. "Some Distribution Patterns for the Georgia Death Sentence." UNIVERSITY OF CALIFORNIA-DAVIS LAW REVIEW 18 (1985): 1327-74.

Reanalyzes some of the Georgia homicide cases used in the research of David Baldus (see item 63 above). Using a classification procedure, rather than statistical analysis, the author presents a theory for use in understanding sentencing outcomes.

71. Barnhill, D.S. "Administering the Death Penalty." WASHINGTON AND LEE LAW REVIEW 39 (1982): 101-24.

Examines the proposal by Judge Clement Haynsworth to create a new national court of criminal appeals to review federal issues in criminal cases. It is argued that such a court would provide more prompt and thorough review of constitutional claims by capital defendants and clarify the constitutional standards involved in the administration of the death penalty.

72. Barry, Rupert V. "Furman to Gregg: The Judicial and Legislative History." HOWARD LAW JOURNAL 22 (1979): 53-117.

Discusses the historical development of the anti-capital punishment movement in America, the constitutional challenges to the death penalty, and changes in the constitutional and legislative status of the death penalty in the 1970's.

73. Bartels, Robert. "Capital Punishment: The Unexamined Issue of Special Deterrence." IOWA LAW REVIEW 68 (1983): 601-7.

A tongue-in-cheek satirical paper showing that people who are executed never murder again.

74. Barzun, Jacques. "In Favor of Capital Punishment." CRIME AND DELINQUENCY 15 (1969): 21-8.

An essay, based on the sanctity of life, criticizing abolitionist arguments against capital punishment.

75. Batey, Robert. "Federal Habeas Corpus and the Death Penalty: 'Finality with a Capital F'." UNIVERSITY OF FLORIDA LAW REVIEW 36 (1984): 252-72.

Reviews procedural doctrines that limit the availability of habeas corpus relief in federal courts. The author argues these procedural doctrines should be disregarded in death penalty cases.

76. Bayer, Ronald. "Lethal Injections and Capital Punishment: Medicine in Service of the State." JOURNAL OF PRISON AND JAIL HEALTH 4 (1984): 7-15.

Examines the ethical issues raised for physicians by the use of lethal injection.

77. Bealey, William F. "The Aggravating Circumstances of Arizona's Death Penalty Statute: A Review." ARIZONA LAW REVIEW 26 (1984): 661-80.

A brief description of Arizona's capital sentencing statute, and of rulings by the Arizona Supreme Court in death penalty cases.

78. Bechdolt, Burley V., Jr. "Capital Punishment and Homicide and Rape Rates in the United States: Time Series and Cross Sectional Regression Analyses." JOURNAL OF BEHAVIORAL ECONOMICS 6 (1977): 33-66.

Presents time series data on deterrence and, using state data from 1970, cross-section data. In neither case is evidence of a deterrent effect found.

79. Beckman, Gail McKnight. "The First 200 Years
     of American Legal Thought on Capital
     Punishment." WOODROW WILSON JOURNAL OF LAW 3
     (1981): 35-47.

     A brief overview of the history of legal
     thought on and the legal status of the death
     penalty.

80. Bedau, Hugo Adam. "A Survey of the Debate on
     Capital Punishment in Canada, England, and the
     United States, 1948-1958." PRISON JOURNAL 38
     (1958): 35-45.

     An examination of then-current capital
     punishment laws and debates. Of particular
     interest is a bibliography, with 119 entries
     on the death penalty, covering the period
     1948-58.

81. Bedau, Hugo Adam. "Death Sentences in New
     Jersey, 1907-1960." RUTGERS LAW REVIEW 19
     (1964): 1-64.

     A comprehensive history of the death penalty
     in the twentieth century in New Jersey,
     including data on all those sentenced to
     death, their characteristics, and the final
     dispositions of their cases. Includes, as an
     Appendix, the essay by Wolf, cited below as
     item 924.

82. Bedau, Hugo Adam. "Capital Punishment in
     Oregon, 1903-1964." OREGON LAW REVIEW 45
     (1965): 1-39.

     A comprehensive overview of the death penalty
     in Oregon in this century, including a
     discussion of executions, commutations, and
     how these two outcomes are affected by race.

83. Bedau, Hugo Adam (ed.). THE DEATH PENALTY IN
     AMERICA: AN ANTHOLOGY, Revised edition. New
     York: Doubleday, 1967.

     Slightly revised from its original version in
     1964, this book contains 39 classic essays.
     An extensive bibliography is also included.
     The book is divided into nine sections: 1) An

introduction, 2) An overview of crimes, laws,
and executions, including an essay on
juveniles and the death penalty, 3) Arguments
for the death penalty, 4) Arguments against
it, 5) Public opinion and the death penalty,
including an essay on attitudes of the
directors of 27 state police departments, 6) A
section on deterrence (including the effect of
the death penalty on murders of police
officers), 7) A look at the successes and
failures of abolition in Oregon, Missouri, and
Delaware, and an essay on the recidivism of
capital murderers, 8) Other issues, such as
errors of justice and commutations in New
Jersey and North Carolina, and 9) Case
histories (including a paper on rehabilitation
on death row).

84. Bedau, Hugo Adam. "Deterrence and the Death
     Penalty: A Reconsideration." JOURNAL OF
     CRIMINAL LAW, CRIMINOLOGY AND POLICE SCIENCE
     61 (1970): 539-48. A similar version was
     published in ETHICS 80 (1970): 205-17.

     Refutes the arguments about deterrence posited
     by van den Haag, cited below as item 869.

85. Bedau, Hugo Adam. "The Death Penalty in
     America: Review and Forecast." FEDERAL
     PROBATION 35 (1971): 32-43.

     Reviews the recent history and then-current
     status of the death penalty in the United
     States.

86. Bedau, Hugo Adam. "The Politics of Death."
     TRIAL 8 (March-April, 1972): 44-6.

     A general discussion of the status of the
     death penalty and recent relevant Supreme
     Court decisions.

87. Bedau, Hugo Adam. "The Nixon Administration
     and the Deterrent Effect of the Death
     Penalty." UNIVERSITY OF PITTSBURGH LAW REVIEW
     34 (1973): 557-66.

     Examines statements made by members of the
     Nixon administration on deterrence in support
     of a federal death penalty and finds that the

statements rely on personal beliefs, not
factual data. Included is an important review
and critique of various efforts to prove
through the use of hearsay anecdotes that the
death penalty deters.

88. Bedau, Hugo Adam. "Challenging the Death
     Penalty." HARVARD CIVIL RIGHTS - CIVIL
     LIBERTIES LAW REVIEW 9 (1974): 626-43.

     A review of Michael Meltsner's book, cited
     below as item 620. Stands on its own as an
     excellent discussion of the history of Furman
     and its immediate effects.

89. Bedau, Hugo Adam. "Problems of Capital
     Punishment." CURRENT HISTORY 71 (July 1976):
     14-8+.

     A brief overview of the history of the
     abolition movement and the fight to abolish
     the death penalty in the decade preceding
     1972. A table gives the status of the death
     penalty by state, 1846-1972. The Furman
     decision and reactions to it are described.

90. Bedau, Hugo Adam. "Social Science Research in
     the Aftermath of Furman v. Georgia: Creating
     New Knowledge About Capital Punishment in the
     United States." Pp. 75-86 in Marc Riedel and
     Duncan Chappell (eds.), ISSUES IN CRIMINAL
     JUSTICE: PLANNING AND EVALUATION. New York:
     Praeger, 1976.

     Discusses the need for social science research
     on the death penalty, and the role of the
     Russell Sage Foundation in trying to develop
     the research agenda.

91. Bedau, Hugo Adam. "Felony Murder Rape and the
     Mandatory Death Penalty: A Study in
     Discretionary Justice." SUFFOLK UNIVERSITY
     LAW REVIEW 10 (1976): 493-520. A revised
     version of this paper appears in Bedau and
     Pierce, 1976, in item 110 below.

     Discusses the nation's only law (in
     Massachusetts) providing for a mandatory death
     penalty for homicides resulting from rape or
     attempted rape; includes discussion of

mandatory death sentences in general.
Analyzes homicides by males with female
victims (N=128) in two Massachusetts counties,
1946-1970, that resulted in a first-degree
murder indictment. No executions occurred for
felony-murder-rape, indicating that in
practice, the mandatory death penalty was
actually discretionary.

92. Bedau, Hugo Adam. THE COURTS, THE
CONSTITUTION, AND CAPITAL PUNISHMENT.
Lexington, Mass.: Lexington Books, 1977.

A collection of previously published essays by
the author (includes items 80, 81, 84, and 86
above). Gives an overview of constitutional
challenges to the death penalty, recent
decisions on this issue by the Supreme Court,
deterrence research, and a discussion of the
mandatory death penalty.

93. Bedau, Hugo Adam. "The Death Penalty: Social
Policy and Social Justice." ARIZONA STATE LAW
JOURNAL 1977 (1977): 767-802.

An examination of the constitutional, ethical,
and philosophical foundations of the death
penalty. Examines mandatory and discretionary
death penalty statutes, and summarizes the
abolitionist perspective. Followed by a
response from Ernest van den Haag, cited below
as item 871.

94. Bedau, Hugo Adam. "Rough Justice: The Limits
of Novel Defenses." HASTINGS CENTER REPORT
(Dec., 1978): 8-11.

A discussion of novel defenses in recent
homicide trials, such as "television
intoxication."

95. Bedau, Hugo Adam. "Retribution and the Theory
of Punishment." THE JOURNAL OF PHILOSOPHY 75
(1978): 601-20.

An examination of the concept of retribution,
the difficulties in defining it, and its role,
scope, and limitations.

96. Bedau, Hugo Adam. "The Death Penalty in the

United States: Imposed Law and the Role of
Moral Elites." Pp. 45-68 in Sandra B. Burman
and Barbara E. Harrell-Bond (eds.), THE
IMPOSITION OF THE LAW. New York: Academic
Press, 1979.

Reviews the trend toward the abolition of the
death penalty. Rejects the hypothesis that
this trend results from a moral elite imposing
its will on the majority.

97. Bedau, Hugo Adam. "A Condemned Man's Last
Wish: Organ Donation and a 'Meaningful'
Death." HASTINGS CENTER REPORT 9 (Feb.,
1979): 16-7.

Should a condemned prisoner be able to choose
his method of dying so his organs can be
donated? In their separate commentaries on a
case raising this question, Bedau answers
negatively, while Michael Zeik answers
positively.

98. Bedau, Hugo Adam. "The 1964 Death Penalty
Referendum in Oregon: Some Notes from a
Participant-Observer." CRIME AND DELINQUENCY
26 (1980): 528-36.

Explains how anti-death penalty activists in
Oregon were successful in convincing the
voters to abolish the death penalty by a wide
margin.

99. Bedau, Hugo Adam. "Capital Punishment." Pp.
147-82 in Tom Regan (ed.), MATTERS OF LIFE AND
DEATH. New York: Random House, 1980.

Develops an argument against the death penalty
based on the idea of the sanctity of life.
Discusses capital punishment as social defense
and the limits of retributive justifications.

100. Bedau, Hugo Adam (ed.). THE DEATH PENALTY IN
AMERICA. 3rd Edition. New York: Oxford
University Press, 1982.

The most comprehensive overview of the death
penalty in print. Included are twenty
essays, excerpts from five Supreme Court
decisions, and long introductions to the book

and to six subsections written by Bedau.
Major topics included are 1) An overview of
the laws, crimes, and executions, 2)
Attitudes toward the death penalty, 3)
Deterrence, 4) Problems of racism, costs,
miscarriages of justice, 5) Debates on
whether executions are "cruel and unusual,"
and 6) Arguments for and against capital
punishment.

101.   Bedau, Hugo Adam.   "Witness to a Persecution:
The Death Penalty and the Dawson Five."
BLACK LAW JOURNAL 8 (1983): 7-28.

Recounts the trial of the "Dawson Five"--five
black men accused of a robbery-murder of a
Georgia white woman in 1977. The author
describes the case, his participation in it,
and the surprising decision of the
prosecution to drop all charges against the
defendants.

102.   Bedau, Hugo Adam.   "Bentham's Utilitarian
Critique of the Death Penalty."   JOURNAL OF
CRIMINAL LAW AND CRIMINOLOGY 74 (1983):
1033-66.

A discussion of Jeremy Bentham's (1748-1832)
powerful critique of the death penalty. The
essay describes Bentham's work, points out
its strengths and weaknesses, and discusses
the implications of his work for contemporary
audiences.

103.   Bedau, Hugo Adam. "Berger's Defense of the
Death Penalty: How Not to Read the
Constitution."   MICHIGAN LAW REVIEW 81
(1983): 1152-65.

A review of Raoul Berger's book, cited below
as item 119. Berger's response is cited
below as item 120.

104.   Bedau, Hugo Adam.   "Toward a Comparative
Jurisprudence on Capital Punishment." HARVARD
CIVIL RIGHTS - CIVIL LIBERTIES LAW REVIEW 19
(1984): 235-43.

A review of David Pannick's book, cited below
as item 671.

105. Bedau, Hugo Adam. THE CASE AGAINST THE DEATH
      PENALTY. New York: American Civil Liberties
      Union (132 W. 43rd St., New York 10036),
      1984.

      A short, well-documented pamphlet that
      systematically and concisely summarizes the
      abolitionists' position against the death
      penalty.

106. Bedau, Hugo Adam. "Thinking of the Death
      Penalty as Cruel and Unusual Punishment."
      UNIVERSITY OF CALIFORNIA-DAVIS LAW REVIEW 18
      (1985): 873-925.

      A philosophical inquiry examining how we can
      determine whether certain punishments are
      excessively severe. Reviews several
      different theories of punishment.

107. Bedau, Hugo Adam. "Gregg v. Georgia and the
      New Death Penalty." CRIMINAL JUSTICE ETHICS
      4 (1985): 3-17.

      An examination of recent Supreme Court
      decisions on the death penalty, particularly
      Gregg. Closely considers the attempts in
      Gregg to address the question of whether the
      death penalty is too severe and how to
      structure discretion in death penalty
      decisions. The issues of whether judge or
      jury should sentence, and of predicting
      dangerousness, are also discussed.

108. Bedau, Hugo Adam. DEATH IS DIFFERENT:
      STUDIES IN THE MORALITY, LAW AND POLITICS OF
      CAPITAL PUNISHMENT. Boston: Northeastern
      University Press, 1987.

      A collection of previously published essays,
      all thoroughly reedited (and some rewritten)
      for this publication. The author examines
      the meaning of the Eighth Amendment, how
      death penalty laws have changed, mandatory
      death penalties, and state constitutional law
      as it relates to capital punishment.
      Includes items 91, 96, 98, 99, 101, 102, 106,
      and 107.

109.   Bedau, Hugo Adam.   "Justice in Punishment and
        Assumption of Risks: Some Comments in
        Response to van den Haag."   WAYNE LAW REVIEW
        33 (1987): 1423-33.

        A critique of an essay by van den Haag, cited
        below as item 878.   Followed by a rejoinder
        by van den Haag.

110.   Bedau, Hugo Adam, and Chester M. Pierce
        (eds.).   CAPITAL PUNISHMENT IN THE UNITED
        STATES.   New York: AMS Press, 1976.

        Published for the American Orthopsychiatric
        Association.   Contains items 40, 42, 160,
        260, 305, 354, 366, 415, 485, 526, 578, 675,
        676, 741, 761, 820, 852, 885, 899, 905, 932,
        and 958.

111.   Bedau, Hugo Adam, and Michael L. Radelet.
        "Miscarriages of Justice in Potentially
        Capital Cases."   STANFORD LAW REVIEW 40
        (1987): 21-179.

        Identifies and describes 350 twentieth-
        century American cases in which people later
        proved to be innocent were convicted of
        homicide or sentenced to death for rape.

112.   Beichman, Arnold.   "The First Electrocution."
        COMMENTARY 35 (1963): 410-9.

        Reviews the history of the world's first
        electrocution, involving William Kemmler in
        New York in 1890.   The feud between Thomas
        Edison and George Westinghouse is described,
        with Edison's argument that the electrocution
        would be painless.

113.   Beeman, Lamar (ed.).   SELECTED ARTICLES ON
        CAPITAL PUNISHMENT.   New York: W.H. Wilson
        Co., 1925.

        An informative, though very dated, collection
        of articles and facts on capital punishment.
        Includes an outline on the debate over the
        death penalty and a 38-page bibliography.

114.   Bendremer, Frederick J., Gale Bramnick,
        Joseph C. Jones III, and Steven N. Lippman.

"McCleskey v. Kemp: Constitutional Tolerance for Racially Disparate Capital Sentencing." UNIVERSITY OF MIAMI LAW REVIEW 41 (1986): 295-355.

An examination of the McCleskey case and how it was handled by the Eleventh Circuit, published before the Supreme Court ruled on the case. The paper attempts to explain why the Eleventh Circuit erected insurmountable barriers to McCleskey's claims. Examines statistical means to demonstrate discrimination in other types of cases.

115. Benjamin, Michael. "Extent of Procedural Due Process Required to Adjudge the Competency of a Condemned Prisoner." UNIVERSITY OF FLORIDA LAW REVIEW 38 (1986): 681-91.

An analysis of the Ford decision, arguing that the Court gave the states little guidance in restructuring their procedures for adjudicating the competency of condemned prisoners.

116. Bennett, Edward W. "The Reasons for Michigan's Abolition of Capital Punishment." MICHIGAN HISTORY 62 (Nov.-Dec., 1978): 42-55.

An overview of the efforts to abolish the death penalty in Michigan.

117. Benson, David J. "Constitutionality of Ohio's New Death Penalty Statute." UNIVERSITY OF TOLEDO LAW REVIEW 14 (1982): 77-97.

Examines Ohio's death penalty statute and evaluates it according to criteria specified by the U.S. Supreme Court. Concludes the statute is constitutionally sound.

118. Bentele, Ursula. "The Death Penalty in Georgia: Still Arbitrary." WASHINGTON UNIVERSITY LAW QUARTERLY 62 (1985): 573-646.

An extensive examination of capital sentencing in Georgia, with detailed discussions of prosecutorial discretion and clemency. Concludes that the Georgia statute has failed to bring about fairness in death sentencing.

119.	Berger, Raoul. DEATH PENALTIES: THE SUPREME COURT'S OBSTACLE COURSE. Cambridge, Mass.: Harvard University Press, 1982.

A book on the limits of Supreme Court authority. Argues that the Court does not have the right to overrule capital statutes duly enacted by state legislatures. The book also includes a long discussion of the history of the Eighth Amendment. Reviewed by Bedau in item 103 above and by Cottrol in item 229 below.

120.	Berger, Raoul. "Death Penalties and Hugo Bedau: A Crusading Philosopher Goes Overboard." OHIO STATE LAW JOURNAL 45 (1984): 863-81.

Comments on Bedau's review (cited above as item 103) of Berger's book (cited above as item 119). Calls Bedau's review "a propagandistic diatribe."

121.	Berger, Vivian. "Born-Again Death." COLUMBIA LAW REVIEW 87 (1987): 1301-24.

A positive review of Welsh White's THE DEATH PENALTY IN THE EIGHTIES (cited below as item 911). Includes a discussion of arbitrariness in modern death sentencing, the challenges the penalty poses for attorney-client relations, and some thoughts about capital punishment in the future.

122.	Bergwerk, Ron. "Step Toward Uniformity: Review of Life Sentences in Capital Cases." FLORIDA STATE UNIVERSITY LAW REVIEW 6 (1978): 1015-27.

Proposes that in order to improve proportionality review, the Florida Supreme Court should review potential death cases that ended in a life sentence, as well as cases resulting in a death sentence.

123.	Beristain, Antonio. "Capital Punishment and Catholicism." INTERNATIONAL JOURNAL OF

CRIMINOLOGY AND PENOLOGY 5 (1977): 321-33.

Discusses the death penalty in light of
contemporary Catholic theology, and concludes
the penalty must be abolished.

124. Berkson, Larry Charles. THE CONCEPT OF CRUEL
AND UNUSUAL PUNISHMENT. Lexington, Mass.:
D.C. Heath, 1975.

Discusses the origins and judicial
interpretations of the Eighth Amendment, and
its relevance to both capital and corporal
punishment.

125. Berlage, Derick P. "Pleas of the Condemned:
Should Certiorari Petitions from Death Row
Receive Enhanced Access to the Supreme
Court?" NEW YORK UNIVERSITY LAW REVIEW 59
(1984): 1120-49.

Argues that enhanced access to the Court is
justified for capital defendants and suggests
criteria the Court can use to select cases
for review.

126. Bernard, J.L., and W.O. Dwyer. "Witherspoon
v. Illinois: The Court was Right." LAW AND
PSYCHOLOGY REVIEW 8 (1984): 105-14.

An examination of the attitudes about capital
punishment expressed by mock jurors and their
consistency with their actual votes in the
penalty phase of a mock capital trial. Finds
that preexisting attitudes do not affect
votes on guilt determination, but do have an
impact on sentencing determinations.

127. Berns, Walter. FOR CAPITAL PUNISHMENT: CRIME
AND THE MORALITY OF THE DEATH PENALTY. New
York: Basic Books, 1979.

Argues for the retention of the death penalty
on moral grounds, basing his position on a
retributive model of justice. An excellent
statement of the pro-death penalty position.
Reviewed by Hughes in item 450 below.

128. Berns, Walter. "Defending the Death Penalty."
CRIME AND DELINQUENCY 26 (1980): 503-11.

A thoughtful defense of capital punishment, based primarily on the morality of retribution and the idea that executions for homicide promote respect for human life.

129. Berry, James. MY EXPERIENCES AS AN EXECUTIONER (H. Snowden Ward (ed.)). Newton Abbott, Devon: David and Charles Reprints, 1972.

First published in 1891, this book presents a biography of Berry, who served as executioner in England and Scotland from 1884 to 1892 (and later became an abolitionist).

130. Berry, Robert M. "Remedies to the Dilemma of Death-Qualified Juries." UNIVERSITY OF ARKANSAS AT LITTLE ROCK LAW JOURNAL 8 (1985): 479-501.

Written shortly before the Supreme Court's decision in Lockhart v. McCree, reviews remedies to the bias created by death qualification, including having the sentence decided by the judge, a new jury, or by the original jury with replacements for its anti-death penalty members.

131. Bersoff, Donald M. "Social Science Data and the Supreme Court: Lockhart As a Case in Point." AMERICAN PSYCHOLOGIST 42 (1987): 52-8.

Examines Lockhart v. McCree and the social science research used in it to show that death qualified jurors are conviction prone. The case is used as an example of how psychologists can influence judicial behavior with well-designed studies.

132. Beyleveld, Deryck. "Ehrlich's Analysis of Deterrence: Methodological Strategy and Ethics in Isaac Ehrlich's Research and Writing on the Death Penalty as a Deterrent." BRITISH JOURNAL OF CRIMINOLOGY 22 (1982): 101-23.

Reviews the controversy caused by Isaac Ehrlich's research on deterrence. The author

argues that Ehrlich's work was either naive
or deliberately designed to support the death
penalty. Responded to by Ehrlich in item 294
below.

133. Beyleveld, Deryck. A BIBLIOGRAPHY OF GENERAL
DETERRENCE RESEARCH. Westmead, England:
Saxon House, 1980.

A comprehensive bibliography of deterrence
research published in English, 1946-78.
Includes abstracts and reviews of categories
of entries.

134. Bishop, Thomas P., and Abby L. Martin.
"Statutory Aggravating Circumstances and the
Death Penalty: What Lies Beyond the Threshold
after Zant v. Stephens?" MERCER LAW REVIEW
35 (1984): 1443-68.

The authors criticize the decision in
Stevens, in which the Supreme Court failed to
reverse a Georgia death sentence even though
one of the aggravating circumstances found at
trial was unconstitutional. This article
sketches the Eighth Amendment issues relating
to the death penalty and analyzes the impact
of Stevens on that history.

135. Black, Charles L., Jr. "The Crisis in
Capital Punishment." MARYLAND LAW REVIEW 31
(1971): 289-311.

An excellent and passionate statement against
the death penalty; one of the best that has
ever been written.

136. Black, Charles L., Jr. "Due Process for
Death: Jurek v. Texas and Companion Cases."
CATHOLIC UNIVERSITY LAW REVIEW 26 (1976):
1-16.

Sharply criticizes the Texas death penalty
statute and the Supreme Court's approval of
that and other death penalty statutes.

137. Black, Charles L., Jr. "Death Penalty Now."
TULANE LAW REVIEW 51 (1977): 429-45.

A lecture delivered at Tulane discussing the

Ohio case of Sandra Lockett, who refused a
negotiated plea and was sentenced to death
despite the fact that she never killed
anyone. The case is used to demonstrate the
arbitrariness of the death penalty.

138. Black, Charles L., Jr. "Reflections on
Opposing the Penalty of Death." ST. MARY'S
LAW JOURNAL 10 (1978): 1-12.

Argues the administration of the death
penalty is characterized by arbitrariness and
mistakes. This essay reflects on that theme
and how it has made the author an ardent
abolitionist.

139. Black, Charles L., Jr. "Governors' Dilemma."
THE NEW REPUBLIC 180 (April 25, 1979): 12-3.

As the number of death row inmates increases,
governors have to decide whether they want to
execute or commute. This essay explores the
options available to those governors who want
to grant clemency to some or all condemned
prisoners in their state.

140. Black, Charles L., Jr. CAPITAL PUNISHMENT:
THE INEVITABILITY OF CAPRICE AND MISTAKE.
2nd Edition. New York: W.W. Norton and Co.,
1981.

A strong argument opposing the death penalty,
largely because of unavoidable arbitrariness,
discrimination, imprecision, and mistakes in
its administration. Of particular interest
is the discussion on charging and plea
bargaining and his critical comments about
the Texas statute. One of the most important
books on capital punishment published in the
last 15 years.

141. Black, Charles L., Jr. "The Death Penalty: A
National Question." UNIVERSITY OF
CALIFORNIA-DAVIS LAW REVIEW 18 (1985):
867-71.

An introduction to a special issue on the
death penalty, arguing that capital
punishment should be treated as a national,
rather than as a state-by-state issue.

142. Black, Theodore, and Thomas Orsagh. "New
     Evidence of the Efficacy of Sanctions as a
     Deterrent to Homicide." SOCIAL SCIENCE
     QUARTERLY 58 (1978): 616-31.

     Develops a neoclassical model of deterrence,
     and tests it using log-linear analysis on
     data from 43 states in 1950 and 47 states in
     1960. The authors are unable to find, a
     consistent relationship between the severity
     of punishment and homicide rates.

143. Blaine, Quentin. "'Shall Surely be Put to
     Death:' Capital Punishment in New Hampshire,
     1623-1985." NEW HAMPSHIRE BAR JOURNAL 27
     (1986): 131-54.

     An extensive examination of the history of
     the death penalty in New Hampshire. Includes
     a list of those executed, and a discussion of
     relevant issues in the state constitution.

144. Bland, James. THE COMMON HANGMAN: ENGLISH
     AND SCOTTISH HANGMEN BEFORE THE ABOLITION OF
     PUBLIC EXECUTIONS. Hornchurch, Essex: Ian
     Henry Publications, 1984.

     An examination of public executions and their
     festive atmosphere, the jobs performed by
     executioners, and a description of the
     executioners who worked in England and
     Scotland from approximately 1500 until the
     abolition of public hanging in the nineteenth
     century.

145. Block, E.B. WHEN MEN PLAY GOD: THE FALLACY
     OF CAPITAL PUNISHMENT. San Francisco:
     Cragmont Publishers, 1983.

     A general statement of the abolitionist
     position, with chapters on deterrence, the
     conviction of innocents, the position of the
     United Nations and other countries, and the
     history of capital punishment.

146. Block, Richard A. "'Death, Thou Shalt Die':
     Reform Judaism and Capital Punishment."
     JOURNAL OF REFORM JUDAISM 30 (Spring, 1983):
     1-10.

Reviews Jewish doctrine in opposition to the
death penalty.

147. Bluestone, Harvey, and Carl L. McGahee.
"Reaction to Extreme Stress: Impending Death
by Execution." THE AMERICAN JOURNAL OF
PSYCHIATRY 119 (1962): 393-6.

Studies 18 men and one woman under sentence
of death in New York, documenting the
inmates' troubled backgrounds and their
efforts to cope with the stresses of death
row confinement.

148. Boaz, Julia E. "Summary Process and the Rule
of Law: Expediting Death Penalty Cases in the
Federal Courts." YALE LAW JOURNAL 95 (1985):
349-70.

In Barefoot v. Estelle, the Supreme Court
held that federal courts may provide
defendants under death sentence with
abbreviated versions of the process afforded
to other prisoners seeking habeas corpus
relief. The author reviews the debate this
ruling inspired, and argues that the ruling
distorts the adjudication process.

149. Bockle, Franz, and Jacques Pohiers (eds.).
THE DEATH PENALTY AND TORTURE. New York:
The Seabury Press, 1979.

A collection of thirteen essays on the death
penalty and torture. Written from various
religious perspectives, essays are included
from Catholic, Protestant, Jewish, and
Islamic viewpoints.

150. Boehm, Virginia R. "Mr. Prejudice, Miss
Sympathy, and the Authoritarian Personality:
An Application of Psychological Measuring
Techniques to the Problem of Jury Bias."
WISCONSIN LAW REVIEW 1968 (1968): 734-50.

Trial lawyers usually select juries using
intuition and experience to guide their
choices. This article attempts to make the
process more systematic. The author, a
psychologist, shows how certain attitudinal

measures can be used to predict jurors'
voting patterns.

151. Bohm, Robert. "American Death Penalty
      Attitudes: A Critical Examination of Recent
      Evidence." CRIMINAL JUSTICE AND BEHAVIOR 4
      (1987): 380-96.

      An examination of attitudes toward the death
      penalty, with a critical discussion of the
      reasons most often given for support and how
      people arrive at their decisions to support
      the punishment.

152. Bok, Curtis. STAR WORMWOOD. New York:
      Knopf, 1959.

      A powerful, fictional account of a young boy
      who is convicted of murder and executed,
      written by a Justice of the Pennsylvania
      State Supreme Court.

153. Bolsen, Barbara. "Strange Bedfellows: Death
      Penalty and Medicine." JOURNAL OF THE
      AMERICAN MEDICAL ASSOCIATION 248 (Aug. 6,
      1982): 518-9.

      Reviews the motivations and work of
      physicians in fighting the death penalty,
      including their concerns about lethal
      injection, the epidemic of homicide, and the
      shortage of psychiatrists available to
      testify in death penalty cases.

154. Bonner, Raymond A. "Death Penalty." ANNUAL
      SURVEY OF AMERICAN LAW 1984 (1984): 493-513.

      Argues the Supreme Court has recently tried
      to speed up executions by eliminating
      procedural safeguards. Also discusses the
      unreliability of psychiatric testimony.
      Major cases analyzed are Zant v. Stephens and
      Barefoot v. Estelle.

155. Bonnie, Richard J. "Psychiatry and the Death
      Penalty: Emerging Problems in Virginia."
      VIRGINIA LAW REVIEW 66 (1980): 167-89.

      Analyzes the constitutional history of death
      sentencing in Virginia, with a special

emphasis on the role and limits of
psychiatric involvement. Concern about
psychiatric predictions of dangerousness is
voiced. It is recommended that indigent
defendants be provided with access to
psychiatric examinations at state expense.

156. Bowers, William J. EXECUTIONS IN AMERICA.
Lexington, Mass.: Lexington Books, 1974.

A review of the history of the death penalty
in the United States, and a discussion of the
characteristics of the condemned. The
Teeters-Zibulka data, which listed all known
executions under state authority in America,
is included. A special concern of the book
is the problem of racial bias. The book was
expanded into a second edition, under a
different title, which is cited below as item
159.

157. Bowers, William J. "The Pervasiveness of
Arbitrariness and Discrimination Under Post-
Furman Capital Statutes." JOURNAL OF
CRIMINAL LAW AND CRIMINOLOGY 74 (1983):
1067-1100.

Focuses on the effects of race on charging,
sentencing, and appellate decisions in
Florida and Georgia. Includes data from
interviews with Florida prosecutors about
their charging decisions. Shows that
arbitrariness is widespread, and links it to
race, region, and other non-legal factors.

158. Bowers, William J. "The Effect of the Death
Penalty is Brutalization, not Deterrence."
In Haas and Inciardi, 1988, cited below as
item 413.

Reanalyzes several studies on the effects of
executions and finds that most show a slight
increase in the murder rate following an
execution.

159. Bowers, William J., with Glenn L. Pierce and
John F. McDevitt. LEGAL HOMICIDE: DEATH AS
PUNISHMENT IN AMERICA, 1864-1982. Boston:
Northeastern University Press, 1984.

One of the most important books on the death
penalty published in the last fifteen years,
this book is also arguably the best source
for data on executions during the last
century and the racial bias the author
contends still pervades the system today.
The historical parts of the book were
included in EXECUTIONS IN AMERICA, cited
above as item 156.   Includes an extensive
bibliography.

160.   Bowers, William J., and Glenn L. Pierce.
"The Illusion of Deterrence in Isaac
Ehrlich's Research on Capital Punishment."
YALE LAW JOURNAL 85 (1975): 187-208.
Reprinted in Bedau and Pierce, 1976, in item
110 above.

A critique of Isaac Ehrlich's research on
deterrence, arguing that the findings are
unreliable, and showing that Ehrlich's
results can not be replicated if post-1964
data are eliminated from the analysis.
Responded to by Ehrlich in item 290 below.

161.   Bowers, William J., and Glenn L. Pierce.
"Arbitrariness and Discrimination Under Post-
Furman Capital Statutes."   CRIME AND
DELINQUENCY 26 (1980): 563-635.

An extensive examination of death-sentencing
patterns in Ohio, Texas, Florida, and
Georgia.   Defendant's and victim's race are
found to be related to sentencing, and
significant intra-state geographic variations
are documented.   Presentencing, sentencing,
and appellate decisions are all examined.

162.   Bowers, William J., and Glenn L. Pierce.
"Deterrence or Brutalization: What is the
Effect of Executions?"   CRIME AND DELINQUENCY
26 (1980): 453-84.

Finds that in New York, over the period
1907-63, there were on average two more
homicides than would have been expected in
the month following an execution.   These data
are interpreted in a more general discussion
of the brutalizing effects of the death
penalty.

163. Boyd, Joseph A., Jr., and James J. Logue.
      "Developments in the Application of Florida's
      Capital Felony Sentencing Law." UNIVERSITY
      OF MIAMI LAW REVIEW 34 (1980): 441-97.

      The authors, a Florida Supreme Court Justice
      and his clerk, discuss the construction and
      application of Florida's death penalty
      statute. Particular attention is directed to
      a discussion of the aggravating circumstances
      found in the law.

164. Boyles, William J., and Lee R. McPheters.
      "Capital Punishment as a Deterrent to Violent
      Crime: Cross Section Evidence." JOURNAL OF
      BEHAVIORAL ECONOMICS 6 (1977): 67-86.

      Examining 1960 data from 47 states, the
      authors find the deterrent effect of capital
      punishment is insignificant.

165. Bradley, Lisa Gayle. "Proportionality in
      Capital and Non-Capital Sentencing: An
      Eighth Amendment Enigma." IDAHO LAW REVIEW
      23 (1986-87): 195-217.

      An examination of the proportionality issue,
      and how the standard is applied differently
      in capital and noncapital cases. Argues that
      proportionality enters in capital cases
      through evaluation of "evolving standards of
      decency," and develops an Eighth Amendment
      proportionality argument.

166. Braithwaite, Lloyd. "Executive Clemency in
      California: A Case Study Interpretation of
      Criminal Responsibility." ISSUES IN
      CRIMINOLOGY 1 (1965): 77-107.

      Twelve case studies are presented of
      California inmates whose sentences were
      commuted by Governor Edmund Brown because of
      doubts about the inmates' sanity.

167. Brasfield, Philip, with Jeffrey M. Elliot.
      DEATHMAN PASS ME BY: TWO YEARS ON DEATH ROW.
      San Bernardino, CA: Borgo Books, 1983.

The autobiography of a man who spent two
years on death row in Texas. The book
describes the author's life before, during,
and after his experience among the condemned.

168. Brennan, Justice William J., Jr.
"Constitutional Adjudication and the Death
Penalty: A View from the Court." HARVARD LAW
REVIEW 100 (1986): 313-31.

A discussion of how the author (an Associate
Justice on the Supreme Court) has dealt with
death row cases over the last thirty years.
Discusses Arthur Goldberg's memo in Rudolph
v. Alabama and Goldberg's dissent from the
denial of certiorari in the case, in which
Justice Brennan and Justice Douglas joined.
The Court's actions in other death penalty
cases are also discussed.

169. Bright, Stephen B. "Judicial System
Inconsistent in Doling Out Death." NATIONAL
PRISON PROJECT JOURNAL 6 (Winter, 1985):
12-5.

A brief review of the current status of
executions and condemnations in the U.S.
Argues that statutorily defined aggravating
circumstances are so vague that they invite
inconsistent application. Racism and the
quality of defense attorneys are also
discussed.

170. Brinkmann, Beth S. "The Presumption of Life:
A Starting Point for a Due Process Analysis
of Capital Sentencing." YALE LAW JOURNAL 94
(1984): 351-73.

Argues that defendants are being sentenced to
death without procedural safeguards and
appellate courts' efforts to correct this are
inadequate and misguided. The author
contends that we should presume from the
start that the defendant will not be
executed, just as we presume he or she is
innocent, and thus should place a heavier
burden of proof on the prosecution.

171. Broderick, Daniel J. "Insanity of the
Condemned." YALE LAW JOURNAL 88 (1979):

533-64.

Reviews the history of the exemption of the
insane from execution. Concludes that the
procedures for assessing sanity of prisoners
are inadequate.

172. Brody, Richard J. "Should Juvenile Murderers
be Sentenced to Death? Don't Kill Children."
AMERICAN BAR ASSOCIATION JOURNAL 72 (June 1,
1986): 32-3.

In a debate with James Anders (see item 22
above), Brody argues that restrictions
against executing juveniles should be
established.

173. Bronson, Edward J. "On the Conviction
Proneness and Representativeness of the
Death-Qualified Jury: A Study of Colorado
Veniremen." UNIVERSITY OF COLORADO LAW
REVIEW 42 (1970): 1-32.

An examination of the effects of excluding
scrupled jurors from service in capital
cases. Questionnaires were completed by 718
prospective jurors. The excluded jurors were
slightly less conviction prone, and the two
groups were found to differ on several
demographic variables (e.g., race and
gender).

174. Bronson, Edward J. "Does the Exclusion of
Scrupled Jurors in Capital Cases Make the
Jury More Likely to Convict? Some Evidence
from California." WOODROW WILSON JOURNAL OF
LAW 3 (1981): 11-34.

Supplementing data gathered for the author's
earlier work in Colorado with data from
California (resulting in a sample of over
2,000 people selected for jury service), the
author finds that the exclusion of scrupled
jurors makes the jury more conviction prone
and less representative.

175. Brown, Teresa A. "Who's Qualified to Decide
Who Dies?" NEBRASKA LAW REVIEW 65 (1986):
558-83.

A comment on the decision in <u>Wainwright</u> <u>v.</u>
<u>Witt</u>, which broadened the prevailing standard
for exclusion of death penalty opponents from
capital juries. The author argues this
holding is contrary to previous rulings of
the Court, and further reduces the
constitutional protections afforded capital
defendants.

176. Browning, James R. "The New Death Penalty
Statutes: Perpetuating a Costly Myth."
GONZAGA LAW REVIEW 9 (1974): 651-705.

The author, a judge on the U.S. Court of
Appeals (Ninth Circuit), examines the
attempts to reinstate the death penalty, and
concludes that the new statutes do not reduce
the problems of the older statutes. He also
states his belief in the uselessness of the
death penalty.

177. Bruck, David. "The Four Men Strom Thurmond
Sent to the Chair." WASHINGTON POST, April
26, 1981 (Available from NAACP Legal Defense
and Educational Fund, Inc., 99 Hudson St.,
New York 10013).

Reviews four South Carolina cases presided
over by now-Senator Strom Thurmond which
resulted in death sentences. Argues that
these cases were, by contemporary standards,
barbaric and unfair.

178. Bruck, David. "Decisions of Death." THE NEW
REPUBLIC 189 (December 12, 1983): 18-25.

Based on his experiences in defending death
row inmates, the author argues that
sentencing decisions are arbitrary and
influenced by race.

179. Bruck, David. "The Death Penalty: An
Exchange." THE NEW REPUBLIC 192 (May 20,
1985): 20-1.

A response to the article by Mayor Koch,
cited below as item 518. Includes a rebuttal
by Koch.

180. Bruck, David. "On Death Row in Pretoria

Central." THE NEW REPUBLIC (July 13 and 20, 1987): 18-25.

Examines the death penalty in South Africa. Interviews of judges and lawyers involved in capital cases are presented. Several similarities with the administration of the death penalty in the United States are discussed.

181. Buchman, Roberta L. "The Final Sentence: Nebraska's Death Penalty." CREIGHTON LAW REVIEW 14 (1980): 256-71.

Examines Nebraska's legislative and supreme court's efforts to reduce arbitrariness in death penalty cases. Finds the state has failed in its efforts to administer the death penalty even handedly.

182. Burt, Robert A. "Disorder in the Court: The Death Penalty and the Constitution." MICHIGAN LAW REVIEW 85 (1987): 1741-819.

This article gives the history of the Supreme Court's rulings in death penalty cases from the 1930's through McCleskey v. Kemp (1987). It describes the legal events before the execution of John Spenkelink and the effects of capital punishment cases on judges and lawyers.

183. BULLETIN OF THE NEW YORK ACADEMY OF MEDICINE. "Homicide: The Public Health Perspective." Published as a special issue in vol. 65 (July, 1986).

Includes 24 papers by eminent scholars. Sections include 1) The epidemiology of homicide, 2) Causes, predictability, intervention, and prevention (includes discussions of domestic violence and mass and serial murders, and drugs and homicide), and 3) Strategies for prevention.

184. Bureau of Justice Statistics. CAPITAL PUNISHMENT, 1984. Washington, D.C.: U.S. Department of Justice, 1986.

Though usually delayed in publication by as

much as two years, this is an extremely useful collection of statistics on persons on death row, movements on and off death row, and statistical summaries of American executions since 1930. Published annually.

185. Burris, Scott. "Death and a Rational Justice: A Conversation on the Capital Jurisprudence of Justice John Paul Stevens." YALE LAW JOURNAL 96 (1987): 521-46.

A fictional conversation on the death penalty between Justices Stevens, Marshall, Brennan, and Berger. Brings out the views of the participants, especially those of Justice Stevens.

186. Bye, Raymond T. CAPITAL PUNISHMENT IN THE UNITED STATES. Philadelphia: The Committee of Philanthropic Labor of Philadelphia Yearly Meeting of Friends, 1919.

A pioneering examination of the evolution of the death penalty, its value as a deterrent, relation to lynching, and the possibility of errors.

187. Byrne, Jane. "Lockhart v. McCree: Conviction-Proneness and the Constitutionality of Death-Qualified Juries." CATHOLIC UNIVERSITY LAW REVIEW 36 (1986): 287-318.

Summarizes the McCree case and the data submitted in support of his claim of bias due to jury death qualification.

188. Callans, Patrick J. "Assembling a Jury Willing to Impose the Death Penalty: A New Disregard for a Capital Defendant's Rights." JOURNAL OF CRIMINAL LAW AND CRIMINOLOGY 76 (1985): 1027-50.

A comment on Wainwright v. Witt, arguing that the decision will prevent defendants from having a fair and impartial jury.

189. Campbell, Ruth. "Sentence of Death by Burning for Women." JOURNAL OF LEGAL HISTORY 5 (1984): 44-59.

Examines the punishment of burning women at the stake in England until this method of execution was abolished in 1790. Burning at the stake was used to execute women (but not men) who were found guilty of killing their spouses (petty treason).

190. Camus, Albert. "Reflections on the Guillotine." Pp. 173-234 in Albert Camus, RESISTANCE, REBELLION AND DEATH. New York: Alfred A. Knopf, 1966. Also published separately in Michigan City, Indiana by Fridtjof-Karla Publishers in 1959.

A powerful essay rejecting the death penalty on moral and philosophical grounds. A classic statement of the abolitionist position.

191. Canada. Department of Justice. CAPITAL PUNISHMENT--NEW MATERIAL 1965-1972. Ottawa: Information Canada, 1972.

This report discusses new developments relating to capital punishment around the world and in Canada since 1965, reviews arguments in favor of abolition and retention, and examines how crime rates in Canada have changed since 1967, when the death penalty was abolished for a five-year trial period.

192. Capote, Truman. IN COLD BLOOD: THE TRUE ACCOUNT OF A MULTIPLE MURDER AND ITS CONSEQUENCES. New York: Random House, 1965.

An account of the murder of a Kansas family in 1959, and the capture, trial, and execution of two men for the crime. Based on interviews and official records, this "nonfiction novel" is an in-depth study of a multiple homicide, its effects on the victims' family and community, and the legal response.

193. Cardarelli, Albert P. "An Analysis of Police Killed by Criminal Action, 1961-1963." JOURNAL OF CRIMINAL LAW, CRIMINOLOGY AND POLICE SCIENCE 59 (1968): 447-53.

A descriptive profile of 140 police officers killed, 1961-63. Little difference is found in the proportion of officers murdered in abolition and in death penalty states.

194.   Carney, Francis J., and Ann L. Fuller. "A Study of Plea Bargaining in Murder Cases in Massachusetts." SUFFOLK UNIVERSITY LAW REVIEW 3 (1969): 292-307.

All cases involving an indictment for first- or second-degree murder in Massachusetts, 1956-65, that ended in a final disposition of guilt or innocence are studied (N=326). 87 percent pled not guilty at the indictment stage, but 68 percent pled guilty at trial (93 percent to a less serious charge). Of the 105 defendants who went to trial, 59 percent were convicted.

195.   Carr, James R. "At Witt's End: The Continuing Quandary of Jury Selection in Capital Cases." STANFORD LAW REVIEW 39 (1987): 427-60.

A discussion of the process of death qualification, especially as affected by Wainwright v. Witt. The article looks at how death qualification has changed and become muddled since Witherspoon, and criticizes the decision in Witt for several shortcomings.

196.   Carrington, Frank G. NEITHER CRUEL NOR UNUSUAL. New Rochelle, New York: Arlington House, 1978.

A defense of capital punishment and a point-by-point critique of the abolitionists' arguments.

197.   Carrington, Frank G. "Deterrence, Death, and the Victims of Crime: A Common Sense Approach." VANDERBILT LAW REVIEW 35 (1982): 587-605.

Discusses the central role of the deterrence question in the area of victim advocacy, and argues, from a common sense approach, that increases in severity of punishment lead to more deterrence. Suggests we should not wait until the deterrence issue is settled before we recognize its importance from the victims' point of view, and thus should continue to have executions.

198.   Carroll, John L.   "The Defense Lawyer's Role in the Sentencing Process: You've Got to Accentuate the Positive and Eliminate the Negative."   MERCER LAW REVIEW 37 (1986): 981-1004.

Using capital cases as examples, the author discusses how to minimize the negative (e.g., working with the preparer of the Pre-Sentence Investigation (PSI) report, dealing with the victim), and how to maximize mitigation.

199.   Carroll, John L.   "Death Row--Hope for the Future."   In Haas and Inciardi, 1988, cited below as item 413.

This paper reviews recent litigation on the constitutionality of death row living conditions in the U.S.   State-by-state variations in the quality of life and living conditions are described.

200.   Carter, Dan T.   SCOTTSBORO: A TRAGEDY OF THE AMERICAN SOUTH.   Baton Rouge: Louisiana State University Press, 1969.

A detailed history of the Scottsboro case, in which nine innocent black men were convicted of the rape of two white women in Alabama.

201.   Carter, Robert, and A. LaMont Smith.   "The Death Penalty in California: A Statistical and Composite Portrait."   CRIME AND DELINQUENCY 15 (1969): 62-76.

Reviews the case records of 194 people executed in the gas chamber at San Quentin, 1938-63.   Demographic data on the offenders are presented, and a composite portrait of the typical inmate is developed and described.

202.   Casscells, Ward, and William J. Curran.   "Doctors, the Death Penalty, and Lethal Injection: Recent Developments."   NEW ENGLAND

JOURNAL OF MEDICINE 307 (Dec. 9, 1982): 1532-3.

Describes the action of various medical organizations in opposing participation of physicians in executions by lethal injection.

203. Catz, Robert S. "Federal Habeas Corpus and the Death Penalty: Need for a Preclusion Doctrine Exception." UNIVERSITY OF CALIFORNIA-DAVIS LAW REVIEW 18 (1985): 1177-219.

Criticizes the recent erosion of the right of death row prisoners to secure federal habeas corpus relief, on the grounds that death is different from other punishments.

204. Cederblom, J.B., and Gonzalo Munevar. "The Death Penalty: The Relevance of Deterrence." CRIMINAL JUSTICE REVIEW 7 (1982): 63-6.

Argues that deterrence is a relevant consideration in the debate over whether death is a justifiable punishment.

205. Cederblom, J.B., and William L. Blizek (eds.). JUSTICE AND PUNISHMENT. Cambridge, Mass.: Ballinger, 1977.

Nine essays, originally presented in a symposium on "Criminal Justice and Punishment" at the University of Nebraska-Omaha, are included. A central issue is retribution, and essays by Hugo Adam Bedau, Norval Morris, and James Q. Wilson are among those included.

206. Chandler, David B. CAPITAL PUNISHMENT IN CANADA: A SOCIOLOGICAL STUDY OF REPRESSIVE LAW. Toronto: McClelland and Stewart, 1976.

A sociological overview of the capital punishment debate in Canada, focusing primarily on the legislative debates of 1967 and 1973. The role of public opinion and how the members of Parliament reacted to it are described. Included is a theoretical approach to the legislative behavior, based primarily on Durkheim.

207. Chapman, Frank. "The Death Penalty, U.S.A.: Racist and Class Violence." POLITICAL AFFAIRS 66 (July, 1987): 17-9.

A brief review of the race and class biases in the administration of the death penalty, written from a Marxist perspective.

208. Cheatwood, Derral. "Capital Punishment and Corrections: Is There an Impending Crisis?" CRIME AND DELINQUENCY 31 (1985): 461-79.

Examines the crisis created by the growing numbers of death row inmates, and explores three solutions: executions, commutations with continued segregation of these prisoners, and commutations followed by dispersal of the inmates throughout the prison system. Argues that many states will soon enact a life-without-release option.

209. Chessman, Caryl. CELL 2455, DEATH ROW. Englewood Cliffs, N.J.: Prentice-Hall, Inc., 1954.

A description of life on death row and the lives of the condemned men, by the famous California death row inmate who was executed in 1960.

210. Chessman, Caryl. TRIAL BY ORDEAL. Englewood Cliffs, N.J.: Prentice Hall, 1955.

Continues Chessman's account of his life on death row, describing his execution dates, legal battles, and the emotional costs of death row to the prisoners, their attorneys, and their families.

211. Chipman, E. Nelson, Jr. "Indiana Death Penalty: An Exercise in Constitutional Futility." VALPARAISO UNIVERSITY LAW REVIEW 15 (1981): 409-51.

An examination of Indiana's death penalty statute reveals significant defects. The statute fails to provide for proper appellate review, and, more importantly, allows too much prosecutorial discretion in determining eligibility for the death penalty.

212. Christianson, Scott. "Execution by Lethal
Injection." CRIMINAL LAW BULLETIN 15 (1979):
69-78.

Documents the history of the adoption of
lethal injection as a means of execution in
Texas and Oklahoma.

213. Clark, Karen Frances. "Narrowing the Rights
of Future Indigent Criminal Defendants in the
Name of Due Process." MEMPHIS STATE
UNIVERSITY LAW REVIEW 16 (1986): 417-29.

A comment on Ake v. Oklahoma, arguing that
the case should have been decided on an equal
protection ground rather than on due process,
as the former would have been more helpful to
indigent defendants.

214. Clark, Ramsey. "The Death Penalty and
Reverence for Life." Pp. 308-15 in Ramsey
Clark, CRIME IN AMERICA. New York: Simon and
Schuster, 1970.

An explanation of why the author, a former
U.S. Attorney General, is opposed to the
death penalty.

215. Clark, Ramsey. "Rush to Death: Spenkelink's
Last Appeal." THE NATION 229 (October 27,
1979): 385, 400-4.

An account of the flurry of appeals in the 48
hours preceding the execution of John
Spenkelink in Florida in 1979. Spenkelink
was the first man to be executed against his
will in the U.S. since 1967.

216. Clarke, Alan W. "Virginia's Capital Murder
Sentencing Proceeding: A Defense
Perspective." UNIVERSITY OF RICHMOND LAW
REVIEW 18 (1984): 341-59.

An analysis of the role of defense attorneys
in the sentencing phase of capital trials,
with particular relevance to Virginia.
Tactics that can be used in obtaining a life
sentence for the client are discussed.

217.   Cloninger, Dale O. "Deterrence and the Death
        Penalty: A Cross Sectional Analysis."
        JOURNAL OF BEHAVIORAL ECONOMICS 6 (1977):
        87-105.

        Examining 1960 data from 48 states, the
        author finds evidence that supports the
        hypothesis that executions have a deterrent
        effect.

218.   Cohen, Neil P. "Can They Kill Me If I'm
        Gone: Trial in Absentia in Capital Cases."
        UNIVERSITY OF FLORIDA LAW REVIEW 36 (1984):
        273-87.

        Argues that trial in absentia in capital
        cases is probably barred, and not a good
        idea, since if condemned the defendant has no
        incentive not to take other lives.

219.   Cohen, William. "Justice Douglas and the
        Rosenberg Case: Setting the Record Straight."
        CORNELL LAW REVIEW 70 (1985): 211-52.

        Defends Justice Douglas against accusations
        that Douglas was responsible for the Supreme
        Court's refusal to halt the executions of the
        Rosenbergs. Serves as a general overview of
        the role of appellate courts in the Rosenberg
        case.

220.   Cohn, Haim H. "The Penology of the Talmud."
        ISRAEL LAW REVIEW 5 (1970): 53-74.

        A general discussion of punishment, including
        capital punishment, from the perspective of
        Talmudic law.

221.   Colquitt, Joseph A. "The Death Penalty Laws
        of Alabama." ALABAMA LAW REVIEW 33 (1982):
        213-351.

        Describes the Alabama capital statutes passed
        in both 1975 and 1981. The trial of a
        capital case is described. Serves as a
        blueprint for both defense and state
        attorneys handling capital cases in Alabama.

222. Colussi, Joseph A. "The Unconstitutionality of Death Qualifying a Jury Prior to the Determination of Guilt: The Fair Cross-Section Requirement in Capital Cases." CREIGHTON LAW REVIEW 15 (1982): 595-617.

Argues that the states are engaging in the unjustified systematic exclusion of a distinct group by the process of death qualification.

223. Combs, Michael W., and John C. Comer. "Race and Capital Punishment: A Longitudinal Analysis." PHYLON 43 (1982): 350-9.

During the 1960's, blacks were more opposed to the death penalty than whites. This difference still remains, though support for the death penalty has increased among both groups.

224. Conners, Cynthia Swarthout. "The Death Penalty in Military Courts: Constitutionally Imposed?" U.C.L.A. LAW REVIEW 30 (1982): 366-404.

Examines the death penalty provisions in the Uniform Code of Military Justice, which have not been revised since 1950. Argues the provisions are fair and defense-oriented. Some changes are suggested to bring the Code into line with recent Supreme Court decisions.

225. Coody, D.W. "Fifth and Sixth Amendments -- Privilege Against Self Incrimination and Right to Counsel -- Compelled Competency Examinations in Capital Punishment Cases: Estelle v. Smith." AMERICAN JOURNAL OF CRIMINAL LAW 10 (1982): 65-78.

Reviews the Supreme Court's ruling that information gained by a psychiatric interview of a defendant who had not been advised of his right to remain silent could not be used in court.

226. Cook, Earleen H. DEATH PENALTY SINCE WITHERSPOON AND FURMAN. Monticello, Ill.: Vance Bibliographies, 1979.

A useful, though unannotated, 27-page listing of citations to articles and books written on the death penalty between 1968 and 1979.

227. Cooper, David D. THE LESSON OF THE SCAFFOLD: THE PUBLIC EXECUTION CONTROVERSY IN VICTORIAN ENGLAND. Athens, Ohio: Ohio University Press, 1974.

Examines the efforts to abolish public executions in Victorian England, revealing several aspects of popular conduct, fears, and attitudes during the nineteenth century in England. Included is an excellent chapter on the "Bloody Code," the term used to describe the large number of capital offenses in the statutes of England in the seventeenth, eighteenth, and nineteenth centuries.

228. Cortner, Richard C. A SCOTTSBORO CASE IN MISSISSIPPI: THE SUPREME COURT AND BROWN V. MISSISSIPPI. Jackson, Miss.: University Press of Mississippi, 1986.

Describes the arrest, near lynching, trial, and condemnation of three probably innocent black men in Mississippi for the murder of a white man. The case was appealed to the Supreme Court, which ruled that confessions obtained by torture could not be used as a basis for convictions.

229. Cottrol, Robert J. "Static History and Brittle Jurisprudence: Raoul Berger and the Problem of Constitutional Methodology." BOSTON COLLEGE LAW REVIEW 26 (1985): 353-87.

A critique of Berger's work (cited above as item 119). Argues Berger does not have an accurate view of the intent of the Constitution's framers, and that Berger has uncritically accepted his own assumptions about the framers' intent in order to prove his points.

230. Cowan, Claudia L., William C. Thompson, and Phoebe C. Ellsworth. "The Effects of Death Qualification on Jurors' Predisposition to

Convict and on the Quality of Deliberation."
LAW AND HUMAN BEHAVIOR 8 (1984): 53-79.

A videotape of a simulated homicide trial was
shown to 288 subjects. Those who would be
qualified to sit on capital juries because of
their support for the death penalty were more
likely to vote for conviction.

231. Craig, Joel M. "Capital Punishment in North
      Carolina: The 1977 Death Penalty Statute and
      the North Carolina Supreme Court." NORTH
      CAROLINA LAW REVIEW 59 (1981): 911-42.

      Explains the development and content of the
      present North Carolina death penalty statute,
      including the aggravating and mitigating
      circumstances, and how appellate courts have
      interpreted them.

232. Cullen, Francis T., Gregory A. Clark, John B.
      Cullen, and Richard A. Mathews.
      "Attribution, Salience, and Attitudes Toward
      Criminal Sanctioning." CRIMINAL JUSTICE AND
      BEHAVIOR 12 (1985): 305-31.

      Questionnaires were sent to 290 lawyers,
      judges, and community residents. No
      relationship was found between attitude
      toward capital punishment and having been a
      victim of crime.

233. Culver, John H. "The Politics of Capital
      Punishment in California." Pp. 14-26 in
      Stuart Nagel, Erika Fairchild, and Anthony
      Champagne (eds.), THE POLITICAL SCIENCE OF
      CRIMINAL JUSTICE. Springfield, Ill.:
      Charles C. Thomas, 1983.

      A discussion of the legislative,
      gubernatorial, and judicial politics in
      California death penalty decisions. Views of
      Ronald Reagan, George Deukmejian, and Rose
      Bird (among others) are described.

234. Culver, John H. "The States and Capital
      Punishment: Executions From 1977-1984."
      JUSTICE QUARTERLY 2 (1985): 567-78.

      Describes the characteristics of 32 inmates

executed between 1977 and 1984.

235. Curran, William J. "Psychiatric Evaluations
      and Mitigating Circumstances in Capital
      Punishment Sentencing." NEW ENGLAND JOURNAL
      OF MEDICINE 307 (Dec. 2, 1982): 1431-2.

      Discusses Eddings v. Oklahoma, in which the
      Supreme Court ruled that the trial court must
      consider the emotional history of the
      defendant in sentencing.

236. Curran, William J. "Uncertainty in Prognosis
      of Violent Conduct: The Supreme Court Lays
      Down the Law." NEW ENGLAND JOURNAL OF
      MEDICINE 310 (June 21, 1984): 1651-2.

      Criticizes the Supreme Court for allowing
      psychiatrists to testify about the likelihood
      of future dangerousness during the sentencing
      phase of capital trials.

237. Curran, William J., and Ward Casscells. "The
      Ethics of Medical Participation in Capital
      Punishment by Intravenous Drug Injection."
      NEW ENGLAND JOURNAL OF MEDICINE 302 (Jan. 24,
      1980): 226-30.

      Contends that the ethical principles of
      medicine forbid medical participation in
      lethal injection.

238. Dahlstrom, W. Grant, James H. Panton, Kenneth
      P. Bain, and Leona E. Dahlstrom. "Utility of
      Megargee-Bohn MMPI Typological Assignments:
      Study with a Sample of Death Row Inmates."
      CRIMINAL JUSTICE AND BEHAVIOR 13 (1986):
      5-17.

      In 1976, 115 North Carolina death row inmates
      were transferred to the general prison
      population after the Supreme Court
      invalidated the state's capital statute. The
      prisoners were administered the MMPI before
      and after the Court's decision. The findings
      indicated the Megargee-Bohn MMPI measure has
      a high degree of reliability.

239. Dake, Norman P. "Who Deserves to Live? Who
      Deserves to Die? Reflections on Capital

Punishment." CURRENTS IN THEOLOGY AND MISSON
10 (April, 1983): 67-77.

A non-denominational Christian perspective
against the death penalty, written by the
Chaplain of the St. Louis County jail.

240.   Dance, Daryl Cumber. LONG GONE: THE
MECKLENBURG SIX AND THE THEME OF ESCAPE IN
BLACK FOLKLORE. Knoxville: University of
Tennessee Press, 1987.

An account of the escape of six condemned
prisoners in Virginia in 1984, public
reaction to the escape, and the recapture of
all the men, against the background of black
folklore. Describes the executions of James
and Linwood Briley, two of the escapees.

241.   Daniels, Stephen. "Social Science and Death
Penalty Cases: Reflections on Change and the
Empirical Justification of Constitutional
Policy." LAW AND POLICY QUARTERLY (July
1979): 336-72.

Examines the use of social science empirical
data in the justification for declaring the
death penalty unconstitutional. Argues that
these data have played a major role, and that
both sides of the debate used them. The
author concludes, however, that social
science research cannot justify a change in
constitutional policy.

242.   Daniels, William J. "Non Occides: Thurgood
Marshall and the Death Penalty." TEXAS
SOUTHERN LAW REVIEW 4 (1977): 243-60.

Examines Justice Marshall's opinions on the
death penalty and the reasoning behind them.

243.   Darrow, Clarence. ATTORNEY FOR THE DAMNED.
Arthur Weinberg (ed.). New York: Simon and
Schuster, 1957.

A book of speeches and addresses to juries by
the great defense lawyer. Of particular
interest is "The Crime of Compulsion" (pp.
16-88), which is his summary argument in the
Leopold and Loeb case, and "Is Capital

58

Punishment a Wise Policy?" (pp. 89-103),
which reprints the transcript of a 1924
debate in which he answered the question
negatively.

244.   Davidow, Robert P., and George D. Lowe.
"Attitudes of Potential and Present Members
of the Legal Profession Toward Capital
Punishment: A Survey and Analysis."   MERCER
UNIVERSITY LAW REVIEW 30 (1979): 585-614.

Surveyed law students from throughout the
country (N=1081), 50 young Houston attorneys,
and 170 judges. The majority, especially the
students, opposed capital punishment. There
was a strong relationship between region and
political party and the responses.

245.   Davis, Christopher. WAITING FOR IT. New
York: Harper and Row, 1980.

A biography of Georgia death row inmate Troy
Gregg, whose death penalty appeal was denied
by the Supreme Court in 1976, thereby
upholding the Georgia death penalty statute
and the constitutionality of executions
generally.

246.   Davis, David Brion.   "The Movement to Abolish
Capital Punishment in America, 1787-1861."
AMERICAN HISTORICAL REVIEW 63 (1957): 23-46.

An examination of the abolition movement
between the American Revolution and Civil
War, its successes and failures, and the
people whose ideas inspired it.

247.   Davis, Michael.   "Death, Deterrence, and the
Method of Common Sense."   SOCIAL THEORY AND
PRACTICE 7 (1981): 145-77.

A philosophical essay on deterrence. Using
"the method of common sense," the author
concludes that death is the most effective
deterrent.

248.   Davis, Michael.   "Is the Death Penalty
Irrevocable?"   SOCIAL THEORY AND PRACTICE 10
(1984): 143-56.

In part because we cannot return a single day
of imprisonment wrongly served, the author
argues the irrevocability of the death
penalty and the risk of executing the
innocent is not a strong anti-death penalty
argument.

249. Davis, Peggy C. "The Death Penalty and the
Current State of the Law." CRIMINAL LAW
BULLETIN 14 (1978): 7-17.

Discusses recent Supreme Court decisions on
the death penalty and the Court's efforts to
reduce arbitrariness in death sentencing.

250. Davis, Peggy C. "Texas Capital Sentencing
Procedures: The Role of the Jury and the
Restraining Hand of the Expert." JOURNAL OF
CRIMINAL LAW AND CRIMINOLOGY 69 (1978):
300-10.

Reviews the Texas death penalty statute,
criticizing it for several reasons,
particularly because it allows psychiatrists
to have a major role in assessing future
dangerousness.

251. Dawson, Patrick A., and J. David Putnal.
"Ford v. Wainwright: Eighth Amendment
Prohibits Execution of the Insane." MERCER
LAW REVIEW 38 (1987): 949-68.

An examination of the issue of competence for
execution in both legal philosophy and in
Supreme Court decisions, in the context of a
summary and review of the Ford decision.

252. Dayan, Marshall. "Payment of Costs in Death
Penalty Cases." CRIMINAL LAW BULLETIN 22
(1986): 18-28.

This article discusses the shortage of
qualified attorneys who volunteer to
represent death row inmates. The commitment
involved in taking such cases is described,
as are various approaches that have been
suggested to address this problem.

253. Decker, Scott H., and Carol W. Kohfeld. "A
Deterrence Study of the Death Penalty in

Illinois, 1933-1980." JOURNAL OF CRIMINAL JUSTICE 12 (1984): 367-77.

Focusing on Illinois, the authors find no deterrent effect of the death penalty on homicide rates.

254. Delahanty, Mary Lou. "Constitutional Infirmities of the Capital Punishment Act." SEATON HILL LAW REVIEW 13 (1983): 515-48.

Examines the 1982 New Jersey capital punishment statute. After reviewing the constitutional framework for capital punishment statutes, concludes the statute's inability to deter homicide, among other things, makes it unconstitutional.

255. Deparle, Jason. "Louisiana Diarist: Killing Folks." THE NEW REPUBLIC 190 (Jan. 30, 1984): 43.

The author describes his feelings after watching Robert Wayne Williams die in the Louisiana electric chair in 1983 and attending his funeral.

256. Deparle, Jason. "Executions Aren't News." WASHINGTON MONTHLY 18 (Feb., 1986): 12-21.

After witnessing an execution, talking with death row inmates, and visiting with the families of murder victims, the author explains why he is opposed to the death penalty.

257. Devine, Edward, Marc Feldman, Lisa Giles-Klein, Cheryl A. Ingram, and Robert F. Williams. "Special Project: The Constitutionality of the Death Penalty in New Jersey." RUTGERS LAW JOURNAL 15 (1984): 261-397.

Outlines the history and status of the death penalty in New Jersey. Argues the current statute may be in violation of the state constitution. Finds inappropriate prosecutorial discretion, argues the process of jury death qualification violates the defendant's rights, and suggests that the

state has not documented a compelling need to
resume executions.

258. Devine, Philip E. THE ETHICS OF HOMICIDE.
Ithaca, New York: Cornell University Press,
1978.

Examines the moral rules against homicide,
their logic, and the arguments that support
exceptions to these rules. Includes
discussions of abortion, capital punishment,
euthanasia, suicide, and war.

259. DeVries, Brian, and Lawrence J. Walker.
"Moral Reasoning and Attitudes Toward Capital
Punishment." DEVELOPMENTAL PSYCHOLOGY 22
(1986) 509-13.

Applies Kohlberg's theory of moral
development (see item 526 below) to capital
punishment. Examining the attitudes of 72
university students, the authors find that
individuals at higher moral stages tend to
oppose capital punishment.

260. Diamond, Bernard L. "Murder and the Death
Penalty: A Case Report." AMERICAN JOURNAL OF
ORTHOPSYCHIATRY 45 (1975): 712-22. Reprinted
in Bedau and Pierce, 1976, cited above as
item 110.

Reports on the examination of a California
convict in 1959, shortly before his
execution, who said he committed three
murders just so he could die in the gas
chamber. The defendant pled guilty to his
crimes, and attempted to prevent appeals and
a clemency investigation in his case.

261. Dike, Sarah T. CAPITAL PUNISHMENT IN THE
UNITED STATES: A CONSIDERATION OF THE
EVIDENCE. Hackensack, N.J.: National Council
on Crime and Delinquency, 1982.

Originally published in 1981 as three review
articles in CRIMINAL JUSTICE ABSTRACTS, this
work is a comprehensive overview of the major
issues in contemporary death penalty debates.
Included are well-documented discussions of
history, the abolitionist movement, pre-

Furman judicial opinions, the Furman and
Coker cases, post-Furman statutes,
deterrence, discrimination, attempts to guide
prosecutorial discretion and judicial
decisions, and public attitudes.

262. Dikijian, Armine. "Capital Punishment: A
Selected Bibliography, 1940-1968." CRIME AND
DELINQUENCY 15 (1969): 162-4.

Lists 38 books and 20 articles published over
the preceding 28 years.

263. Dillon, Richard G. "Capital Punishment in
Egalitarian Society: The Meta' Case."
JOURNAL OF ANTHROPOLOGICAL RESEARCH 36
(1980): 437-52.

An anthropological study of the use of
capital punishment by the Meta', an
egalitarian society in Cameroon (West
Africa).

264. DiSalle, Michael V. "Comments on Capital
Punishment and Clemency." OHIO STATE LAW
JOURNAL 25 (1964): 71-83.

Outlines the reasons why the author, a former
Governor of Ohio, opposes the death penalty.
The Ohio rules for clemency are reviewed, and
examples of commuted death sentences are
given.

265. DiSalle, Michael V. THE POWER OF LIFE OR
DEATH. New York: Random House, 1965.

Written by a former Governor of Ohio, this
book describes his struggles with the death
penalty and the power to grant clemency while
he was in office, and the reasons why he so
strongly believes the death penalty should be
abolished.

266. Dix, George E. "The Death Penalty,
'Dangerousness,' Psychiatric Testimony, and
Professional Ethics." AMERICAN JOURNAL OF
CRIMINAL LAW 5 (1977): 151-224.

Examines a Texas case in which the author
believes professional ethics were violated by

a psychiatrist's testimony, and the failure
of appellate courts to challenge this
testimony. The author attempts to develop
ethical standards for acceptable expert
testimony in capital cases.

267. Dix, George E. "Administration of the Texas
Death Penalty Statutes: Constitutional
Infirmities Related to the Prediction of
Dangerousness." TEXAS LAW REVIEW 55 (1977):
1343-414.

A crucial element of the Texas death penalty
statute is the determination of whether the
offender will be "dangerous." This article
examines the problems involved in making that
assessment and the constitutional questions
it raises. The author concludes that the
practice violates constitutional protections.

268. Dix, George E. "Participation by Mental
Health Professionals in Capital Murder
Sentencing." INTERNATIONAL JOURNAL OF LAW
AND PSYCHIATRY 1 (1978): 283-308.

Examines efforts to individualize capital
sentencing decisions, with specific attention
to the role of mental health professionals in
the decisions. The statutes of Texas, Ohio,
and Arizona are specifically discussed.

269. Dix, George E. "Appellate Review of the
Decision to Impose Death." GEORGETOWN LAW
JOURNAL 68 (1979): 97-161.

An analysis of appellate decisions in death
penalty cases in Florida, Georgia, and Texas.
Concludes that, in all three states, the
appellate reviews have failed to achieve
their goal of ensuring consistency in
sentencing.

270. Dix, George E. "Constitutional Validity of
the Texas Capital Murder Scheme: A Continuing
Question." TEXAS BAR JOURNAL 43 (1980):
627-34.

Examines several issues relating to the Texas
death penalty statute, including the
admissibility of mitigating evidence and

appellate review. Figures on the number of cases reversed by the Court of Criminal Appeal are given.

271. Dix, George E. "Expert Prediction Testimony in Capital Sentencing: Evidentiary and Constitutional Consideration." AMERICAN CRIMINAL LAW REVIEW 19 (1981): 1-48.

Because of the inaccuracy of psychiatric predictions of dangerousness, the author concludes the use of such predictions in capital trials is unconstitutional.

272. Dix, George E. "A Legal Perspective on Dangerousness: Current Status." PSYCHIATRIC ANNALS 13 (1983): 243+.

A brief overview of the concept of dangerousness, its ambiguities, and the uncritical assumption in legal proceedings that dangerousness can be accurately predicted.

273. Dix, George E. "Psychological Abnormality and Capital Sentencing: The New 'Diminished Responsibility'." INTERNATIONAL JOURNAL OF LAW AND PSYCHIATRY 7 (1984): 249-67.

The mental status of the defendant is a factor in capital sentencing. Consideration of this factor presents a unique area of law by defining partial or diminished responsibility. This paper reviews the concept of diminished responsibility and its use in capital sentencing.

274. Dolinko, David. "Foreward: How to Criticize the Death Penalty." JOURNAL OF CRIMINAL LAW AND CRIMINOLOGY 77 (1986): 546-601.

Reviews procedural and substantive (moral) attacks on capital punishment. Argues that most contemporary challenges to the death penalty fail because they rest only on procedural grounds, sidestepping the underlying moral issues.

275. Donnelly, Samuel J.M. "A Theory of Justice, Judicial Methodology, and the

Constitutionality of Capital Punishment:
Rawls, Dworkin, and a Theory of Criminal
Responsibility." SYRACUSE LAW REVIEW 29
(1978): 1109-74.

Relates the theories of Rawls and Dworkin on
rights and justice to legal decisions on
capital punishment.

276. Donohue, John J. III. "Godfrey v. Georgia:
Creative Federalism, the Eighth Amendment,
and the Evolving Law of Death." CATHOLIC
UNIVERSITY LAW REVIEW 30 (1980): 13-64.

Criticizes the Supreme Court's decision in
Godfrey, and the Georgia Supreme Court's
response to the decision, because both Courts
seem to be allowing arbitrariness in death
sentencing.

277. Dorin, Dennis D. "Two Different Worlds:
Criminologists, Justices and Racial
Discrimination in the Imposition of Capital
Punishment in Rape Cases." JOURNAL OF
CRIMINAL LAW AND CRIMINOLOGY 72 (1982):
1667-98.

Discusses the 1977 ruling in which the
Supreme Court abolished the death penalty for
rape. Suprisingly, the Court did so with
only brief reference to the research that had
shown the death penalty for rape to be
discriminatorily applied. Grounds the
discussion in a general treatment of the role
of social science research in influencing
judicial decisions, and suggests ways of
improving communication between judges and
social scientists.

278. Dorin, Dennis D. "A Case Study of the Misuse
of Social Science in Capital Punishment
Cases: The Massachusetts Supreme Judicial
Court's Findings of Racial Discrimination in
Watson (1980)." In Haas and Inciardi, 1988,
cited below as item 413.

Criticizes the Massachusetts decision that
struck the state's death penalty law because
of a fear that the law would lead to
discriminatory sentencing, despite no

empirical documentation of such racism in the state.

279. Dorius, Earl F. "Personal Recollections of the Gary Gilmore Case." WOODROW WILSON JOURNAL OF LAW 3 (1981): 49-129.

An account in the form of a diary of the various events preceding the Utah execution of Gary Gilmore (1977), written by a Utah Assistant Attorney General who was one of the main attorneys for the state in the case.

280. Drahozal, Christopher R. "Wainwright v. Witt and Death-Qualified Juries: A Changed Standard But an Unchanged Result." IOWA LAW REVIEW 71 (1986): 1187-208.

Analyses the Witt decision and strongly criticizes the Court for making easier the exclusion of anti-death penalty citizens from service on capital juries. Concludes, however, that the impact of this decision will not be great, as the jurors it excuses would probably have been removed anyway by prosecutorial peremptory challenges.

281. Draper, Thomas (ed.). CAPITAL PUNISHMENT. New York: W.H. Wilson, 1985 (The Reference Shelf, Vol. 57, No. 2).

A collection of essays, mostly from the popular press, that cover different aspects of the death penalty debate. Includes several essays that discuss lethal injection.

282. Dreiser, Theodore. AN AMERICAN TRAGEDY. Cleveland: World Publishing Co., 1953.

This novel, loosely based on an actual case (Chester Gillette), describes the crime, trial, condemnation, and execution of a young man in New York. Contains excellent descriptions of death row and the experiences of the victim's and defendant's families.

283. Dressler, Joshua. "The Jurisprudence of Death by Another: Accessories and Capital Punishment." UNIVERSITY OF COLORADO LAW REVIEW 51 (1979): 17-75.

Can the death penalty be imposed on those who
assist in but do not perpetrate murders? The
author argues that this is constitutionally
permissible only in some cases--where the
accessory actually causes the killing to
occur. The author also reports data on all
executions, 1935-71, broken down by whether
the case was appealed and the role (i.e.,
perpetrator or accessory) of the defendant in
the crime.

284. Drinan, Robert F., S.J. "The State and
      Insane Condemned Criminals." JURIST 12
      (1952): 92-6.

      An argument against executing the insane, by
      a lawyer-priest who later was elected to
      Congress from Massachusetts.

285. Duff, Charles. A HANDBOOK ON HANGING.
      London: Putnam, 1928.

      This famous little book was written
      ostensibly to praise the art of hanging but
      is really a satire of the pro-death penalty
      position.

286. Duffy, Clinton T., with A. Hirshberg. 88 MEN
      AND 2 WOMEN. New York: Doubleday, 1962.

      The accounts of 90 executions presided over
      by the author while he was warden at San
      Quentin, and a powerful abolitionist's
      perspective on capital punishment.

287. Edison, Michael. "The Empirical Assault on
      Capital Punishment." JOURNAL OF LEGAL
      EDUCATION 23 (1971): 2-15.

      The author reviews the literature on the
      effects of death qualification on jury
      behavior, and describes a study being done on
      this issue for the NAACP Legal Defense Fund.

288. Ehrhardt, Charles W., and L. Harold Levinson.
      "Florida's Legislative Response to Furman:
      An Exercise in Futility?" JOURNAL OF
      CRIMINAL LAW AND CRIMINOLOGY 64 (1973):
      10-21.

An excellent summary of the judicial,
legislative, and gubernatorial reactions to
Furman in Florida, and description of how
Florida became the first state after _Furman_
to reenact the death penalty.

289.   Ehrhardt, Charles W., Philip A. Hubbart, L.
Harold Levinson, William McKinley Smiley,
Jr., and Thomas A. Wills. "The Future of
Capital Punishment in Florida: Analysis and
Recommendations." JOURNAL OF CRIMINAL LAW
AND CRIMINOLOGY 64 (1973): 2-10.

Examines the constitutionality of the Florida
death penalty statute enacted in 1972.
Predicts the provision in the law allowing a
judge to impose death over a jury's vote for
life will be found unconstitutional.

290.   Ehrlich, Isaac. "Deterrence: Evidence and
Inference." YALE LAW JOURNAL 85 (1975):
209-27.

An answer to the criticisms of his work
offered by Baldus and Cole (see item 60
above) and, especially, Bowers and Pierce
(see item 160 above). Argues that Bowers and
Pierce misinterpret his framework, and that
his original conclusions, though "tentative
and inconclusive," still stand.

291.   Ehrlich, Isaac. "The Deterrent Effect of
Capital Punishment: A Question of Life and
Death." AMERICAN ECONOMIC REVIEW 65 (1975):
397-417.

An important and controversial analysis of
American homicides, 1933-67, which finds that
each execution reduces the number of expected
homicides by eight.

292.   Ehrlich, Isaac. "Rejoinder." YALE LAW
JOURNAL 85 (1975): 368-9.

A comment on the remarks of Peck, cited below
as item 684.

293.   Ehrlich, Isaac. "Capital Punishment and
Deterrence: Some Further Thoughts and

Additional Evidence." JOURNAL OF POLITICAL
ECONOMY 85 (1977): 741-88.

Examines cross-sectional patterns of murders
and executions in the U.S. in 1940 and 1950,
and finds support for deterrence theory.

294. Ehrlich, Isaac. "Of Positive Methodology,
Ethics, and Polemics in Deterrence Research."
BRITISH JOURNAL OF CRIMINOLOGY 22 (1982):
124-39.

A response to the paper by Beleveld, cited as
item 132 above.

295. Ehrlich, Isaac, and Joel C. Gibbons. "On the
Measurement of the Deterrent Effect of
Capital Punishment and the Theory of
Deterrence." JOURNAL OF LEGAL STUDIES 6
(1977): 35-50.

Accuses Passel and Taylor, in a paper cited
below as item 677, of seriously flawed
reasoning when they concluded that Ehrlich's
data actually show that executions increase,
rather than decrease, homicide rates.

296. Ehrlich, Isaac, and Randall Mark. "Fear of
Deterrence: A Critical Evaluation of the
'Report of the Panel on Research on Deterrent
and Incapacitative Effects.'" JOURNAL OF
LEGAL STUDIES 6 (1977): 293-316.

A response to (and strong criticism of) the
critique of Ehrlich's work prepared by a
panel that was appointed by the National
Academy of Sciences (item 511 below).

297. Ehrmann, Herbert B. THE CASE THAT WILL NOT
DIE: COMMONWEALTH VS. SACCO AND VANZETTI.
Boston: Little Brown, 1969.

An overview of the case of Sacco and Vanzetti
and their execution in 1927 for a crime they
did not commit, written by one of their
attorneys.

298. Ehrmann, Sara R. "For Whom the Chair Waits."
FEDERAL PROBATION 26 (1962): 14-25.

An overview of the risks of executing the innocent and the insane. Argues that only the poor and friendless are executed, and that murderers would pose no threat if their death sentences were commuted. Argues that those convicted of murder do well on parole.

299.   Elliot, Robert G. AGENT OF DEATH: THE MEMOIRS OF AN EXECUTIONER. New York: Dutton, 1940.

An autobiography and statement against the death penalty by the man who carried out executions in the electric chair in New York (and some other states) for the first third of the twentieth century.

300.   Ellis, Harvey D., Jr. "Constitutional Law: The Death Penalty: A Critique of the Philosophical Bases Held to Satisfy the Eighth Amendment Requirements for its Justification." OKLAHOMA LAW REVIEW 34 (1981): 567-613.

An examination of Gregg v. Georgia, arguing the U.S. Supreme Court distorted the views of different schools of thought on the question of how punishments can be justified. The positions of the members of the Court in Gregg are described and critiqued. The author argues that the only legitimate justification for the death penalty is incapacitation.

301.   Ellison, W. James. "State Executions for Juveniles: Defining 'Youth' as a Mitigating Factor for Imposing a Sentence of Less than Death." LAW AND PSYCHOLOGY REVIEW 11 (1987): 1-38.

Examines the constitutional significance of "youth" as a mitigating factor in death penalty cases. Examines the issue in common law and current state laws. The principal justifications for sentencing youth to death are reviewed and examined, and the concept of "egocentrism" is developed and applied as a mitigating factor.

302.   Elliston, Frederick A. "Deadly Force and

Capital Punishment: A Comparative Appraisal."
Pp. 153-67 in William C. Heffernan and
Timothy Stroup (eds.), ETHICS: HARD CHOICES
IN LAW ENFORCEMENT. New York: John Jay
Press, 1985.

Argues the same principles used to justify
capital punishment can be used in studying
the question of when police can be justified
in using deadly force.

303.   Ellsworth, Phoebe C.   "Juries on Trial."
PSYCHOLOGY TODAY 19 (July 1985): 44-6.

Reviews recent research that indicates those
who support the death penalty are more likely
than abolitionists to find the defendant
guilty.

304.   Ellsworth, Phoebe C.   "Unpleasant Facts: The
Supreme Court's Response to Empirical
Research on Capital Punishment."   In Haas and
Inciardi, 1988, cited below as item 413.

Discusses the refusal of the Supreme Court to
acknowledge the validity of social science
research done on deterrence, racial
discrimination, and the fairness of juries in
capital cases.   In particular, the author
criticizes the decision in Lockhart v.
McCree.

305.   Ellsworth, Phoebe C., and Lee Ross.   "Public
Opinion and Judicial Decision Making: An
Example from Research on Capital Punishment."
Pp. 152-171 in Bedau and Pierce, 1976, cited
above as item 110.

A reflective essay intended for psychologists
who want to do research that might influence
legal decisions.   How to formulate research
questions, choose an audience, collect data
of use to that audience, and avoid bias are
among the questions explored.   A 4-page
questionnaire surveying attitudes about
capital punishment is included.

306.   Ellsworth, Phoebe C., and Lee Ross.   "Public
Opinion and Capital Punishment: A Close
Examination of the Views of Abolitionists and

Retentionists." CRIME AND DELINQUENCY 29
(1983): 116-69.

A survey designed to measure the attitudinal
and informational basis for beliefs about the
death penalty was administered to 500
respondents in California. While most knew
little about the death penalty, few indicated
that their positions on it would change if
their beliefs about deterrence were
incorrect. Opinions are found to stem more
from general values than from specific
reasoning.

307. Ellsworth, Phoebe C., Raymond M. Bukaty,
Claudia L. Cowan, and William C. Thompson.
"The Death Qualified Jury and the Defense of
Insanity." LAW AND HUMAN BEHAVIOR 8 (1984):
81-93.

Subjects (N=35) were classified as death
qualified or excludable jurors, and read four
summaries of cases in which defendants
entered a plea of insanity. In the two cases
involving schizophrenia, the death qualified
jurors were more likely to vote for guilt.
In the other two cases (involving organic
problems), there were no differences in the
voting patterns.

308. Endres, Michael E. THE MORALITY OF CAPITAL
PUNISHMENT: EQUAL JUSTICE UNDER LAW? Mystic,
Conn.: Twenty-Third Publications, 1985.

A moral and legal argument against the death
penalty, arguing that the punishment serves
no valid purpose and is unfairly applied.

309. England, Jane C. "Capital Punishment in the
Light of Constitutional Evolution: An
Analysis of Distinctions between Furman and
Gregg." NOTRE DAME LAWYER 52 (April, 1977):
596-610.

Discusses the views of the Supreme Court
Justices articulated in the Furman and Gregg
decisions.

310. Erdahl, Lowell O. PRO-LIFE/PRO-PEACE: LIFE-
AFFIRMING ALTERNATIVES TO ABORTION, WAR,

MERCY KILLING, AND THE DEATH PENALTY.
Minneapolis: Augsburg Publishing House,
1986.

Written by a Lutheran bishop, this book calls
for a consistent, pro-life Christian ethic on
all of these issues.

311. Erez, Edna. "Thou Shalt not Execute: Hebrew
Law Perspective on Capital Punishment."
CRIMINOLOGY 19 (1981): 25-43.

Discusses historical developments in Hebrew
law regarding capital punishment, and various
legal and moral requirements that make the
imposition of the death penalty nearly
impossible.

312. Erickson, Maynard L., and Jack P. Gibbs.
"The Deterrence Question: Some Alternative
Methods of Analysis." SOCIAL SCIENCE
QUARTERLY 54 (1973): 534-51.

Argues that the deterrence hypothesis has
been prematurely dismissed. Data are
presented for all states for 1960 on the
severity and certainty of imprisonment for
homicide (any possible effect of the death
penalty is not taken into account). It is
concluded that the relationship between
severity of imprisonment and homicide rates
is contingent upon the certainty of
punishment.

313. Erskine, Hazel. "The Polls: Capital
Punishment." PUBLIC OPINION QUARTERLY 34
(1970): 290-307.

Summarizes several major public opinion polls
on capital punishment taken since 1936,
documenting a sharp decline in support.

314. Eshelman, Byron, with Frank Riley. DEATH ROW
CHAPLAIN. Englewood Cliffs: Prentice Hall,
1962.

The author was chaplain at San Quentin
Prison, and provides an eyewitness account of
life on death row, executions, and a critical
analysis of the death penalty.

315. Espy, M. Watt, Jr. "Capital Punishment and
      Deterrence: What the Statistics Cannot Show."
      CRIME AND DELINQUENCY 26 (1980): 537-44.

      Gives examples of executions in American
      history that took the lives of those who
      should have been deterred, such as police
      officers, relatives of other condemned
      inmates, and persons who had previously
      witnessed an execution.

316. Espy, M. Watt, Jr. "The Historical Per-
      spective." In Magee, 1980, cited below as
      item 585, pp. 163-74.

      A paper originally published in CRISIS AND
      CHRISTIANITY. Describes the author's work in
      documenting the history of executions in
      America. Case examples of executing the
      insane, the innocent, and those who should
      have been deterred are given.

317. Espy, M. Watt, Jr. "Executions Under State
      Authority: An Inventory." In Bowers, 1984
      (cited above as item 159), pp. 395-525.

      Originally compiled by Negley Teeters and
      Charles Zibulka (and published in Bowers,
      1974, cited as item 159 above), and updated
      and corrected by Espy, this list gives the
      names, counties, and dates of execution of
      every person put to death under state
      authority since 1864.

318. Ewing, Charles P. "Psychologists and
      Psychiatrists in Capital Sentencing: Experts
      or Executioners?" SOCIAL ACTION AND THE LAW 8
      (1982): 67-70.

      Reviews the literature on the validity of
      predictions of dangerousness, and concludes
      that such predictions are inaccurate. Argues
      that such predictions violate ethical
      principles.

319. Ewing, Charles P. "'Dr. Death' and the Case
      for an Ethical Ban on Psychiatric and
      Psychological Predictions of Dangerousness in
      Capital Sentencing Proceedings." AMERICAN

JOURNAL OF LAW AND MEDICINE 8 (1983): 407-28.

Examines the reliability of psychiatric
predictions of dangerousness and their
current use in death penalty cases, and
condemns their use on the grounds of
professional ethics.

320. Ewing, Charles P. "Diagnosing and Treating
'Insanity' on Death Row: Legal and Ethical
Perspectives." BEHAVIORAL SCIENCES AND THE
LAW 5 (1987): 175-85.

A discussion of whether mental health
professionals can meet both legal and ethical
demands by diagnosing and treating insane
inmates on death row. After reviewing the
laws and procedures, the author argues that
any participation violates the ethical norms
of the profession.

321. Exum, James G., Jr. "The Death Penalty in
North Carolina." CAMPBELL LAW REVIEW 8
(1985): 1-28.

The author is an Associate Justice of the
North Carolina Supreme Court and heads a
committee established by the American Bar
Association to study the costs of the death
penalty. The Judge voted against the death
penalty while a member of the state
legislature, but does not believe that the
punishment is unconstitutional. In this
article, he reviews how the death penalty
functions in North Carolina.

322. Fagan, Ronald W. "Police Attitudes Toward
Capital Punishment." JOURNAL OF POLICE
SCIENCE ADMINISTRATION 14 (1986): 193-201.

In a survey of 78 police officers in
Washington State, it was found that 85
percent "strongly favor" and an additional 9
percent "favor" capital punishment.

323. Farmer, Millard C. "Jury Composition
Challenges." LAW AND PSYCHOLOGY REVIEW 2
(1976): 43-74.

An examination of the difficulty of selecting

a fair jury in capital cases. Law and
controversies pertaining to jury selection
are reviewed, as are some of the practical
aspects of challenging a list of prospective
jurors.

324. Farris, Kelton. "Statistical Evidence of
Discrimination in Eleventh Circuit Death
Penalty Appeal: Will Spinkellink Ever Die?"
STETSON LAW REVIEW 15 (1986): 489-514.

An examination of the McCleskey case in the
Eleventh Circuit, and comparison to an
earlier, similar attempt to prove racial bias
by John Spenkelink (whose name is frequently
misspelled, even in the court records of his
case).

325. Fattah, Ezzat A. "The Canadian Experiment
with Abolition of the Death Penalty." In
Bowers, 1974, (cited above as item 156), pp.
121-35.

Examines crime statistics in Canada since the
last execution there in 1962, and finds no
support for the contention that abolition
would lead to an increase in homicides.

326. Fattah, Ezzat A. "Perceptions of Violence,
Concern about Crime, Fear of Victimization
and Attitudes to the Death Penalty."
CANADIAN JOURNAL OF CRIMINOLOGY 21 (1979):
22-38.

Are high levels of violent crime, growing
concern about crime, and fears of
victimization correlated with support for the
death penalty? By examining Gallup Poll
data, the author answers these questions
negatively. He instead posits that support
for the death penalty arises from personality
characteristics.

327. Fattah, Ezzat A. "Is Capital Punishment a
Unique Deterrent? A Dispassionate Review of
Old and New Evidence." CANADIAN JOURNAL OF
CRIMINOLOGY 23 (1981): 291-311.

A review of the major issues and empirical
evidence in deterrence research, from which

the author concludes that there is no support
for the deterrence hypothesis.

328. Fattah, Ezzat A. "Canada's Successful
      Experience with the Abolition of the Death
      Penalty." CANADIAN JOURNAL OF CRIMINOLOGY 25
      (1983): 421-31.

      Canada's last hanging was in 1962 and the
      country formally abolished the death penalty
      in 1976. A history of the abolition movement
      is presented, and the predictions of the
      retentionists are reviewed and shown to be
      erroneous. Neither police killings nor
      general homicide rates have increased since
      abolition.

329. Finch, Michael, and Mara Ferraro. "The
      Empirical Challenge to Death Qualified
      Juries: On Further Examination." NEBRASKA
      LAW REVIEW 65 (1986): 21-74.

      Examines the research on the effects of
      excluding those who oppose the death penalty
      from capital juries. Argues there is no
      compelling reason for death qualification,
      and on that basis alone it should not be
      permitted. Shows how death qualified jurors
      are attitudinally and demographically (on
      race and sex) different from other jurors.

330. Finks, Thomas O. "Lethal Injection: An
      Uneasy Alliance of Law and Medicine."
      JOURNAL OF LEGAL MEDICINE 4 (1983): 383-403.

      Examines the problems in medical ethics
      associated with lethal injection. Describes
      the gubernatorial veto of a bill in Illinois
      that would have adopted lethal injection.

331. Fisher, Jim. THE LINDBERGH CASE. New
      Brunswick: Rutgers University Press, 1987.

      An examination of the kidnapping of the
      Lindbergh baby and the 1936 execution of
      Bruno Richard Hauptmann, written from the
      perspective of the New Jersey State Police,
      arguing that Hauptmann was guilty as charged.

332. Fitzgerald, Robert C., and Phoebe C.

Ellsworth. "Due Process vs. Crime Control: Death Qualification and Jury Attitudes." LAW AND HUMAN BEHAVIOR 8 (1984): 31-51.

Reviews previous research on juror attitudes to the death penalty and to the guilt of the defendant. Also surveys 811 eligible jurors in Alameda County, California, and finds that 17.2 percent stated they could be fair in determining guilt, but would never impose a death sentence. Those who would be excluded from capital juries were more likely to be black, female, and less favorable to the prosecution.

333. Fogelson, Robert M. (Advisory Editor). CAPITAL PUNISHMENT: NINETEENTH CENTURY ARGUMENTS. New York: Arno Press (Criminal Justice in America Series), 1974.

A collection of nineteenth century reports made in the Massachusetts House and Senate on the subject of capital punishment.

334. Foley, Linda A. "Florida After the Furman Decision: The Effect of Extralegal Factors on the Processing of Capital Offense Cases." BEHAVIORAL SCIENCES AND THE LAW 5 (1987): 457-65.

Data from 829 Florida murder cases, 1972-78, are examined. Defendant's age and gender, victim's race, and the county of trial are all found to predict trial outcome, degree of murder convicted of, and the imposition of the death penalty.

335. Foley, Linda A., and Richard S. Powell. "The Discretion of Prosecutors, Judges, and Juries in Capital Cases." CRIMINAL JUSTICE REVIEW 7 (1982): 16-22.

Examines 829 cases involving first-degree murder indictments in Florida, 1972-78. Concludes that prosecutors, judges, and jurors are all influenced by the gender of the defendant, and judges are influenced by the race of the victim.

336. Fong, Ivan K. "Ineffective Assistance of

Counsel at Capital Sentencing." STANFORD LAW
REVIEW 39 (1987): 461-97.

A discussion of procedural safeguards at
capital sentencing, and an argument that
Strickland v. Washington fails to ensure that
capital defendants will receive adequate
counsel at sentencing.

337.   Forst, Brian E.   "The Deterrent Effect of
Capital Punishment: A Cross-State Analysis of
the 1960's." MINNESOTA LAW REVIEW 61 (1977):
743-67.

Discusses the strengths and weaknesses of
time-series and cross-sectional approaches to
the deterrence question, evaluates Ehrlich's
research, and proposes a new approach.
Examines state-by-state changes in the
homicide rate between 1960 and 1970, and
concludes that the death penalty does not add
any deterrent effects over and above the
effects exerted by imprisonment.

338.   Forst, Brian E.   "Capital Punishment and
Deterrence: Conflicting Evidence?" JOURNAL OF
CRIMINAL LAW AND CRIMINOLOGY 74 (1983):
927-42.

Examines recent work that has found a
deterrent effect of executions and the
criticisms of that work. Analyzes data on
homicides and the death penalty for
retentionist and abolitionist states for 1960
and 1970. Several different approaches to
the data fail to find any support for the
argument that the death penalty is superior
to long imprisonment in its deterrent
effects.

339.   Forster, George.   "Resurrection of the Death
Penalty: The Validity of Arizona's Response
to Furman v. Georgia." ARIZONA STATE LAW
JOURNAL 1974 (1974): 257-96.

An examination of the new Arizona death
penalty statute. Concludes, in part because
of the ambiguity of its aggravating and
mitigating circumstances, that the statute is
unconstitutional.

340. Fortas, Abe.   "The Case Against Capital
     Punishment."   THE NEW YORK TIMES MAGAZINE
     (January 23, 1977): 8-9+.

     Written shortly after Gary Gilmore's
     execution, this article, by a former
     Associate Justice of the U.S. Supreme Court,
     outlines the reasons why he opposes the death
     penalty.

341. Fox, James Alan.   "The Identification and
     Estimation of Deterrence: An Evaluation of
     Yunker's Model."   JOURNAL OF BEHAVIORAL
     ECONOMICS 6 (1977): 225-242.

     A critique of the work of James Yunker on
     capital punishment, cited below in item 945.

342. Fox, James Alan.   "Persistent Flaws in
     Econometric Studies of the Death Penalty: A
     Discussion of Layson's Findings."   Testimony
     before the Subcommittee on Criminal Justice,
     U.S. House of Representatives, May 7, 1986
     (Printed at pp. 334-47 of item 961 below).

     Identifies a host of problems in the work of
     Stephen Layson (cited below as item 543),
     including measurement error, aggregation
     bias, temporal shifts, and causal ambiguity.

343. Frankel, David S.   "The Constitutionality of
     the Mandatory Death Penalty for Life-Term
     Prisoners Who Murder."   NEW YORK UNIVERSITY
     LAW REVIEW 55 (1980): 636-70.

     Argues that a mandatory death sentence for
     murders by inmates already serving a life
     term invites the admission of arbitrariness
     into sentencing decisions, as it may affect
     the willingness of juries to convict.

344. Frankfurter, Felix.   OF LAW AND MEN.   New
     York: Harcourt, 1956.

     A collection of papers by the late Supreme
     Court Justice.   Includes his 1950 statement,
     "The Problem of Capital Punishment," which he
     presented as a witness before the Royal
     Commission on Capital Punishment in London.

In this essay, he states his personal
opposition to the death penalty.

345. Frankfurter, Marion Denman, and Gardner
Jackson (eds.). THE LETTERS OF SACCO AND
VANZETTI. New York: Octagon Books, 1971.

A collection of letters written by Sacco and
Vanzetti while in prison. Includes speeches
the men made in court and accounts of their
final visits and executions.

346. Freeman, M.D.A. "Retributivism and the Death
Sentence." Pp. 405-22 in M.A. Stewart (ed.),
LAW, MORALITY, AND RIGHTS. Dordrecht,
Holland: Reidel, 1983.

A discussion of the history and concepts of
retribution in philosophical literature.
Argues that retributivism always has limits,
and that it cannot justify the death penalty.

347. French, Lawrence A. "Blacks and Capital
Punishment: An Assessment of Latent
Discriminatory Justice in the United States."
JOURNAL OF SOCIOLOGY AND SOCIAL WELFARE 6
(1979): 231-44.

A general overview of discriminatory use of
the death penalty, particularly in North
Carolina, arguing that the Supreme Court
should acknowledge the latent discrimination
that typifies the system.

348. French, Lawrence A. "Boundary Maintenance
and Capital Punishment: A Sociological
Perspective." BEHAVIORAL SCIENCES AND THE
LAW 5 (1987): 423-32.

After observing that there are major regional
differences (South/non-South) in executions
and in racial bias in executions, the author
develops a societal reaction/boundary
maintenance model to explain these
differences.

349. Friedlander, Robert A. "Punishing
Terrorists: A Modest Proposal." OHIO
NORTHERN UNIVERSITY LAW REVIEW 13 (1986):
149-55.

Calls for public executions of terrorists.

350. Friedlander, Robert A. "Socrates was Right: Propositions in Support of Capital Punishment." NEW ENGLAND JOURNAL ON CRIMINAL AND CIVIL CONFINEMENT 13 (1987): 1-9.

A discussion of the U.S. Justice Department's efforts in 1987 to authorize death sentences by administrative action through the U.S. Sentencing Commission, and a general argument that capital punishment is necessary and desirable.

351. Friedman, Lee S. "The Use of Multiple Regression Analysis to Test for a Deterrent Effect of Capital Punishment: Prospects and Problems." Pp. 61-87 in Sheldon Messinger and Egon Bittner (eds.), CRIMINOLOGY REVIEW YEARBOOK, Vol. 1. Beverly Hills: Sage, 1979.

Reviews the recent research on the deterrent effect of capital punishment done with multiple regression procedures, and the problems that are encountered by this method. Criticizes Ehrlich's work and argues that there is no conclusive evidence showing the death penalty is a deterrent.

352. Friedman, Robert. "Death Row." ESQUIRE 93 (April 1980): 84-92.

A brief report of interviews with 18 condemned Florida prisoners. Includes more detailed portraits of seven of the men.

353. Gale, Mary Ellen. "Retribution, Punishment, and Death." UNIVERSITY OF CALIFORNIA-DAVIS LAW REVIEW 18 (1985): 973-1035.

Argues that neither retributive nor utilitarian theories can justify capital punishment.

354. Gallemore, Johnnie L., and James H. Panton. "Inmate Responses to Lengthy Death Row Confinement." AMERICAN JOURNAL OF PSYCHIATRY 129 (1972): 167-71. Reprinted in Bedau and Pierce, 1976, in item 110 above.

The authors (one of whom is a psychiatrist) interviewed and conducted psychological tests on eight death row prisoners in North Carolina. Over time, five adjusted adequately, but three of the inmates became significantly less functional.

355. Gallup, George. "The Death Penalty." GALLUP REPORTS 244 and 245 (Jan./Feb., 1986): 10-6.

Reports national poll data on support for the death penalty and support of the penalty by different demographic groups. While 70 percent of the population favors the death penalty, only 55 percent does so given an alternative of life imprisonment, and 56 percent voices support if the death penalty is not a deterrent. Given life imprisonment and no deterrent effects, only 43 percent supports capital punishment.

356. Gardner, Martin R. "Executions and Indignities--An Eighth Amendment Assessment of Methods of Inflicting Capital Punishment." OHIO STATE LAW JOURNAL 39 (1978): 96-130.

A review of the evolution of the Supreme Court's definition of "cruel and unusual punishment," with a discussion of the constitutionality of various methods of execution.

357. Gardner, Martin R. "Mormonism and Capital Punishment: A Doctrinal Perspective, Past and Present." DIALOGUE: A JOURNAL OF MORMON THOUGHT 12 (1979): 9-26.

Reviews the history of Mormon support for capital punishment, and finds little doctrinal basis for it.

358. Gardner, Martin R. "Illicit Legislative Motivation as a Sufficient Condition for Unconstitutionality Under the Establishment Clause: A Case for Consideration: The Utah Firing Squad." WASHINGTON UNIVERSITY LAW QUARTERLY 1979 (1979): 435-99.

The use of the firing squad as a means of

execution in Utah has a sectarian motivation:
Mormons believe that blood must be shed in
executions. Because the religious motive is
illicit, the author argues the statute must
be invalidated.

359. Gardner, Romaine L. "Capital Punishment: The
Philosophers and the Court." SYRACUSE LAW
REVIEW 29 (1978): 1175-216.

Shows the roots in traditional philosophical
theory of the views of Justices in recent
Supreme Court decisions on capital
punishment.

360. Garey, Margot. "The Cost of Taking a Life:
Dollars and Sense of the Death Penalty."
UNIVERSITY OF CALIFORNIA-DAVIS LAW REVIEW 18
(1985): 1221-73.

A comparison of the costs of the death
penalty vs. life imprisonment, finding that
the former is much more expensive than the
latter.

361. Garfinkle, Harold. "Research Note on Inter-
and Intra-Racial Homicides." SOCIAL FORCES
27 (1949): 369-81.

A classic investigation of the significance
of race of offender and of victim in the
severity of punishment meted out. Reports
data on 821 homicide offenders from ten North
Carolina counties, 1930-1940. Finds black
defendant/white victim crimes are treated
most harshly.

362. Garrett, Steven M. "Applying the Frye Test
to Psychiatric Predictions of Dangerousness
in Capital Cases." CALIFORNIA LAW REVIEW 70
(1982): 1069-90.

Discusses a 1981 California death penalty
case in which the state Supreme Court held
that the use of a psychiatric prediction of
dangerousness during a penalty phase
constitutes reversible error. Only if such
testimony could be proved reliable could it
be used, and this proof could come only
through a defendant's long history of

criminality or a long relationship with the
psychiatrist. The author argues that these
exceptions are unwarranted.

363. Gaylord, C.L. "Capital Punishment in Ancient
United States: A Legal-Anthropological
Perspective From 12,000 A.D." CASE AND
COMMENT 82 (Jan.-Feb., 1977): 3-10.

A novel attempt to envision how people will
look back at our (by then) primitive process
of executions in 10,000 years.

364. Geiger, Anthony L., and Scott Selbach. "S.B.
1: Ohio Enacts Death Penalty Statute."
UNIVERSITY OF DAYTON LAW REVIEW 7 (1982):
532-66.

Examines three attempts by the Ohio
legislature to pass a constitutionally
permissible post-Furman death penalty
statute. Discusses the reasons why the first
two bills failed to withstand constitutional
challenges.

365. Geimer, William S. "Death At Any Cost: A
Critique of the Supreme Court's Recent
Retreat from its Death Penalty Standards."
FLORIDA STATE UNIVERSITY LAW REVIEW 12
(1985): 737-80.

Reviews recent Supreme Court decisions, and
criticizes the Court for retreating from the
standards it announced in 1976 for death
penalty cases. Argues the Court has
abandoned its previous death penalty
standards, which had included strict due
process guarantees.

366. Gelles, Richard J., and Murray A. Straus.
"Family Experience and Public Support of the
Death Penalty." AMERICAN JOURNAL OF
ORTHOPSYCHIATRY 45 (1975): 596-613.
Reprinted in Bedau and Pierce, 1976, cited
above as item 110.

Do early family experiences explain people's
opinions about capital punishment? The
authors' research leads them to conclude that
support is based on authoritarianism and

prejudice, and that these attitudes have their roots in early family relationships.

367. Georgia Journal of Corrections. "Capital Punishment: Positions and Opinion." GEORGIA JOURNAL OF CORRECTIONS 3 (1974): 26-40.

A series of brief opinion statements on capital punishment by Karl Menninger, American Bar Association, Liberty Lobby, Hugo Adam Bedau, the John Birch Society, and the American Civil Liberties Union.

368. Gerber, Rudolph J. "A Death Penalty We Can Live With." NOTRE DAME LAWYER 50 (1974): 251-72.

An analysis of the history, use, and effects of capital punishment, and an argument that the death penalty should be abolished.

369. Gerstein, Robert S. "Capital Punish-ment--'Cruel and Unusual'?: A Retributivist Response." ETHICS 85 (1974): 75-9.

A response to the article by Long, cited below as item 573. Argues that Long rejects the death penalty because he relies solely on utilitarian justifications. The author argues that the role of retributivism also needs to be considered in death penalty debates.

370. Gettinger, Stephen H. SENTENCED TO DIE: THE PEOPLE, THE CRIMES, AND THE CONTROVERSY. New York: Macmillan, 1979.

Recounts the stories of eight death row inmates, using each to illustrate different issues in the debate on capital punishment. A very informative and readable presentation of such issues as deterrence, criminal responsibility, racism, consensual execution, post-Furman death penalty statutes, lethal injection, etc.

371. Gettinger, Stephen H. "Robert A. Sullivan." ROLLING STONE (Feb. 2, 1984): 60.

A eulogy for Bob Sullivan, executed in

Florida on November 30, 1983, and a
description of his last hours.

372. Gibbs, Jack P. CRIME, PUNISHMENT AND
DETERRENCE. New York: Elsevier, 1975.

A general discussion of deterrence theories
and other possible preventive consequences of
punishment, including a review of research
findings.

373. Gibbs, Jack P. "A Critique of the Scientific
Literature on Capital Punishment and
Deterrence." JOURNAL OF BEHAVIORAL ECONOMICS
6 (1977): 279-309.

Criticizes existing studies of deterrence
because they fail to reflect awareness of the
various mechanisms, other than deterrence,
through which legal punishments may prevent
crimes.

374. Gibbs, Jack P. "Preventive Effects of
Capital Punishment Other than Deterrence."
CRIMINAL LAW BULLETIN 14 (1978): 34-50.

Shows there are several ways other than
deterrence through which legal punishment may
prevent crimes (e.g., normative validation,
incapacitation).

375. Gibbs, Jack P. "The Death Penalty,
Retribution, and Penal Policy." JOURNAL OF
CRIMINAL LAW AND CRIMINOLOGY 69 (1978):
291-9.

A concise summary of the retribution
justification for capital punishment and its
shortcomings.

376. Gibbs, Jack P. "Deterrence Theory and
Research." Pp. 87-130 in Gary B. Melton
(ed.) (Nebraska Symposium on Motivation), THE
LAW AS A BEHAVIORAL INSTRUMENT. Lincoln:
University of Nebraska Press, 1986.

An examination of deterrence theory,
conceptualization of terms within it, and
discussion of types of deterrence. Overviews
research on general deterrence.

377. Gillers, Stephen. "Deciding Who Dies."
UNIVERSITY OF PENNSYLVANIA LAW REVIEW 129
(1980): 1-124.

Argues that juries, not judges, should decide
who dies, and that those opposed to the death
penalty should not be removed from capital
juries. Includes as an Appendix a state-by-
state listing of procedures used in capital
sentencing.

378. Gillers, Stephen. "Proving the Prejudice of
Death-Qualified Juries After Adams v. Texas."
UNIVERSITY OF PITTSBURGH LAW REVIEW 47
(1985): 219-55.

A review of Welsh White's LIFE IN THE BALANCE
(see item 910 below); points out that much
death penalty scholarship is outdated soon
after it is published. The paper challenges
the practice of death qualification of juries
in capital cases.

379. Gillers, Stephen. "The Quality of Mercy:
Constitutional Accuracy at the Selection
Stage of Capital Sentencing." UNIVERSITY OF
CALIFORNIA-DAVIS LAW REVIEW 18 (1985):
1037-111.

Reviews judicial and legislative searches for
systematic death sentencing procedures.
Argues that any systematic theory of
sentencing must weigh community standards of
both retribution and mercy, but that
contemporary death sentencing procedures fail
to balance these two values.

380. Gilloon, Thomas J. "Capital Punishment and
the Burden of Proof: The Sentencing
Decision." CALIFORNIA WESTERN LAW REVIEW 17
(1981): 316-53.

Examines the burden of proof at the
sentencing phase required to impose the death
penalty. Argues the standard should be
"proof beyond a reasonable doubt." The
author focuses on California; he argues a
person can, today, be condemned on the basis

of a lesser burden-of-proof standard in that state.

381. Glaser, Daniel. "A Response to Bailey: More Evidence on Capital Punishment as a Correlate of Tolerance for Murder." CRIME AND DELINQUENCY 22 (1976): 40-3.

Replies to William Bailey's critique (cited above as item 41) of an earlier paper by Glaser and Zeigler (cited below as item 384).

382. Glaser, Daniel. "The Realities of Homicide Versus the Assumptions of Economists in Assessing Capital Punishment." JOURNAL OF BEHAVIORAL ECONOMICS 6 (1977): 243-68.

A critique of the work of James Yunker and Isaac Ehrlich on capital punishment.

383. Glaser, Daniel. "Capital Punishment-- Deterrent or Stimulus to Murder? Our Unexamined Deaths and Penalties." UNIVERSITY OF TOLEDO LAW REVIEW 10 (1979): 317-33.

Discusses the work of Hans Mattick (see article by Lamb, cited below as item 533) on the death penalty. Argues that the available evidence indicates capital punishment reduces the certainty that murderers will be convicted, increases plea bargaining, may stimulate murder, and thus produces less deterrence than imprisonment.

384. Glaser, Daniel, and Max S. Zeigler. "Use of the Death Penalty v. Outrage at Murder." CRIME AND DELINQUENCY 20 (1974): 333-8.

Explanation is offered as to why states with the highest execution rates also have the highest murder rates. The authors argue that both rates reflect a low valuation of life. This article was critiqued by Bailey, cited above as item 41.

385. Glover, Jonathan. CAUSING DEATH AND SAVING LIVES. New York: Penguin, 1977.

A discussion of the moral problems involved in abortion, suicide, euthanasia, capital punishment, and other life-or-death choices. Outlines how various moral perspectives approach these problems.

386. Godbold, John C. "Pro Bono Representation of Death Sentenced Inmates." RECORD OF THE ASSOCIATION OF THE BAR OF THE CITY OF NEW YORK 42 (1987): 859-76.

This lecture, by a judge on the Eleventh Circuit Court of Appeals, discusses the critical shortage of competent attorneys for death row inmates in post-conviction hearings.

387. Goldberg, Arthur J. "Death Penalty and the Supreme Court." ARIZONA LAW REVIEW 15 (1973): 355-68.

Points out that there were only ten cases prior to Furman in which the Supreme Court discussed the Eighth Amendment. These decisions are discussed, and the author, a former Supreme Court Justice, concludes the death penalty violates the Amendment's protections.

388. Goldberg, Arthur J. "The Death Penalty for Rape." HASTINGS CONSTITUTIONAL LAW QUARTERLY 5 (1978): 1-13.

Examines the history of the Supreme Court rulings on the Eighth Amendment through the Coker decision, and makes a plea to the Court to overturn Gregg.

389. Goldberg, Arthur J., and Alan M. Dershowitz. "Declaring the Death Penalty Unconstitutional." HARVARD LAW REVIEW 83 (1970): 1773-819.

Examines Eighth Amendment cases that have been heard by the Supreme Court (the senior author is a former Supreme Court Justice), and argues the Court should hold the death penalty unconstitutional.

390. Goldberg, Steven. "On Capital Punishment." ETHICS 85 (1974): 67-74.

Argues that the central issue in capital
punishment debates concerns deterrence, and
shows how both proponents and opponents have
used this argument in bolstering their
positions.

391. Goodman, Daniel S. "Demographic Evidence in
Capital Sentencing." STANFORD LAW REVIEW 39
(1987): 499-543.

A lengthy examination of the use of
statistical evidence of recidivism in capital
cases. Argues that while one cannot use race
or gender to make predictions, statistical
predictions can be useful in some cases.

392. Goodpaster, Gary. "Judicial Review of Death
Sentences." JOURNAL OF CRIMINAL LAW AND
CRIMINOLOGY 74 (1983): 786-826.

Argues that rigorous appellate review of
death sentences, including proportionality
review, is constitutionally required. The
paper describes how this is done to some
extent in certain jurisdictions, and outlines
ways in which the review procedure should be
improved.

393. Goodpaster, Gary. "The Trial for Life:
Effective Assistance of Counsel in Death
Penalty Cases." NEW YORK UNIVERSITY LAW
REVIEW 58 (1983): 299-362.

Assesses the requirement that defendants
facing the death penalty be given effective
assistance of counsel. Argues that the
courts should pay particular attention to the
quality of defense in the penalty phase, and
suggests standards and procedures for its
assessment.

394. Gordon, Robert Wayne. "Crystal-balling
Death?" BAYLOR LAW REVIEW 30 (1978): 35-64.

With specific reference to Texas, this
article challenges the validity and
reliability of psychiatric predictions of
dangerousness at the penalty phase of capital
trials.

395.   Gorecki, Jan. CAPITAL PUNISHMENT: CRIMINAL
       LAW AND SOCIAL EVOLUTION. New York: Columbia
       University Press, 1983.

       An argument against the death penalty,
       positing that as societies evolve, the
       exercise of violence by the state declines.

396.   Gottlieb, Gerald H.   "Testing the Death
       Penalty." SOUTHERN CALIFORNIA LAW REVIEW 34
       (1961): 268-81.

       A pioneering article that was the first to
       lay out the modern Eighth Amendment challenge
       to the death penalty because of the ambiguity
       of the phrase "cruel and unusual" and the
       necessity to consider changing standards of
       decency in interpreting the clause.

397.   Gottlieb, Gerald H.   "Capital Punishment."
       CRIME AND DELINQUENCY 15 (1969): 1-20.

       A general essay in opposition to capital
       punishment. Argues that the purpose of the
       death penalty is torture, and that this
       purpose makes the death penalty unconstitu-
       tional.

398.   Gowers, Sir Ernest. A LIFE FOR A LIFE? THE
       PROBLEM OF CAPITAL PUNISHMENT. London:
       Chatto and Windus, 1956.

       Written by the chairman of the 1953 Royal
       Commission on Capital Punishment, this is an
       account of issues raised by the death penalty
       in England and of the author's eventual
       support for complete abolition.

399.   Granuci, Anthony F.   "'Nor Cruel and Unusual
       Punishments Inflicted': The Original
       Meaning." CALIFORNIA LAW REVIEW 57 (1969):
       839-65.

       Examines the views of the framers of the
       American Bill of Rights on cruel and unusual
       punishment, and traces the legal developments
       behind the English Bill of Rights. Argues
       the American framers misinterpreted English
       law.

400. Gredd, Helen. "<u>Washington</u> <u>v</u>. <u>Strickland</u>: Defining Effective Assistance of Counsel at Capital Sentencing." COLUMBIA LAW REVIEW 83 (1983): 1544-81.

Discusses the 1982 case in which the Eleventh Circuit defined standards for effective assistance of counsel. Argues the court's approach is misguided, because it failed to require higher standards for effective assistance at capital sentencing than in noncapital contexts.

401. Green, William. "Capital Punishment, Psychiatric Experts, and Predictions of Dangerousness." CAPITAL UNIVERSITY LAW REVIEW 13 (1984): 533-53.

Argues that because of problems of definition and predictions, psychiatrists should not be allowed to answer questions about hypothetical situations in death penalty cases. Recommends that psychiatric testimony including the diagnosis of antisocial personality disorder should not be permitted because it misleads the jury into believing the defendant must die.

402. Greenberg, Jack. "Capital Punishment as a System." YALE LAW JOURNAL 91 (1982): 908-36.

Argues that the large number of appellate court reversals of death sentences demonstrates the need for extraordinary care in deciding who dies. The necessary system of appellate review, however, destroys the two primary goals of capital punishment, deterrence and retribution, and leads to more disparities in the death sentencing process.

403. Greenberg, Jack. "Against the American System of Capital Punishment." HARVARD LAW REVIEW 99 (1986): 1670-80.

A critique of the death penalty, based primarily on the inability of contemporary systems of death sentencing to isolate the worst criminals (and only the worst) for condemnation.

404. Greenberg, Jack, and Jack Himmelstein.
      "Varieties of Attack on the Death Penalty."
      CRIME AND DELINQUENCY 15 (1969): 112-20.

      Describes the efforts and strategy of the
      NAACP Legal Defense and Educational Fund to
      challenge the death penalty. Their first
      involvement (in a case in Groveland, Florida)
      and current motivations are outlined.

405. Greene, Enid. "Double Jeopardy and
      Resentencing in Bifurcated Criminal
      Proceedings." BRIGHAM YOUNG UNIVERSITY LAW
      REVIEW (Winter, 1982): 192-204.

      A comment on <u>Bullington</u> <u>v</u>. <u>Missouri</u>, in which
      the Supreme Court ruled that a death sentence
      could not be imposed at retrial if the
      sentence rendered at the original trial was
      not death. The author argues the Court's
      reasoning for this holding does not withstand
      close scrutiny.

406. Greenland, Cyril. "The Last Public Execution
      in Canada: Eight Skeletons in the Closet of
      the Canadian Justice System." CRIMINAL LAW
      QUARTERLY 29 (1987): 415-20.

      Despite the fact that public executions in
      Canada were banned by legislation in 1869,
      eight Indians were publicly hanged (for
      treason) in 1885. This article examines the
      case and its numerous violations of the
      defendants' rights.

407. Greenwald, Helene B. "Capital Punishment for
      Minors: An Eighth Amendment Analysis."
      JOURNAL OF CRIMINAL LAW AND CRIMINOLOGY 74
      (1983): 1471-517.

      Discusses whether the execution of juveniles
      is excessive punishment under the Eighth
      Amendment. After discussing the history and
      present status of this practice, the author
      concludes that such executions are
      unconstitutional.

408. Griggs, Larry T. "Harmless Error, Cause and
      Prejudice, Comity and Federalism: 'Legal
      Magic' and the Florida Death Penalty."

STETSON LAW REVIEW 13 (1983): 83-114.

Discusses the Eleventh Circuit's 1983
decision in the case of Florida death row
inmate Alvin Ford. Among the issues
discussed are the use of non-record
information by the Florida Supreme Court in
its review, the failure of that court to
remand the case for resentencing after
invalidating the finding of some of the
aggravating circumstances, and the limitation
on the jury to consider only statutorily-
defined mitigating circumstances.

409. Gross, Samuel R. "Determining the Neutrality
of Death-Qualified Juries: Judicial Appraisal
of Empirical Data." LAW AND HUMAN BEHAVIOR 8
(1984): 7-30.

Reviews the legal history of the exclusion
from capital juries of those opposed to the
death penalty, and the questions that social
scientists can address in evaluating the
impact of this exclusion.

410. Gross, Samuel R. "Race and Death: The
Judicial Evaluation of Evidence of
Discrimination in Capital Sentencing."
UNIVERSITY OF CALIFORNIA-DAVIS LAW REVIEW 18
(1985): 1275-325.

Reviews research on racial discrimination in
the death penalty and the response of the
Supreme Court to that research. Discusses
the background of the Eleventh Circuit's
decision in McCleskey v. Kemp and criticizes
the Eleventh Circuit Court's decision in the
case.

411. Gross, Samuel R., and Robert Mauro. "Patterns
of Death: An Analysis of Racial Disparities
in Capital Sentencing and Homicide
Victimization." STANFORD LAW REVIEW 37
(1984): 27-153.

An extensive analysis of death sentencing
patterns in eight states: Georgia, Florida,
Illinois, Oklahoma, North Carolina,
Mississippi, Virginia, and Arkansas.
Compares FBI records of all homicides in the

state to characteristics of those sentenced
to death. Finds "remarkably stable and
consistent" discrimination, based on race of
victim, in all states.

412.   Grupp, Stanley. "Some Historical Aspects of
the Pardon in England." THE AMERICAN JOURNAL
OF LEGAL HISTORY 7 (1963): 51-62.

Examines historical aspects of the pardon in
pre-eighteenth century England. Discusses
how the pardon power evolved and was limited
and abused.

413.   Haas, Kenneth C., and James A. Inciardi
(eds.). CHALLENGING CAPITAL PUNISHMENT:
LEGAL AND SOCIAL SCIENCE APPROACHES. Newbury
Park, Calif: Sage (forthcoming, 1988).

Contains items 158, 199, 278, 304, 422, 681,
713, 733, 838, and an introductory essay.

414.   Hadley, Lord Carr of, and David Burnham.
"The Capital Punishment Debate 1979: A
Review." JOURNAL OF CRIMINAL LAW 44 (1980):
111-8.

An examination of the capital punishment
debate in Parliament in 1979. Written by one
of the participants in the debate, this essay
explains why the effort to restore the death
penalty in England failed.

415.   Hamilton, V. Lee, and Laurence Rotkin.
"Interpreting the Eighth Amendment: Perceived
Seriousness of Crime and Severity of
Punishment." Pp. 502-24 in Bedau and Pierce,
1976, cited above as item 110.

Examines the relationship between perceived
seriousness of crime and severity of
punishment. The authors find huge gaps in
the perceived severity of three punishments:
life imprisonment, life without parole, and
the death penalty. The substantial gap
between the two types of life sentences,
according to the authors, provides support
for the argument that the death penalty could
be replaced by life without parole.

416. Hamilton, V. Lee and Laurence Rotkin. "The Capital Punishment Debate: Public Perceptions of Crime and Punishment." JOURNAL OF APPLIED SOCIAL PSYCHOLOGY 9 (1979): 350-76.

Using a sample from the Boston area, the authors find that capital and noncapital crimes are intermingled in severity ratings, that the death penalty is not seen as significantly more severe than life imprisonment without parole, and that extra-legal factors influence what types of offenders are believed to deserve death.

417. Hammer, Richard. BETWEEN LIFE AND DEATH. New York: Macmillan, 1969.

Describes John Brady's trial, time on death row, and the appeal of his case which resulted in the U.S. Supreme Court's 1963 ruling of Brady v. Maryland.

418. Haney, Craig. "Juries and the Death Penalty: Readdressing the Witherspoon Question." CRIME AND DELINQUENCY 26 (1980): 512-27.

Reviews the Supreme Court's decisions on the issue of excluding those who oppose the death penalty from capital juries. The effects of this exclusion on jury decision-making are described, and a number of reforms are suggested.

419. Haney, Craig. "On the Selection of Capital Juries: The Biasing Effects of the Death-Qualification Process." LAW AND HUMAN BEHAVIOR 8 (1984): 121-32.

Subjects were exposed either to a regular voir dire or to one that included questions about death qualification. The latter group was found to be more conviction prone, suggesting that the process of death qualification itself tends to make jurors more likely to believe the defendant is guilty.

420. Haney, Craig. "Examining Death Qualification: Further Analysis of the Process Effect." LAW AND HUMAN BEHAVIOR 8

(1984): 133-51.

Describes the biasing effect of the process of death qualification, arguing that the process itself makes jurors more conviction prone.

421. Haney, Craig. "Epilogue: Evolving Standards and the Capital Jury." LAW AND HUMAN BEHAVIOR 8 (1984): 153-8.

A reflection on the necessity to reexamine the question of death qualification and some thoughts about the role of social science in informing and influencing legal change.

422. Hans, Valerie P. "Death by Jury." In Haas and Inciardi, 1988, cited above as item 413.

Discusses penalty phase juries in the context of social science research on jury decision making, raising several questions about how this context can cause jurors to become misled, confused, or influenced by legally irrelevant factors.

423. Hardman, Dale G. "Notes at an Unfinished Lunch." CRIME AND DELINQUENCY 23 (1977): 365-71.

A fictional luncheon conversation between a legislator, a judge, and a prosecutor. Argues that the only way that death can be a deterrent is to have public executions (but the group soon realizes that our history amply demonstrates that public executions, when used, never had deterrent effects).

424. Hare, John H. "The Death Penalty." SOUTH CAROLINA LAW REVIEW 33 (1981): 53-73.

An examination of South Carolina's death penalty statute and recent decisions by its Supreme Court in death penalty cases.

425. Harris, Philip W. "Over-Simplification and Error in Public Opinion Surveys on Capital Punishment." JUSTICE QUARTERLY 3 (1986): 429-55.

Reports results of a 1984 national public
opinion poll, conducted by the author and
Associated Press. Finds that 12 percent of
the respondents opposed the death penalty in
all cases and 27 percent supported it for all
homicides. Problems in interpreting poll
data are discussed.

426. Hartman, Joan F. "'Unusual' Punishment: The
Domestic Effects of International Norms
Restricting the Application of the Death
Penalty." UNIVERSITY OF CINCINNATI LAW
REVIEW 52 (1983): 655-99.

Examines the issue of executing juveniles in
light of international human rights norms
that condemn such punishment. The question
of executing juveniles is used to raise
larger questions about the purpose and
relevance of international law.

427. Havlena, Thomas. "Abolishing the Death
Penalty -- Why? How? When?" WESTERN STATE
LAW REVIEW 15 (1987): 127-78.

Explores a variety of issues that support
those who argue for abolition, and discusses
different ways that abolition might occur and
the preconditions (especially a change in
public opinion) that will have to be met
before abolition can happen.

428. Hazard, Geoffrey C., Jr., and David W.
Louisell. "Death, the State, and the Insane:
Stay of Execution." UCLA LAW REVIEW 9
(1962): 381-405.

Reviews the history and purposes of exempting
the insane from punishment. Criticizes
procedures used to evaluate the sanity of
death row prisoners, with specific attention
directed toward the procedures used in
California.

429. Hazard, John W., Jr. "Gardner v. Florida:
Pre-Sentence Reports in Capital Sentencing
Procedures." OHIO NORTHERN UNIVERSITY LAW
REVIEW 5 (1978): 175-89.

Examines the case in which the Supreme Court

refused to uphold the validity of the Florida
Supreme Court's use of presentence
investigation reports that had been withheld
from the defense.

430. Heilbrun, Alfred B., Jr., Lynn C. Heilbrun,
and Kim L. Heilbrun. "Impulsive and
Premeditated Homicide: An Analysis of
Subsequent Parole Risk of the Murderer."
JOURNAL OF CRIMINAL LAW AND CRIMINOLOGY 69
(1978): 108-14.

Examines records of 164 Georgia males, all of
whom had been imprisoned for murder and
paroled. Finds that 44 percent successfully
completed parole. Concludes the impulsive
murderers did worse on parole than the
premeditated murderers.

431. Heilbrun, Kirk S. "The Assessment of
Competency for Execution: An Overview."
BEHAVIORAL SCIENCES AND THE LAW 5 (1987):
383-96.

A thoughtful overview of the issue of
competency for execution, including a listing
of each state's statute governing exemptions
from execution because of insanity.

432. Hellwig, Leonie G. "The Death Penalty in
Washington: A Historical Perspective."
WASHINGTON LAW REVIEW 57 (1982): 525-49.

A discussion of the death penalty statute
enacted in Washington state in 1981 and the
events and court decisions that led up to it.
The state's earlier death penalty statute had
been invalidated because it allowed the death
penalty only in cases in which the defendant
pled not guilty.

433. Henry, William O.E. "Representation of Death
Sentenced Inmates." FLORIDA BAR JOURNAL 59
(December, 1985): 53-6.

Describes the problem of the lack of
attorneys willing to handle collateral
appeals for Florida death row inmates.
Describes a program established by the
Florida Bar to recruit volunteer attorneys.

434. Herron, Roy Brasfield. "Defending Life in
     Tennessee Death Penalty Cases." TENNESSEE
     LAW REVIEW 51 (1984): 681-768.

     A comprehensive overview of the Tennessee
     death penalty law, and description of tactics
     used by defense attorneys at various stages
     in a capital or potentially capital case.

435. Hertz, Randy, and Robert Weisberg. "In
     Mitigation of the Penalty of Death: Lockett
     v. Ohio and the Capital Defendant's Right to
     Consideration of Mitigating Circumstances."
     CALIFORNIA LAW REVIEW 69 (1981): 317-76.

     Argues that the implications for the defense
     of the Supreme Court's decision in Lockett
     have not been fully appreciated. One
     mitigating factor alone may be sufficient
     reason to impose a noncapital sentence.
     Defendants may also be able to show that, in
     their individual cases, the deterrent and
     retributive goals of the death penalty would
     not be served.

436. Hester, Reid K., and Ronald E. Smith.
     "Effects of a Mandatory Death Penalty on the
     Decisions of Simulated Jurors as a Function
     of Heinousness of the Crime." JOURNAL OF
     CRIMINAL JUSTICE 1 (1973): 319-26.

     A description of a fictional gang-war
     homicide case was read by 150 students.
     Given identical evidence, subjects were less
     likely to render a guilty verdict if it
     carried a mandatory death sentence. These
     differences were significant in the study of
     the gang-war killing, but not in a study
     using a description of a fictional heinous
     murder.

437. Hewing, Margaret S. "Stare Decisis and the
     Illinois Death Penalty." UNIVERSITY OF
     ILLINOIS LAW REVIEW 1986 (1986): 177-98.

     Describes the doctrine of stare decisis and
     concludes its role in capital cases should be
     diminished.

438. Hibbert, Christopher. THE ROOTS OF EVIL.
Boston: Little, Brown and Co., 1963.

A book on the history and growth of
punishment and the changes in the ways in
which criminal offenders are viewed. Of
particular relevance is a chapter on capital
punishment, which discusses its history (with
a British emphasis), then-current status, and
the author's reasons for concluding it should
be abolished.

439. Hicks, Peggy L. "Compelled Election Between
Constitutional Rights in Capital Sentencing
Proceedings." COLUMBIA LAW REVIEW 87 (1987):
327-43.

A defendant testifies at a pretrial hearing
on a motion to suppress evidence. He is
subsequently convicted of capital murder.
Can the statements made at the pretrial
hearing be used against him at the sentencing
phase? The conflict between the Fourth
Amendment right to challenge evidence and the
Fifth Amendment right against self-
incrimination is discussed in this paper.

440. Hill, Christopher M. "Can the Death Penalty
be Imposed on Juveniles: The Unanswered
Question in Eddings v. Oklahoma." CRIMINAL
LAW BULLETIN 20 (1984): 5-33.

Reviews the Eddings decision, in which the
Supreme Court left open the question of the
constitutionality of the death penalty for
minors. Argues a ruling on this issue would
be premature, as public opinion on the matter
is still unclear.

441. Hoenack, Stephen A., and William C. Weiler.
"A Structural Model of Murder Behavior and
the Criminal Justice System." AMERICAN
ECONOMIC REVIEW 70 (1980): 327-41.

Discusses the statistical problems of
identification in the research on deterrence
of Isaac Ehrlich. An alternative model is
suggested for the one posited by Ehrlich.

442. Hoenack, Stephen A., Robert T. Kudrel, and

David L. Sjoquist. "The Deterrent Effect of Capital Punishment: A Question of Identification." POLICY ANALYSIS 4 (1978): 491-527.

An important examination of Ehrlich's work. Ehrlich's research is found to be faulty because of his failure to recognize the importance of the statistical problem of identification.

443. Hogan, Brian. "Killing Ground, 1964-1973." CRIMINAL LAW REVIEW 1974 (1974): 387-401.

The last execution in England was in 1964. This paper examines the abolition of the death penalty in England, and discusses the mens rea of murder and manslaughter and various defenses used in homicide cases.

444. Holland, Nancy. "Death Row Conditions: Progression Toward Constitutional Protections." AKRON LAW REVIEW 19 (1985): 293-310.

Examines the evolution of judicial attention to prison conditions, focusing on a narrow body of case law affecting the quality of life on America's death rows.

445. Horowitz, Irwin A., and David G. Seguin. "The Effects of Bifurcation and Death Qualification on Assignment of Penalty in Capital Crimes." JOURNAL OF APPLIED SOCIAL PSYCHOLOGY 16 (1986): 165-85.

An experimental examination of 44 twelve-person simulated juries which were assigned to one of five trial conditions. Death qualified, bifurcated juries were found to be more likely to convict and to give the most severe sentences.

446. Horwitz, Elinor Lander. CAPITAL PUNISHMENT, U.S.A. Philadelphia: Lippincott, 1973.

An overview of capital punishment, beginning with a history and discussion of torture and of English law. Chapters on Sacco and Vanzetti, Leopold and Loeb, the Rosenbergs, and Caryl Chessman are included.

447. Hubbard, F. Patrick. "'Reasonable Levels of
      Arbitrariness' in Death Sentencing Patterns:
      A Tragic Perspective on Capital Punishment."
      UNIVERSITY OF CALIFORNIA-DAVIS LAW REVIEW 18
      (1985): 1113-64.

      Argues that arbitrariness is an inevitable
      consequence of judicial review of death
      sentences, and thus some arbitrariness is
      reasonable and necessary.

448. Hubbard, F. Partick, Brenton G. Burry, and
      Robert Widener. "A 'Meaningful' Basis for
      the Death Penalty: The Practice,
      Constitutionality, and Justice of Capital
      Punishment in South Carolina." SOUTH
      CAROLINA LAW REVIEW 34 (1982): 391-582.

      A detailed description of South Carolina's
      procedure for imposing the death penalty,
      from trial through sentencing, appeal, and
      clemency. A discussion of the
      constitutionality of capital punishment and a
      philosophical justification for it are also
      included.

449. Huff, C. Ronald, Arye Rattner, and Edward
      Sagarin. "Guilty Until Proven Innocent:
      Wrongful Conviction and Public Policy."
      CRIME AND DELINQUENCY 32 (1986): 518-44.

      A general discussion of the problem of
      wrongful convictions in felony cases.

450. Hughes, Graham. "License to Kill." NEW YORK
      REVIEW OF BOOKS 26 (June 28, 1979): 22-5.

      One of the leading reviews of the book by
      Walter Berns (cited above as item 127).
      Argues there is no justifiable case for
      capital punishment, and that Berns, while
      disagreeing with this assertion, does a
      "splendid" job of outlining a pro-death
      penalty position.

451. Huie, William Bradford. THE EXECUTION OF
      PRIVATE SLOVIK. New York: Dell, 1954.

The story of the only American soldier to be executed for desertion since the Civil War. Private Slovik's execution took place in 1945.

452. Huie, William Bradford. RUBY MCCOLLUM: WOMAN IN THE SUWANEE JAIL. New York: Signet Books, 1957.

The story of Ruby McCollum, sentenced to death in Florida for the 1952 murder of her alleged lover, a white physician. McCollum was later transferred to a mental hospital, and was never executed.

453. Huie, William Bradford. "The South Kills Another Negro." Pp. 85-91 in Edward McGehee and William Hildebrand, 1964, cited below as item 607.

The story of the trial and 1937 execution of an Alabama black man, Roosevelt Wilson (a.k.a. Collins), who was convicted of the rape of a white woman even though the sexual relationship was consensual.

454. Human Rights. "Why Death Row Needs Lawyers." HUMAN RIGHTS 14 (Winter, 1987): 26-8.

An overview of the goals of the American Bar Association's Death Penalty Representation Project.

455. Hurka, Thomas. "Rights and Capital Punishment." DIALOGUE 21 (1982): 647-60.

A philosophical examination of "rights-based," rather than utilitarian or retributivist, arguments on capital punishment. Concludes that this moral theory does not support the use of the death penalty.

456. Husbands, Robert H. "New Direction for Capital Sentencing or an About-Face for the Supreme Court? Lockett v. Ohio: A recent development." AMERICAN CRIMINAL LAW REVIEW 16 (1979): 317-37.

A discussion of the Lockett case.

457. Ingle, Joseph. "Etiquette of Death."
     SOUTHERN 2 (March, 1988): 19-22.

     A description of Louisiana Governor Edwards'
     refusal to grant clemency to Willie Watson in
     1987.

458. Ingram, T. Robert (ed.). ESSAYS ON THE DEATH
     PENALTY. Houston: St. Thomas Press, 1963.

     Includes eight essays on the death penalty,
     all from various Christian perspectives.

459. Isenberg, Irwin (ed.). THE DEATH PENALTY.
     New York: H.W. Wilson (The Reference Shelf,
     Vol. 49, No. 2), 1977.

     A collection of 21 essays relating to the
     death penalty selected from popular
     newspapers and magazines.

460. Ita, Timothy A. "Habeas Corpus--Expedited
     Appellate Review of Habeas Corpus Petitions
     Brought by Death-Sentenced State Prisoners."
     JOURNAL OF CRIMINAL LAW AND CRIMINOLOGY 74
     (1983): 1404-24.

     A discussion of the Supreme Court's decision
     in Barefoot v. Estelle. Argues this decision
     is not supported by precedents in the area of
     habeas corpus appellate procedures.

461. Jackson, Bruce, and Diane Christian. DEATH
     ROW. Boston: Beacon Press, 1980.

     The authors interviewed 26 Texas death row
     inmates in 1979. Though no citations are
     given and the names of the inmates are
     changed, the book gives useful insights into
     death row conditions. Includes photographs
     of the inmates and of death row.

462. Jackson, Robert T., Jr. "Issues in Capital
     Sentencing." ARMY LAWYER (July, 1986): 54-6.

     Suggests that the Georgia statute looks like
     a blueprint for the death penalty under the
     Uniform Code of Military Justice, and that
     the military should study the Georgia

experience for lessons on what will happen
when military death sentences are appealed.

463.   Jacoby, Joseph E., and Raymond Paternoster.
"Sentencing Disparity and Jury Packing:
Further Challenges to the Death Penalty."
JOURNAL OF CRIMINAL LAW AND CRIMINOLOGY 73
(1982): 379-87.

Examines 205 South Carolina homicide cases,
1977-79, in which the prosecutor could have
asked for the death penalty. Defendants
charged with murdering whites were 3.2 times
more likely than those accused of murdering
blacks to have cases in which the prosecutor
sought death. Also finds that death
qualified juries are biased toward conviction
and death sentences, and disproportionately
exclude blacks.

464.   Jacoby, Susan. WILD JUSTICE: THE EVOLUTION
OF REVENGE. New York: Harper and Row, 1983.

A seminal outline of the meaning of
"justice," which the author argues holds a
place for revenge that is tempered by
compassion. Argues that while revenge is
proper, the death penalty is not, because the
penalty is disproportionate and it distorts
the moral fabric of the society.

465.   Jankovic, Ivan. "Socialism and the Death
Penalty." RESEARCH IN LAW, DEVIANCE, AND
SOCIAL CONTROL, A RESEARCH ANNUAL (Vol. 6).
Greenwich, CT: JAI Press, 1984, pp. 109-37.

An informative examination of the connections
between socialism and abolition and a review
of the history and present status of the
death penalty in certain socialist countries,
especially Yugoslavia. The contradiction
between ideological rejection of the death
penalty and retention in practice is
discussed.

466.   Jayewardene, C.H.S. "The Canadian Movement
Against the Death Penalty." CANADIAN JOURNAL
OF CRIMINOLOGY AND CORRECTION 14 (1972):
366-90.

A description of the history of the abolition
movement in Canada. A comprehensive
bibliography is included.

467.   Jayewardene, C.H.S. THE PENALTY OF DEATH:
        THE CANADIAN EXPERIENCE. Lexington, Mass.:
        D.C. Heath, 1977.

An examination of the moratorium on the death
penalty in Canada and the eventual abolition
of capital punishment. Special attention is
devoted to the question of deterrence; murder
rates and murders of police officers are
examined, and no support is found for the
argument that the removal of the death
penalty would lead to higher homicide rates.

468.   Jeffko, Walter G. "Capital Punishment in a
        Democracy." AMERICA 135 (Dec. 11, 1976):
        413-4.

An argument that in debates over the death
penalty, the burden of proof is on those who
would retain state executions, and that death
penalty proponents have not met this
challenge.

469.   Jester, Jean Catto. "The Abolition of Public
        Executions: A Case Study." INTERNATIONAL
        JOURNAL OF CRIMINOLOGY AND PENOLOGY 4 (1976):
        25-32.

A general discussion of the abolition of
public executions, with a focus on England,
arguing that the ban came from a desire to
ensure the continuation of the death penalty.

470.   Johnson, Elmer H. "Selective Forces in
        Capital Punishment." SOCIAL FORCES 36
        (1957): 165-9.

Studies the records of 660 death row inmates
in North Carolina between 1909 and 1954.
Reports execution rates by race and type of
crime, and finds that race is correlated with
sentencing outcome.

471.   Johnson, Guy B. "The Negro and Crime." THE
        ANNALS OF THE AMERICAN ACADEMY OF POLITICAL
        AND SOCIAL SCIENCE 217 (1941): 93-104.

A classic study of racial characteristics of
murderers and victims, using 1930's data
gathered in Atlanta, Richmond, and five North
Carolina counties. Argues that race affects
crime statistics and criminal justice
processing.

472. Johnson, Kathleen L. "Death Row Right to
Die: Suicide or Intimate Decision?" SOUTHERN
CALIFORNIA LAW REVIEW 54 (1981): 575-631.

Presents the arguments both for and against
consensual executions, and, after emphasizing
the importance of free choice, proposes
procedures that would enable prisoners who
wish to be executed to have their choice
respected.

473. Johnson, Oakley C. "Is the Punishment of
Rape Equally Administered to Negroes and
Whites in the State of Louisiana?" Pp.
216-28 in William Patterson (ed.), WE CHARGE
GENOCIDE. New York: International
Publishers, 1970.

An analysis of Louisiana prison records,
showing that the death penalty for rape was
almost exclusively reserved for blacks.

474. Johnson, Robert. "Under Sentence of Death:
The Psychology of Death Row Confinement."
LAW AND PSYCHOLOGY REVIEW 5 (1979): 141-92.

Examines the psychological impact of death
row confinement on condemned prisoners.
Based on in-depth interviews with 35 Alabama
death row prisoners in 1978.

475. Johnson, Robert. "Warehousing for Death:
Observations on the Human Environment of
Death Row." CRIME AND DELINQUENCY 26 (1980):
545-62.

Based on interviews with Alabama death row
inmates, this paper describes the setting and
adjustment problems faced by condemned
prisoners.

476. Johnson, Robert. CONDEMNED TO DIE: LIFE

UNDER SENTENCE OF DEATH. New York: Elsevier, 1981.

Discusses life and conditions on death row, based on interviews with condemned inmates in Alabama. Describes the experiences of death row prisoners and their families as a crucible of fear and powerlessness.

477. Johnson, Robert. "A Life for a Life?" JUSTICE QUARTERLY 1 (1984): 569-80.

An argument against the death penalty, based primarily on humanitarian respect for the prisoner and recognition of the limits of retribution.

478. Johnson, Robert, and John L. Carroll. "Litigating Death Row Conditions: The Case for Reform." Pp. 8-3 to 8-33 in Ira P. Robbins (ed.), PRISONERS AND THE LAW. New York: Clark Bordman Co., 1987.

A review of death row conditions and litigation over them both before and after the 1972 Furman decision.

479. Jolly, Robert W., Jr., and Edward Sagarin. "The First Eight After Furman: Who Was Executed With the Return of the Death Penalty?" CRIME AND DELINQUENCY 30 (1984): 610-23.

A brief examination of the first eight executions in the United States after 1976, based upon information in newspaper reports.

480. Jones, Ann. WOMEN WHO KILL. New York: Holt, Rinehart and Winston, 1980.

A series of studies, mostly of prominent historical cases, approaching the subject of women and murder from different angles. Included are sections on famous female criminals (or suspected criminals), some of whom were executed, such as Lizzie Borden, Ruth Snyder, and Alice Crimmins.

481. Jones, Hardy, and Nelson Potter. "Deterrence, Retribution, Denunciation and

the Death Penalty." UNIVERSITY OF MISSOURI-
KANSAS CITY LAW REVIEW 49 (1981): 158-69.

Argues that even if the death penalty had
significant deterrent effects, it still could
not be justified. Stresses that
retributivist arguments can be made against
capital punishment, as well as for it.

482. Joseph, Seth Parker. "The Eighth Amendment,
Rape, and Sexual Battery: A Study in Methods
of Judicial Review." UNIVERSITY OF MIAMI LAW
REVIEW 32 (1978): 690-708.

Reviews the Supreme Court's criteria for
determining when the death penalty for a
certain crime category is disproportionate.

483. Joyce, James Avery. CAPITAL PUNISHMENT: A
WORLD VIEW. New York: Thomas Nelson and
Sons, 1961.

Includes discussions of the Chessman case,
the death penalty in history and in different
countries today, why the penalty should be
abolished, and, in particular, the 1958 and
1960 debates in the United Nations concerning
alternatives to capital punishment.

484. Judson, Charles J., James J. Pandell, Jack B.
Owens, James L. McIntosh, and Dale L.
Matschullat. "A Study of the California Jury
in First-Degree Murder Cases." STANFORD LAW
REVIEW 21 (1969): 1297-437.

An analysis of data on numerous variables in
238 cases, between 1958 and 1966, in which
California juries decided whether to impose
death on defendants convicted of first-degree
murder. The study found no race effects, but
the economic status of the defendant was
associated with death sentencing.

485. Jurow, George L. "New Data on the Effect of
a 'Death Qualified' Jury on the Guilt
Determination Process." HARVARD LAW REVIEW
84 (1971): 567-611. Reprinted in Bedau and
Pierce, 1976, cited as item 110 above.

Two hundred eleven factory workers were

administered a questionnaire. The author
concludes that death qualified jurors are
more conviction prone than are other jurors.

486. Kadane, Joseph B. "Juries Hearing Death
Penalty Cases: Statistical Analysis of a
Legal Procedure." JOURNAL OF THE AMERICAN
STATISTICAL ASSOCIATION 78 (1983): 544-51.

Develops a statistical method to measure the
effects of the exclusion of those opposed to
the death penalty (and those always favoring
its use) from capital juries. Concludes that
the exclusion creates substantial bias
against the defense.

487. Kadane, Joseph B. "After Hovey: A Note on
Taking Account of the Automatic Death Penalty
Jurors." LAW AND HUMAN BEHAVIOR 8 (1984):
115-20.

Examines data on jurors to determine if the
exclusion of those who would always vote for
the death penalty would correct the
conviction proneness of death qualified
jurors, and concludes that the impact of
excluding this group is negligible.

488. Kanter, Stephen. "Dealing with Death: The
Constitutionality of Capital Punishment in
Oregon." WILLAMETTE LAW REVIEW 16 (1979):
1-65.

Argues that the death penalty in Oregon is
unconstitutional because retribution is
prohibited under the state constitution, and
that without the justification of
retribution, the U.S. Supreme Court would
declare the penalty to be cruel and unusual.

489. Kaplan, David A. "In Florida, a Story of
Politics and Death: A Governor Controls the
Ultimate Decision." NATIONAL LAW JOURNAL
(July 16, 1984): 1+.

An examination of Florida Governor Bob
Graham's actions on the death penalty.
Argues that the Governor wants to execute
prisoners, but, realizing that too many
executions might not be politically

expedient, is not executing as many as he
could.

490.   Kaplan, John. "The Problem of Capital
        Punishment." UNIVERSITY OF ILLINOIS LAW
        REVIEW 1983 (1983): 555-77.

        Examines and criticizes several pro-death
        penalty arguments (deterrence,
        incapacitation, retribution, cost),
        highlighting some of the major issues
        contained in contemporary death penalty
        debates.

491.   Kaplan, John. "Evidence in Capital Cases."
        FLORIDA STATE UNIVERSITY LAW REVIEW 11
        (1983): 369-86.

        Argues that most restrictions on the
        admissibility of mitigation evidence at the
        penalty phase of capital trials should be
        abandoned.

492.   Kaplan, John. "Administering Capital
        Punishment." UNIVERSITY OF FLORIDA LAW REVIEW
        36 (1984): 177-92.

        An overview of the issue of capital
        punishment, including the problems of
        executing the innocent and arbitrariness. A
        response by van den Haag is cited below as
        item 873, and one by Little is cited below as
        item 567.

493.   Kaplan, Stanley M. "Death, So Say We All."
        PSYCHOLOGY TODAY 19 (July 1985): 48-53.

        The author, a psychiatrist, describes the
        psychological trauma experienced by jurors in
        death penalty cases. Fifteen jurors from
        capital cases were interviewed. Most felt
        extreme stress from the experience.

494.   Karge, Stewart W. "Capital Punishment: Death
        for Murder Only." JOURNAL OF CRIMINAL LAW
        AND CRIMINOLOGY 69 (1978): 179-96.

        The evolution of the Supreme Court's views on
        the constitutionality of the death penalty is
        examined, from its earliest discussion of

Eighth Amendment issues (1878) to today (when death sentences are permitted only for criminal homicides).

495. Karp, David J. "Coker v. Georgia: Disproportionate Punishment and the Death Penalty for Rape." COLUMBIA LAW REVIEW 78 (1978): 1714-30.

A discussion of the Coker case, its legal origins, and implications. Concludes that the arguments against the constitutionality of the death penalty for rape are unconvincing.

496. Kay, Marvin L. Michael, and Loren Lee Cary. "'The Planters Suffer Little or Nothing': North Carolina Compensations for Executed Slaves, 1748-1772." SCIENCE AND SOCIETY 40 (1976): 288-306.

All but the New England colonies provided compensation for the slave owner if a slave was executed or given severe corporal punishment. This paper reviews how the process worked in North Carolina, pointing out the compensations were higher than the cost of replacing the slave.

497. Kelly, Matthew J., and George Schedler. "Capital Punishment and Rehabilitation." PHILOSOPHICAL STUDIES 34 (1978): 329-31.

Proposes the hypothetical argument that we should medically "tinker" with the worst criminals, destroying their humanity without killing them. By showing that such "tinkering" with a person could never be justified, the authors argue that they also show that capital punishment can never be justified.

498. Kennedy, Jonathan. "Florida's 'Cold, Calculated and Premeditated' Aggravating Circumstance in Death Penalty Cases." STETSON LAW REVIEW 17 (1987): 47-107.

A detailed examination of one of the aggravating circumstances specified in Florida's law. The author considers Florida

Supreme Court rulings on the circumstance,
and concludes the court has failed to rule
consistently and coherently.

499. Kennedy, Ludovic. TEN RILLINGTON PLACE. New
York: Simon and Schuster, 1961.

The story of John Reginald Christie, who
committed a murder in England in 1949 for
which an innocent man, Timothy John Evans,
was erroneously executed (and subsequently
pardoned).

500. Kennedy, Ludovic. THE AIRMAN AND THE
CARPENTER: THE LINDBERGH KIDNAPPING AND THE
FRAMING OF RICHARD HAUPTMANN. New York:
Viking, 1985.

An account of the Lindbergh kidnapping in
1932; vigorously argues that the 1936
execution of Hauptmann for the murder was a
miscarriage of justice.

501. Kenner, William D. "Competency on Death
Row." INTERNATIONAL JOURNAL OF LAW AND
PSYCHIATRY 8 (1986): 253-5.

A brief discussion of the issues of
competency to waive appeals and competency to
be executed, with a recommendation that
psychiatrists can best help the courts by
giving functional, not diagnostic,
appraisals.

502. Kerton, Laura L. "Enmund v. Florida: The
Constitutionality of Imposing the Death
Penalty Upon a Co-Felon in Felony Murder."
DEPAUL LAW REVIEW 32 (1983): 713-41.

Applauds the result in the Enmund case, but
argues that in reaching its decision, the
Court stretched the limits of excessiveness
and formulated a new, unclear requirement of
proof of intent.

503. Kevorkian, Jack. "Medicine, Ethics, and
Execution by Lethal Injection." MEDICINE AND
LAW 4 (1985): 407-13.

Argues that the medical profession's

opposition to participation in lethal
injections cannot withstand scrutiny,
especially when physicians also do abortions.
Suggests that physicians are obligated to
perform executions, and should also
transplant the prisoner's organs during and
after the execution.

504. Kevorkian, Jack. "Opinions on Capital
Punishment, Executions, and Medical Science."
MEDICINE AND LAW 4 (1985): 515-33.

A questionnaire was given to 169 respondents,
including some prisoners. The majority,
especially among the inmates, supported
capital punishment, and preferred lethal
injection as the method.

505. King, David. "The Brutalization Effect:
Execution Publicity and the Incidence of
Homicide in South Carolina." SOCIAL FORCES 57
(1978): 683-7.

An examination of South Carolina homicides
during 1950-63 and newspaper reports of
executions during this period. The author
finds no support for either the deterrence or
brutalization hypotheses.

506. Kirk, Michael. "Sixth and Fourteenth
Amendments--the Swain Song of the Racially
Discriminatory Use of Peremptory Challenges."
JOURNAL OF CRIMINAL LAW AND CRIMINOLOGY 77
(1986): 821-43.

A comment on Batson v. Kentucky (1986), in
which the Supreme Court held that whenever a
defendant makes a prima facie case of
purposeful discrimination in the use of
peremptory challenges, the prosecutor must
justify his or her challenges on non-racial
grounds.

507. Kleck, Gary. "Capital Punishment, Gun
Ownership, and Homicide." AMERICAN JOURNAL
OF SOCIOLOGY 84 (1979): 882-910.

Finds a direct and reciprocal relationship
between gun ownership levels and the homicide
rate. The certainty of arrest and conviction

is negatively associated with homicide rates, and imprisonment has an incapacitative effect. However, the 1947-73 data show no deterrent effect of the death penalty.

508. Kleck, Gary. "Racial Discrimination in Criminal Sentencing: A Critical Evaluation of the Evidence with Additional Evidence on the Death Penalty." AMERICAN SOCIOLOGICAL REVIEW 46 (1981): 783-804.

Reviews previous research on race and the death penalty, and concludes that studies which have found race-of-defendant discrimination have been conducted only in the South or have examined only sentencing for rape. Victim's race appears to be the major source of discrimination.

509. Kleck, Gary. "Life Support for an Ailing Hypothesis: Models of Summarizing the Evidence for Racial Discrimination in Sentencing." LAW AND HUMAN BEHAVIOR 9 (1985): 271-85.

Argues that the weight of the evidence contradicts the hypothesis of widespread racial discrimination in sentencing. The author identifies five ways in which many summaries of the literature convey the opposite impression.

510. Kleck, Gary. "Crime Control Through the Private Use of Armed Force." SOCIAL PROBLEMS 35 (1988): 1-21.

Suggests that in 1980, between 1,500-2,800 felons were killed by civilians, 8,700-16,000 were injured, and that guns were used defensively about one million times. Argues that victim resistance with guns is an effective deterrent or prevention device.

511. Klein, Lawrence R., Brian Forst, and Victor Filatov. "The Deterrent Effect of Capital Punishment: An Assessment of the Estimates." Pp. 336-60 in Alfred Blumstein, Jacqueline Cohen, and Daniel Nagin (eds.), DETERRENCE AND INCAPACITATION: ESTIMATING THE EFFECTS OF CRIMINAL SANCTIONS ON CRIME RATES.

Washington, D.C.: National Academy of
Sciences, 1978.

Probably the most influential review of Isaac
Ehrlich's work. Concludes that Ehrlich's
work is so problematic that, although it is
suggestive, it cannot be used as a basis for
policy decisions. Responded to by Ehrlich in
item 296 above.

512. Klein, Robert Anthony. "Juvenile Criminals
and the Death Penalty: Resurrection of the
Question Left Unanswered in Eddings v.
Oklahoma." NEW ENGLAND JOURNAL ON CRIMINAL
AND CIVIL CONFINEMENT 11 (1985): 437-87.

Examines the constitutionality of executing
inmates for crimes committed when under age
18, with a focus on the Maryland case of
James Trimble.

513. Klemm, Margaret Fae. THE DETERMINANTS OF
CAPITAL SENTENCING IN LOUISIANA, 1979-1984.
Ph.D. Dissertation, University of New
Orleans, 1986.

Race of victim, offender-victim relationship,
and geographical location are found to
predict who is sentenced to death, with the
effects of these variables somewhat
attenuated when the defendant's prior record
is considered.

514. Knorr, Stephen J. "Deterrence and the Death
Penalty: A Temporal Cross-Sectional
Approach." JOURNAL OF CRIMINAL LAW AND
CRIMINOLOGY 70 (1979): 235-54.

Critically reviews deterrence research, and
uses regression analysis to model execution
and homicide data from 1950-60. Divides
effects into regional and state models, but
finds no support for the deterrence
hypothesis.

515. Knowlton, Robert E. "Problems of Jury
Discretion in Capital Cases." UNIVERSITY OF
PENNSYLVANIA LAW REVIEW 101 (1953): 1099-136.

A classic paper on the role of juries in

capital sentencing, the rationale for that role, the function of the jury in various states, and what information jurors should have in order to make an informed sentencing decision.

516. Knudsen, Donald P. "Inequities and Abuses of Death Qualification: Causes and Cures." SOUTH DAKOTA LAW REVIEW 32 (1987): 281-99.

Reviews empirical literature that shows death qualified juries to be more conviction prone than other juries, and the rulings of the U.S. and South Dakota Supreme Courts that have approved their use. Discusses the inequities inherent in death qualification and the potential for abuse.

517. Kobbervig, Wayne, James Inverarity, and Pat Lauderdale. "Deterrence and the Death Penalty: A Comment on Phillips." AMERICAN JOURNAL OF SOCIOLOGY 88 (1982): 161-4.

A critique of the research of David Phillips, cited below as item 688. Includes a response by Phillips.

518. Koch, Edward T. "How Capital Punishment Affirms Life--Death and Justice." THE NEW REPUBLIC 192 (April 15, 1985): 12-5.

A short argument by the New York City Mayor, positing that because life is precious, we should execute people who kill. Six principal anti-death penalty arguments are criticized. A response by Bruck is cited above as item 179.

519. Koenig, Dorean M. "Capital Punishment and Crimes of Murder." LOYOLA UNIVERSITY OF CHICAGO LAW JOURNAL 13 (1982): 817-40.

Discusses various definitions of homicide, showing how the concept of willful murder has been narrowed, while the concept of felony murder has been expanded.

520. Koenig, Dorean M. "Freedom or Death: Two Doors in the Criminal Justice System (A Comparison of the Insanity Defense and

Capital Sentencing)." COOLEY LAW REVIEW 2
(1984): 341-62.

An examination of the use of mental health
professionals in making sentencing
determinations and the insanity defense in
capital trials. Criticizes the use of such
professionals in determinations of the
defendant's "ability to control" himself and
future dangerousness.

521. Koeninger, Rupert C. "Capital Punishment in
Texas, 1924-1968." CRIME AND DELINQUENCY 15
(1969): 132-41.

Reports on 483 persons executed in Texas
since the electric chair was first installed.
Background and case characteristics are
given. Concludes the death penalty has been
applied in a discriminatory fashion and has
not reduced crime rates.

522. Koestler, Arthur. REFLECTIONS ON HANGING.
New York: Macmillan and Co., 1957.

A classic treatise opposing the death penalty
by the famous writer (himself condemned to
death during the Spanish Civil War).
Includes discussions of the "Bloody Code" and
the history of capital punishment in England.

523. Koestler, Arthur. DIALOGUE WITH DEATH.
London: Macmillan, 1966.

As a correspondent covering the Spanish Civil
War in 1937, Koestler was captured by
Franco's troops, sentenced to death, and
spent several months on death row witnessing
the executions of his fellow prisoners and
awaiting his own. Written immediately after
his release in 1937, this book gives an
account of that experience and describes the
psychological impact of condemnation.

524. Koestler, Arthur, and C.H. Rolph. HANGED BY
THE NECK: AN EXPOSURE OF CAPITAL PUNISHMENT
IN ENGLAND. London: Penguin, 1961.

An expansion of Koestler's work in
REFLECTIONS ON HANGING (approximately one-

third of this book originally appeared there). A chapter entitled "What About the Victims?" is included.

525. Kofoed, Alan. "Who Shall Live and Who Shall Die?: State v. Osborn and the Idaho Death Penalty." IDAHO LAW REVIEW 18 (1982): 195-213.

Examines the 1981 decision of the Idaho Supreme Court, in its first post-Furman death penalty case, and how that decision interprets and limits the state's death penalty statute.

526. Kohlberg, Lawrence, and Donald Elfenbein. "The Development of Moral Judgments Concerning Capital Punishment." AMERICAN JOURNAL OF ORTHOPSYCHIATRY 45 (1975): 614-40. Reprinted in Bedau and Pierce, 1976, cited as item 110 above.

Data from a 20-year study on the development of moral judgment among American males show that in the most mature stages of development, there is a rejection of capital punishment. The authors contend that this provides a basis for asserting the immorality and unconstitutionality of the death penalty.

527. Kohlberg, Lawrence, and Donald Elfenbein. "Capital Punishment, Moral Development, and the Constitution." Pp. 243-93 in Lawrence Kohlberg, ESSAYS ON MORAL DEVELOPMENT, vol. I. New York: Harper and Row, 1981.

A revised and updated version of the previous paper by the authors.

528. Kopeny, William J. "Capital Punishment -- Who Should Choose?" WESTERN STATE UNIVERSITY LAW REVIEW 12 (1985): 383-416.

Argues that trial judges should use their own powers to fix maximum non-capital sentences before trial, so that certain cases are made ineligible for the death penalty from the start.

529. Kroll, Michael. "The Fraternity of Death."

CALIFORNIA LIVING (Los Angeles Herald), March 25, 1984: 8-12.

A vivid portrait of the men who supervised executions at San Quentin prison. Includes a discussion of the history of the gas chamber and some of its occupants.

530. Kroll, Michael A. "Death Watch: Counsel for the Condemned." CALIFORNIA LAWYER (December, 1987): 24-7, 106-9.

A description of the reactions by California defense attorneys as the numbers on death row and the prospects for executions increase. Many defense attorneys are avoiding capital cases. Changes in the prison atmosphere (among both inmates and guards) are also described.

531. Kunstler, William M. BEYOND A REASONABLE DOUBT?: THE ORIGINAL TRIAL OF CARYL CHESSMAN. New York: William Morrow, 1961.

The story of Caryl Chessman, sentenced to death in California in 1948 and executed in 1960 (for kidnapping for purpose of robbery), and why his case caused worldwide outrage.

532. Kuzma, Susan M. "The Constitutionality of Ohio's Death Penalty." OHIO STATE LAW JOURNAL 38 (1977): 617-75.

An analysis and criticism of the Ohio Supreme Court's decisions in death penalty cases, with particular attention to findings on mitigating circumstances.

533. Lamb, John H. "Dialogue with Hans W. Mattick." UNIVERSITY OF TOLEDO LAW REVIEW 10 (1979): 267-98.

An introduction to a special issue of the journal dedicated to Hans Mattick (see also item 383 above (Glaser) and item 635 below (Morris)). In this interview, Mattick outlines his views about the criminal justice system and why he opposes the death penalty.

534. Landerer, Lilly E. "Capital Punishment as a

Human Rights Issue Before the U.N." HUMAN
RIGHTS JOURNAL 4 (1971): 511-34.

Describes the efforts of the United Nations,
since it was first established, to restrict
or abolish the death penalty.

535. Lanza-Kaduce, Lonn. "Formality, Neutrality,
and Goal-Rationality: The Legacy of Weber in
Analyzing Legal Thought." JOURNAL OF
CRIMINAL LAW AND CRIMINOLOGY 73 (1982):
533-60.

An examination of the Furman decision,
arguing that to understand appellate
decision-making, the personal values of
judges are less important than judicial
perceptions of formal rules about how to
proceed.

536. Larkin, Paul J. "The Eighth Amendment and
the Execution of the Presently Incompetent."
STANFORD LAW REVIEW 32 (1980): 765-805.

Argues that the Eighth Amendment forbids the
execution of the mentally incompetent.
Discusses at length the Utah case of Gary
Gilmore and his competence for execution.

537. Lassers, Willard J. SCAPEGOAT JUSTICE: LLOYD
MILLER AND THE FAILURE OF THE AMERICAN LEGAL
SYSTEM. Bloomington: Indiana University
Press, 1973.

Presents the story of Lloyd Miller, convicted
of a 1955 Illinois murder and sentenced to
death on the basis of prosecutorial
misconduct. Reviews the events leading to
Miller's eventual exoneration.

538. Laurence, John. THE HISTORY OF CAPITAL
PUNISHMENT. Secaucus, N.J.: Citadel Press,
1960.

Originally published in 1932, this book
outlines the history of the death penalty,
prefaced with an essay by Clarence Darrow.
Chapters are included on various methods of
execution (beheading, the guillotine), famous
executioners, and how condemned prisoners

124

faced their fate.

539. Lawes, Lewis. MAN'S JUDGMENT OF DEATH: AN ANALYSIS OF CAPITAL PUNISHMENT BASED ON FACTS, NOT SENTIMENT. New York: Putnam, 1924.

An explanation of why the author, then warden of Sing Sing Prison, opposed the death penalty. Statistics are given on disparities in imposing the death penalty and on its uselessness as a deterrent.

540. Lawrence, Charles E., Jr. "Death as a Punishment for Rape: Disproportional, Cruel and Unusual Punishment." HOWARD LAW JOURNAL 21 (1978): 955-67.

A comment on Coker v. Georgia, which ruled that the sentence of death for rape was disproportionate.

541. Lawson, Steven F., David R. Colburn, and Darryl Paulson. "Groveland: Florida's Little Scottsboro." FLORIDA HISTORICAL QUARTERLY 65 (1986): 1-26.

Describes a classic case of racism involving four black men suspected of rape. One was shot by a mob, one was sentenced to life, and the other two to death, although all were probably innocent. The case, which began in 1949, ultimately involved Thurgood Marshall and the NAACP Legal Defense Fund.

542. Layson, Stephen K. "Homicide and Deterrence: Another View of the Canadian Time-Series Evidence." CANADIAN JOURNAL OF ECONOMICS 16 (1983): 52-73.

Examines Canadian homicides, 1927-77, and finds support for the hypothesis that capital punishment deters homicide.

543. Layson, Stephen K. "Homicide and Deterrence: A Reexamination of the United States Time-Series Evidence." SOUTHERN ECONOMIC JOURNAL 52 (1985): 68-89.

Using Vital Statistics records of homicides

between 1933 and 1967, the author concludes
that each execution deters approximately 18
murders from occurring. Presented as an
attempt to correct some of the faults in the
research of Isaac Ehrlich. Critiqued by
James Fox, cited above as item 342.

544. Layson, Stephen K. "United States Time-
Series Homicide Regressions with Adaptive
Expectations." BULLETIN OF THE NEW YORK
ACADEMY OF MEDICINE 62 (1986): 589-600.

Updates Ehrlich's work to include homicides
through 1984, and thus examines homicides
from 1934-84. He finds that each execution
deters 15 homicides.

545. Leavy, Deborah. "A Matter of Life and Death:
Due Process Protection in Capital Clemency
Proceedings." YALE LAW JOURNAL 90 (1981):
889-911.

Reviews the literature on clemency for death
row inmates, as well as current practices and
procedural problems. Argues that certain due
process practices should be extended to
clemency proceedings.

546. Ledewitz, Bruce S. "The Requirement of
Death: Mandatory Language in the Pennsylvania
Death Penalty Statute." DUQUESNE LAW REVIEW
21 (1982): 103-57.

Defines mandatory statutes as those where a
death sentence is required if certain
conditions are met, and distinguishes them
from automatic death penalty statutes, where
death is automatic if convicted of a certain
offense. Comparing Pennsylvania and Georgia,
the author argues the Pennsylvania statute is
unconstitutional because it does not allow
the sentencer to consider all mitigating
evidence, especially attacks upon the death
penalty itself.

547. Ledewitz, Bruce S. "The New Role of
Statutory Aggravating Circumstances in
American Death Penalty Law." DUQUESNE LAW
REVIEW 22 (1984): 317-96.

Examines the Supreme Court's opinion in <u>Zant</u>
<u>v. Stephens</u>, which changed the role of
aggravating circumstances by holding that
such circumstances must narrow the pool of
defendants eligible for a death sentence.
The article examines current aggravating
circumstances and discusses the issues
involved in evaluating whether they achieve
this new requirement.

548.   Ledewitz, Bruce S. "A Conversation Between a
Judge and His Friend Concerning Whether the
Judge Should Sentence a Defendant to Death."
JUDICATURE 71 (June-July, 1987): 7-12.

A fictional conversation between a judge, who
is about to sentence a person to death
despite reservations about the death penalty,
and a friend. At issue is whether the judge
should apply laws about which he has
conscientious misgivings.

549.   Legal Defense Fund. DEATH ROW, U.S.A.
(Available from NAACP Legal Defense Fund, 99
Hudson St., New York 10013).

Published every two months, this is the best
source of information regarding who is on
death row, their names, gender, race, and
jurisdiction, the characteristics of those
executed since 1977, and recent and pending
cases in the U.S. Supreme Court.

550.   Lehtinen, Marlene W. "The Value of Life: An
Argument for the Death Penalty." CRIME AND
DELINQUENCY 23 (1977): 237-52.

A general overview of capital punishment,
summarizing the retentionist position.
Argues we should have 3,000 executions per
year. Responded to by Smith, listed below as
item 813.

551.   Lempert, Richard O. "Desert and Deterrence:
An Assessment of the Moral Bases of the Case
for Capital Punishment." MICHIGAN LAW REVIEW
79 (1981): 1177-231.

Examines retribution and deterrence as moral
issues. Gives an excellent "common sense"

discussion of the logic of the deterrence
argument and why we can expect little
deterrent effect from the death penalty.
Argues retribution cannot justify the death
penalty, while in theory, deterrence could--
but in practice does not do so because the
evidence of no deterrent effect is so strong.
Critiqued by Alexander in item 9 above.

552.   Lempert, Richard O.   "The Effect of
Executions on Homicides: A New Look in an Old
Light." CRIME AND DELINQUENCY 29 (1983):
88-115.

Compares states on the basis of their
different probabilities of execution-per-
homicide, and finds no support for the
deterrence hypothesis.

553.   Lempert, Richard O.   "Capital Punishment in
the '80's: Reflections on the Symposium."
JOURNAL OF CRIMINAL LAW AND CRIMINOLOGY 74
(1983): 1101-14.

Discusses the dozen papers included in a
special issue of the journal, pointing out
that most of the authors stop short of
outright rejection of capital punishment;
instead they all suggest reforms. The author
also links this body of work to similar work
done in previous decades.

554.   LeSage, Constance R.   "Death Penalty for
Rape: Cruel and Unusual Punishment."
LOUISIANA LAW REVIEW 38 (1978): 868-74.

A critical comment on the Coker decision,
arguing that it departs from previous
treatments of the death penalty and ignores
various justifications for imposing death on
some of the most violent rapists.

555.   Leslie, Jack.   DECATHLON OF DEATH.   Mill
Valley, Calif.: Tarquin Books, 1979.

The story of the crimes, appeals, and 1955
executions in California of Jack Santo, Emmet
Perkins, and Barbara Graham.

556.   Lester, David.   THE DEATH PENALTY: ISSUES AND

128

ANSWERS. Springfield, Ill.: Charles C.
Thomas, 1987.

A very brief and general overview of the
death penalty debate.

557.   Levin, Jack, and James Alan Fox. MASS
MURDER: AMERICA's GROWING MENACE. New York:
Plenum, 1985.

Reviews several recent cases of mass murder
and of the theories that attempt to explain
the occurrences. Examines characteristics of
victims and assailants.

558.   Levine, Murray. "The Adversary Process and
Social Science in the Courts: Barefoot v.
Estelle." JOURNAL OF PSYCHIATRY AND THE LAW
12 (1984): 147-81.

In the Barefoot case, the Supreme Court
refused to prohibit the admission of
psychiatric predictions of future
dangerousness in capital cases, relying on
the adversary process to protect against
unreliable testimony. Evidence of the
unreliability of such predictions, and how
that unreliability is increased by the
adversarial process, is reviewed.

559.   Levine, Stephen (ed.). DEATH ROW. San
Francisco: Glide Publications, 1972.

A collection of a dozen essays, most of which
are by men on death row. Essays by Warden
Clinton Duffy and Chaplain Byron Eshelman are
also included.

560.   Levy, Barbara. LEGACY OF DEATH. Englewood
Cliffs, N.J.: Prentice-Hall, 1973.

The story of the Sanson family, who for
seven generations (1635-1889) served as
France's official executioners.

561.   Lewis, Dorothy Otnow, Jonathan H. Pincus,
Marilyn Feldman, Lori Jackson, and Barbara
Bard. "Psychiatric, Neurological, and
Psychoeducational Characteristics of 15 Death
Row Inmates in the United States." AMERICAN

JOURNAL OF PSYCHIATRY 143 (July, 1986):
838-45.

Reports clinical evaluations conducted on 15
death row inmates. All had histories of
severe head injury, five had major
neurological impairment, and seven had less
serious neurological problems.

562. Lewis, Peter W. "Killing the Killers: A
Post-Furman Profile of Florida's Condemned."
CRIME AND DELINQUENCY 25 (1979): 200-18.

Provides descriptive data on the backgrounds
and characteristics of 83 Florida death row
inmates. Presents data suggesting that
defendants with white victims are more likely
to receive death sentences than those who
kill blacks.

563. Lewis, Peter W., Henry W. Mannle, Harry E.
Allen, and Harold J. Vetter. "A Post-Furman
Profile of Florida's Condemned--A Question of
Discrimination in Terms of the Race of the
Victim and a Comment on Spinkellink v.
Wainwright." STETSON LAW REVIEW 9 (1979):
1-45.

Presents a profile of 83 inmates on Florida's
death row and a description of a typical week
on death row. The authors compare data on
all murders in Florida with murders committed
by prisoners on death row, and conclude that
defendants who kill whites are more likely
than those who kill blacks to be condemned.

564. Liebman, Ellen. "Appellate Review of Death
Sentences: A Critique of Proportionality
Review." UNIVERSITY OF CALIFORNIA-DAVIS LAW
REVIEW 18 (1985): 1433-80.

Argues that proportionality review is
essential in ensuring that death sentences
are not imposed in an arbitrary or capricious
manner, and criticizes the Supreme Court for
failing to require such review in the 1984
Pulley v. Harris case.

565. Liebman, James S., and Michael J. Shepard.
"Guiding Capital Sentencing Beyond the

'Boiler Plate': Mental Disorder As a
Mitigating Factor." GEORGETOWN LAW JOURNAL
66 (1978): 757-836.

Evaluates the U.S. Supreme Court decision in
Gregg, and contends that mental disorder
should be considered a major mitigating
circumstance under Gregg. Some discussion of
mental retardation and sociopathology is also
included.

566. Lindsay, Stephen P. "Prosecutorial Abuse of
Peremptory Challenges in Death Penalty
Litigation: Some Constitutional and Ethical
Considerations." CAMPBELL LAW REVIEW 8
(1985): 71-123.

Examines how peremptory challenges are used
by prosecutors in death penalty cases.
Reviews the empirical research that has
examined the extent and effects of these
challenges, and argues the practice violates
the defendant's constitutional rights by the
creation of juries that strongly favor the
death penalty.

567. Little, Joseph W. "Another View."
UNIVERSITY OF FLORIDA LAW REVIEW 36 (1984):
200-6.

A comment on an article by Kaplan (cited
above as item 492). Argues that Kaplan's
argument fails because it focuses on
procedural, not moral issues. Includes a
criticism of Florida's procedure that allows
judges to impose a death sentence even after
the jury has recommended life imprisonment.

568. Lloyd, James T., Jr. "Questions Surrounding
Virginia's Death Penalty." UNIVERSITY OF
RICHMOND LAW REVIEW 17 (1983): 603-16.

Examines issues raised by Virginia's death
penalty statute, including the issue of the
defendant's right to waive appeals. The 1982
consensual execution of Francis Coppola in
Virginia is discussed in depth.

569. Lobsenz, James E. "Unbridled Prosecutorial
Discretion and Standardless Death Penalty

Policies: The Unconstitutionality of the
Washington Capital Punishment Statutory
Scheme." UNIVERSITY OF PUGET SOUND LAW
REVIEW 7 (1984): 299-353.

Argues that the unchecked power of county
prosecutors to decide in what cases (if any)
to seek the death penalty leads to an
inequitable application of the penalty, and
hence the statute should be found unconstitutional.

570. Loeb, Robert H. CRIME AND CAPITAL
      PUNISHMENT. 2nd Edition. New York: Franklin
      Watts, 1986.

      A brief and general overview of capital
      punishment, intended for high school
      students.

571. Lofland, John. "The Dramaturgy of State
      Executions." Pp. 275-325 in Horace
      Bleackley, STATE EXECUTIONS VIEWED
      HISTORICALLY AND SOCIOLOGICALLY. Montclair,
      N.J.: Patterson Smith, 1977.

      Prepared as an original commentary for the
      republication of Bleackley's 1929 classic,
      The Hangmen of England, Lofland describes the
      rituals of historic and modern executions,
      emphasizing the drama and concealment
      involved.

572. Loh, Wallace D. SOCIAL RESEARCH IN THE
      JUDICIAL PROCESS: CASES, READINGS, AND TEXT.
      New York: Russell Sage Foundation, 1984.

      This is a book of empirical legal studies.
      Chapter 5 (pp. 193-272) uses death penalty
      case studies, and covers equal protection
      challenges, due process challenges
      (Witherspoon), and Eighth Amendment
      challenges (research on "evolving standards
      of decency").

573. Long, Thomas A. "Capital Punishment: 'Cruel
      and Unusual'?" ETHICS 83 (1973): 214-23.

      A discussion of the concepts of "cruel" and
      "unusual," arguing that the death penalty is

both, and that it should be abolished.
Responded to by Gerstein, cited above as item
369.

574.　Lopez-Rey, Manuel.　"General Overview of
Capital Punishment as a Legal Sanction."
FEDERAL PROBATION 44 (March, 1980): 18-23.

Provides a global overview of the status of
the death penalty and the extent of its use.

575.　Lotz, Roy, and Robert M. Regoli.　"Public
Support for the Death Penalty."　CRIMINAL
JUSTICE REVIEW 5 (1980): 55-66.

Three reasons for public support for the
death penalty are identified:　the Rational,
the Systems, and the Traditional Values
model.　A sample of 1,419 residents of
Washington State was surveyed.　The latter
model has the best explanatory value--
supporters of capital punishment believed in
orderliness, discipline, and sexual
restraint.

576.　Lyons, Douglas B.　"Capital Punishment: A
Selected Bibliography."　CRIMINAL LAW
BULLETIN 8 (1972): 783-802.

A useful bibliography, arranged by category
(but not annotated), mainly covering death
penalty materials published after 1968.
Among the more useful categories are listings
of papers relating to _Witherspoon_ issues and
executive clemency.

577.　Mackey, Philip English.　"Reverend George B.
Cheever: Yankee Reformer as Champion of the
Gallows."　PROCEEDINGS OF THE AMERICAN
ANTIQUARIAN SOCIETY 82 (Oct., 1972): 323-42.

Examines the career of the man who was most
instrumental in preventing any reforms in the
New York death penalty law in the nineteenth
century.

578.　Mackey, Philip English.　"The Inutility of
Mandatory Capital Punishment: An Historical
Note."　BOSTON UNIVERSITY LAW REVIEW 54
(1974): 32-5.　Reprinted in Bedau and Pierce,

1976, cited above as item 110.

The author reviews widespread criticism of the mandatory death penalty in different jurisdictions in the nineteenth century.

579. Mackey, Philip English. "'The Result May be Glorious'--Anti-Gallows Movement in Rhode Island, 1838-1852." RHODE ISLAND HISTORY 33 (Feb., 1974): 19-31.

An overview of the successful effort to abolish the death penalty in Rhode Island.

580. Mackey, Philip English. "An All-Star Debate On Capital Punishment, Boston, 1854." ESSEX INSTITUTE HISTORICAL COLLECTIONS 110 (July, 1974): 181-99.

Examines four days of legislative arguments over a bill intended to abolish the Massachusetts death penalty.

581. Mackey, Philip English. "Edward Livingston and the Origins of the Movement to Abolish Capital Punishment in the United States." LOUISIANA HISTORY 16 (Spring, 1975): 145-66.

Examines the efforts to abolish the death penalty in New York and Louisiana by the great abolitionist, Edward Livingston.

582. Mackey, Philip English. VOICES AGAINST DEATH: AMERICAN OPPOSITION TO CAPITAL PUNISHMENT, 1787-1975. New York: Burt Franklin, 1976.

Presents 26 statements against the death penalty by various figures in American history (e.g., Rush, Spear, Whitman, Greeley, Darrow, Chessman, and executioner Robert Elliott).

583. Mackey, Philip English. HANGING IN THE BALANCE: THE ANTI-CAPITAL PUNISHMENT MOVEMENT IN NEW YORK STATE, 1776-1861. New York: Garland Books, 1982.

A history of the capital punishment laws in New York State and the efforts to revise and

restrict them during the first 85 years of
the nation's history. One of the best and
most comprehensive studies of the history of
the death penalty in one state.

584.   MacNamara, Donel E.J. "Convicting the
        Innocent." CRIME AND DELINQUENCY 15 (1969):
        57-61.

        A brief overview of the problem of convicting
        the innocent, with numerous citations to both
        British and American cases.

585.   Magee, Doug. SLOW COMING DARK: INTERVIEWS ON
        DEATH ROW. New York: Pilgrim Press, 1980.

        Interviews with twelve death row inmates,
        focusing on the prisoners' accounts of their
        lives before and since receiving death
        sentences, and their reflections on their
        experiences.

586.   Magee, Doug. WHAT MURDER LEAVES BEHIND: THE
        VICTIM'S FAMILY. New York: Dodd, Mead, 1983.

        An excellent discussion of the experiences of
        families of homicide victims, constructed
        with data obtained from interviews with them.

587.   Mailer, Norman. THE EXECUTIONER'S SONG.
        Boston: Little, Brown, 1979.

        The story of the life and death of Gary
        Gilmore, executed in Utah in 1977. Reviewed
        by Babcock in item 38 above.

588.   Malone, Patrick. "Death Row and the Medical
        Model." HASTINGS CENTER REPORT 9 (October,
        1979): 5-6.

        Reviews physicians' attitudes toward lethal
        injections and the ethical problems this
        method of execution creates.

589.   Mangum, Geoffrey Carlyle. "Vague and
        Overlapping Guidelines: A Study of North
        Carolina's Capital Sentencing Statute." WAKE
        FOREST LAW REVIEW 16 (1980): 765-819.

        Examines how the North Carolina Supreme Court

has interpreted and applied the provisions of
the state's death penalty law. Argues the
aggravating circumstances in the statute are
too broad and vague to be uniformly applied.

590. Manheim, Karl M. "The Capital Punishment
      Cases: A Criticism of Judicial Method."
      LOYOLA OF LOS ANGELES LAW REVIEW 12 (1978):
      85-134.

      Explores the treatment of death penalty cases
      by the Supreme Court since 1971. Argues
      against the Court's reliance on legislative
      and popular opinion to interpret the meaning
      of the Eighth Amendment. Criticizes the
      Court for lacking coherent death penalty
      standards.

591. Marcus, Michael H., and David S. Weissbrodt.
      "The Death Penalty Cases." CALIFORNIA LAW
      REVIEW 56 (1968): 1268-490.

      A comprehensive overview of the California
      death penalty statute. Includes a discussion
      of 1) the state's interest in the death
      penalty, 2) the individual's interest in
      life, 3) California death penalty trials and
      appeals, and 4) the right to counsel after
      the first appeal. Contends that both
      practical experience and constitutional law
      compel an end to the death penalty.

592. Margolis, Joseph. "Punishment." SOCIAL
      THEORY AND PRACTICE 2 (1973): 347-63.

      A philosophical examination of the goals of
      punishment and the success of the death
      penalty in achieving them.

593. Margolis, Joseph. "Capital Punishment."
      JOURNAL OF BEHAVIORAL ECONOMICS 6 (1977):
      269-78.

      A philosophical statement arguing that the
      role of deterrence need not be a central
      question in contemporary death penalty
      debates.

594. Marsel, Robert S. "Mr. Justice Arthur J.
      Goldberg and the Death Penalty: A Memorandum

to the Conference."   SOUTH TEXAS LAW REVIEW
27 (1986): 487-92.

Describes Justice Goldberg's memorandum
proposing that the death penalty should be
found cruel and unusual under all
circumstances. Discusses the influence of
the memorandum on later Supreme Court
decisions.

595.   Marshall, Justice Thurgood.   "Remarks on the
Death Penalty Made at the Judicial Conference
of the Second Circuit." COLUMBIA LAW REVIEW
86 (1986): 1-8.

Sharply criticizes the administration of the
death penalty, outlining why he believes that
death row inmates are not afforded adequate
due process safeguards.

596.   Masur, Louis Paul.   THE CULTURE OF EXECUTIONS
AND THE CONFLICT OVER CAPITAL PUNISHMENT IN
AMERICA, 1776-1860.   Ph.D. Dissertation,
Princeton University, 1985.

Examines the changing rituals of execution
and the debate over the death penalty between
the Revolution and the Civil War.

597.   Mayell, Marvin S.   "Eighth Amendment--
Proportionality Review of Death Sentences Not
Required."   JOURNAL OF CRIMINAL LAW AND
CRIMINOLOGY 75 (1984): 839-54.

Discusses with approval the 1984 case of
Pulley v. Harris, in which the Supreme Court
refused to order proportionality reviews to
determine if similar cases were receiving
similar penalties.

598.   Maynes, Rodger.   "The Death Penalty for
Juveniles--A Constitutional Alternative."
JOURNAL OF JUVENILE LAW 7 (1983): 54-67.

Argues that executing juveniles is
constitutional and an effective means for
protecting society from hardened juvenile
offenders.

599.   McCafferty, James A. (ed.).   CAPITAL

PUNISHMENT. Chicago: Aldine-Atherton, 1972.

Included are sixteen essays by scholars; among them are five supporting and six opposing the death penalty.

600. McCall, Bruce. "Sentencing by Death Qualified Juries and the Right to Jury Nullification." HARVARD JOURNAL ON LEGISLATION 22 (1985): 289-300.

Argues the Supreme Court should recognize a defendant's Sixth Amendment right to a trial by a jury that is not unfairly prejudiced against the exercise of its powers of nullification (i.e., the jury's power to avoid what it sees as a harsh or unjust punishment).

601. McCall, Donn J. "Evolution of Capital Punishment in Wyoming: A Reconciliation of Social Retribution and Humane Concern?" LAND AND WATER LAW REVIEW 13 (1978): 865-907.

An examination and analysis of Wyoming's prior and current death penalty statutes. The author concludes that the current statute is constitutionally valid.

602. McClellan, Grant S. (ed.). CAPITAL PUNISHMENT. New York: Wilson, 1961.

A collection of twenty-eight essays on the death penalty, mostly from popular magazines, debating the pros and cons of capital punishment.

603. McCray, Doug. "Death Watch: The Journal of a Florida Convict Awaiting Execution." ST. PETERSBURG TIMES, (May 27, 1984): D1 (also published in SOUTHERN EXPOSURE, Vol. 13, 45-51).

A Florida death row inmate describes the events that occurred when his death warrant was signed, and his emotional and psychological reactions.

604. McFadden, Gerald T. "Capital Sentencing: Effect of McGautha and Furman." TEMPLE LAW

QUARTERLY 45 (1972): 619-48.

An examination of the McGautha and Furman rulings and their effects on capital sentencing.

605. McFarland, Sam G. "Is Capital Punishment a Short-Term Deterrent to Homicide? A Study of the Effects of Four Recent Executions." JOURNAL OF CRIMINAL LAW AND CRIMINOLOGY 74 (1983): 1014-32.

Examines weekly homicide rates after four executions, 1977-81. No evidence of a deterrent effect is found.

606. McGahey, Richard M. "Dr. Ehrlich's Magic Bullet: Econometric Theory, Econometrics, and the Death Penalty." CRIME AND DELINQUENCY 26 (1980): 485-502.

Reviews the recent studies on deterrence, especially Isaac Ehrlich's, and the criticisms of this body of work. Attempts to explain the statistical issues involved in such work for a lay audience.

607. McGehee, Edward G., and William H. Hildebrand (eds.). THE DEATH PENALTY: A LITERARY AND HISTORICAL APPROACH. Boston: D.C. Heath, 1964.

A collection of fifty selections from well-known authors on the topic of capital punishment. Among the contributors are William Blackstone, Jerome Frank, Aldous Huxley, Will Rogers, William Thackeray, Thomas Hardy, Thomas More, William Wordsworth, Victor Hugo, Charles Dickens, H.L. Mencken, and Theodore Roosevelt.

608. McGovern, James R. ANATOMY OF A LYNCHING: THE KILLING OF CLAUDE NEAL. Baton Rouge: Louisiana State University Press, 1982.

An account of the lynching of Claude Neal in Florida in 1934. The historical setting is outlined, events described and cited, and results of interviews with some of the participants are presented.

609. McGowan, Gailon W., Jr. "The Opportunity to Address the Merits: _Barefoot_ _v_. _Estelle_." COLUMBIA HUMAN RIGHTS LAW REVIEW 17 (1985): 83-102.

An examination of the _Barefoot_ decision, concluding that the effect of the ruling has been to deprive death row prisoners of their Fifth and Fourteenth Amendment rights. Describes the process of appeals for stays of execution, and the experiences of attorneys representing condemned inmates.

610. McKee, David L., and Michael L. Sesnowitz. "Welfare Economic Aspects of Capital Punishment." AMERICAN JOURNAL OF ECONOMICS AND SOCIOLOGY 35 (1976): 41-7.

Using postulates from modern welfare economics, the authors argue the deterrence question is largely irrelevant in the debate about capital punishment. Arguing along lines similar to cost-benefit analysis, the authors conclude that capital punishment is not justifiable. Responded to by Reynolds in item 737 below.

611. McKee, David and Michael Sesnowitz. "Capital Punishment: The Canadian Experience." JOURNAL OF BEHAVIORAL ECONOMICS 6 (1977): 145-52.

Examining Canadian data, 1930-1954, the authors find no support for the deterrence hypothesis.

612. McLean, Rebecca. "Reconstruction of Arizona's Death Penalty Statute Under _Watson_." ARIZONA LAW REVIEW 22 (1980): 1037-53.

In the _Watson_ decision (1978), the Arizona Supreme Court found a portion of the state's statute unconstitutional because of problems under _Lockett_ _v_. _Ohio_. However, it allowed defendants then on death row to be resentenced to death under the reconstructed statute. The author describes and criticizes the decision, arguing that those then on death row should not have been resentenced to death.

613. McMahon, Dennis P. "Rape, Recidivism, and Capital Punishment: Time for the Supreme Court to Re-examine Its Interpretation of the Eighth Amendment." OHIO NORTHERN UNIVERSITY LAW REVIEW 9 (1982): 99-119.

Criticizes the Supreme Court's holding that rapists, regardless of their prior history or the circumstances of their crime, cannot be executed. Instead, the author argues that habitual rapists should be punished by death.

614. McManners, John. DEATH AND THE ENLIGHTMENT: CHANGING ATTITUDES TO DEATH AMONG CHRISTIANS AND UNBELIEVERS IN EIGHTEENTH-CENTURY FRANCE. New York: Oxford University Press, 1981.

Contains an excellent discussion of the changing cultural meanings of death and a similarly fine chapter on public executions.

615. McManus, Walter S. "Estimates of the Deterrent Effect of Capital Punishment: The Importance of the Researcher's Prior Beliefs." JOURNAL OF POLITICAL ECONOMY 93 (1985): 417-25.

Shows how assumptions necessary in deterrence research are influenced by the researcher's prior expectations about which model the data will fit.

616. Mead, Margaret. "A Life for a Life: What that Means Today." REDBOOK (June, 1978): 56-60.

A statement against the death penalty by a pioneering anthropologist.

617. Meador, Roy. CAPITAL REVENGE: 54 VOTES AGAINST LIFE. Philadelphia: Dorrance and Co., 1975.

In 1974, fifty-four U.S. Senators voted in favor of reinstituting the death penalty at the federal level. This book is a series of

essays opposing the death penalty, with one
essay directed to each of the Senators.

618.   Mello, Michael. "Florida's 'Heinous,
       Atrocious or Cruel' Aggravating Circumstance:
       Narrowing the Class of Death-Eligible Cases
       Without Making it Smaller." STETSON LAW
       REVIEW 13 (1984): 523-54.

       Reviews capital cases in which Florida courts
       found the aggravating circumstance that the
       crime was "especially heinous, atrocious, or
       cruel." Argues that this circumstance is a
       catch-all that fails to channel the
       sentencing decisions of judges and juries.

619.   Mello, Michael, and Ruthann Robson. "Judge
       Over Jury: Florida's Practice of Imposing
       Death Over Life in Capital Cases." FLORIDA
       STATE UNIVERSITY LAW REVIEW 13 (1985): 31-75.

       Reviews the provision of Florida law that
       allows judges to sentence defendants to death
       despite a jury recommendation of life
       imprisonment. Argues the override provision
       undermines the jury's historic sentencing
       function, is costly, and increases the
       probability that an innocent defendant will
       be executed.

620.   Meltsner, Michael. CRUEL AND UNUSUAL: THE
       SUPREME COURT AND CAPITAL PUNISHMENT. New
       York: Random House, 1973.

       An outstanding account, by a leading attorney
       in the fight over the death penalty conducted
       by the NAACP Legal Defense Fund between 1963
       and 1972. Describes legal strategies which
       brought about a moratorium on executions, and
       which led to the Furman decision, declaring
       the death penalty unconstitutional as then
       administered. Reviewed by Bedau in item 88
       above.

621.   Meltsner, Michael. "Litigating Against the
       Death Penalty: The Strategy Behind Furman."
       YALE LAW JOURNAL 82 (1973): 1111-39.

       An edited excerpt from the above book, in
       which the author describes the successful

attempts to block executions in Texas and Florida by class action habeas corpus petitions.

622.   Meltsner, Michael. "On Death Row, the Wait Continues." Pp. 169-76 in Herman Schwartz (ed.), THE BURGER COURT: RIGHTS AND WRONGS OF THE SUPREME COURT, 1969-1986. New York: Viking, 1987.

A brief overview and criticism of death penalty decisions made by the Supreme Court while Warren Burger was its Chief Justice.

623.   Meyer, Herman H.B.   SELECT LIST OF REFERENCES ON CAPITAL PUNISHMENT. Washington, D.C.: U.S. Government Printing Office, 1912.

A list of 282 books and articles, including author and subject indices.

624.   Mikva, Abner J., and John C. Godbold. "You Don't Have to be a Bleeding Heart: Representing Death Row." HUMAN RIGHTS 14 (Winter, 1987): 21-5.

A dialogue between two judges (from the D.C. Court of Appeals and the Eleventh Circuit Court of Appeals respectively) on the problem of securing attorneys for death row inmates.

625.   Miller, Arthur S., and Jeffrey H. Bowman. "'Slow Dance on the Killing Ground': The Willie Francis Case Revisited." DEPAUL LAW REVIEW 32 (1982): 1-75.

A history of the case of Willie Francis, who in 1946 was spared death when the electric chair in which he was seated failed to operate properly. Francis then argued that to attempt to execute him again would be "cruel and unusual punishment." The Supreme Court disagreed, and Francis was executed.

626.   Miller, Alan V. CAPITAL PUNISHMENT AS A DETERRENT: A BIBLIOGRAPHY. Monticello, Ill.: Vance Bibliographies, 1980.

A 10-page listing of recent work on deterrence and the death penalty.

627. Miller, Gene. INVITATION TO A LYNCHING.
Garden City, New York: Doubleday, 1975.

Written by a reporter from the Miami Herald,
this book recounts the story of Freddie Pitts
and Wilbert Lee, two innocent men who were
twice sentenced to death in Florida and
ultimately pardoned in 1975.

628. Millman, Michael G. "Financing the Right to
Counsel in Capital Cases." LOYOLA OF LOS
ANGELES LAW REVIEW 19 (1985): 383-90.

Describes the problems of finding qualified
attorneys to represent California death row
inmates, and the office of California
Appellate Project (headed by the author),
which recruits lawyers to handle these cases.

629. Moberly, Walter. THE ETHICS OF PUNISHMENT.
London: Faber and Faber, 1968.

A thorough discussion of penal theory,
including retributive and utilitarian
approaches, and their strengths and
weaknesses. Includes a chapter on moral
questions raised by capital punishment.

630. Monahan, John. "The Prediction of Violent
Criminal Behavior: A Methodological Critique
and Prospectus." Pp. 244-69 in Alfred
Blumstein, Jacqueline Cohen, and Daniel Nagin
(eds.), DETERRENCE AND INCAPACITATION:
ESTIMATING THE EFFECTS OF CRIMINAL SANCTIONS
ON CRIME RATES. Washington, D.C.: National
Academy of Sciences, 1978.

Suggests several ways that the prediction of
dangerousness can be improved through
empirical research. Policies that rely on
predicted dangerousness and the empirical
data on this issue are reviewed.

631. Moore, Michael. "Attitude Toward Capital
Punishment: Scale Validation." PSYCHOLOGICAL
REPORTS 37 (1975): 21-2.

Thurstone's "Attitude Toward Capital
Punishment" scale was found valid and

reliable in predicting 44 students' votes on the California Death Penalty Proposition.

632.   Moran, Gary, and John Craig Comfort. "Neither 'Tentative' nor 'Fragmentary': Verdict Preference of Impaneled Felony Jurors as a Function of Attitude Toward Capital Punishment." JOURNAL OF APPLIED PSYCHOLOGY 71 (1986): 146-55.

Investigates differential inclinations to convict among felony jurors who vary in their approval of capital punishment. Jurors favoring capital punishment were more likely to convict. Characteristics of jurors are given, categorized by their attitude toward capital punishment.

633.   Morgan, Roy B., Jr. "Death Penalty in Tennessee: Recent Developments." MEMPHIS STATE UNIVERSITY LAW REVIEW 8 (1977): 107-20.

Analyzes changes in Tennessee's death penalty law as a result of the U.S. Supreme Court's 1976 death penalty rulings.

634.   Morris, John B., Jr. "The Rush to Execution: Successive Habeas Corpus Petitions in Capital Cases." YALE LAW JOURNAL 95 (1985): 371-89.

Reviews cases of recent executions in which constitutional claims were never decided by the courts. Criticizes the summary disposal of potentially valid claims raised in successive habeas corpus petitions.

635.   Morris, Norval. "Hans Mattick and the Death Penalty: Sentimental Notes on Two Topics." UNIVERSITY OF TOLEDO LAW REVIEW 10 (1979): 299-316.

Expanding on Mattick's work (see article by Lamb, cited above as item 533), Morris argues it would be unreasonable to reintroduce the death penalty because of the undesirable effects it has on society.

636.   Morris, Norval, and Gordon Hawkins. "The Death Penalty and Abortion." Pp. 79-86 in Norval Morris and Gordon Hawkins, LETTER TO

THE PRESIDENT ON CRIME CONTROL. Chicago: University of Chicago Press, 1977.

Argues that capital punishment today is almost completely irrelevant to the problem of controlling crime, and calls for its abolition.

637. Mossman, Douglas. "Assessing and Restoring Competency to be Executed: Should Psychiatrists Participate?" BEHAVIORAL SCIENCES AND THE LAW 5 (1987): 397-410.

Argues that the evaluation and treatment of death row prisoners for competency to be executed is ethical for mental health professionals and emphasizes respect for patients' autonomy and rationality. While the paper does not recommend psychiatric participation, it offers a "moral rationale," based on retributive principles, to support those who choose to participate.

638. Moyer, Joel C. "The Death Penalty in Massachusetts." SUFFOLK UNIVERSITY LAW REVIEW 8 (1974): 632-81.

Briefly reviews the history of capital punishment in Massachusetts, and describes legislative, executive, judicial, and political reactions to the _Furman_ decision.

639. Muller, Eric L. "The Legal Defense Fund's Capital Punishment Campaign: The Distorting Influence of Death." YALE LAW AND POLICY REVIEW 4 (1985): 158-87.

Argues that just as the death penalty distorts decisions of the criminal justice system, it also distorts decisions of lawyers and law firms working against capital punishment. Describes the abolition efforts of the Legal Defense Fund in the context of the organization's commitment to racial equality.

640. Mulligan, William Hughes. "Cruel and Unusual Punishments: The Proportionality Rule." FORDHAM LAW REVIEW 47 (1979): 639-50.

The author, a judge on the U.S. Court of
Appeals (Second Circuit), discusses the
proportionality principle, and argues for
judicial restraint in its application.

641.   Mullin, Courtney. "The Jury System in Death
Penalty Cases: A Symbolic Gesture." LAW AND
CONTEMPORARY PROBLEMS 43 (1980): 137-54.

Argues that social, not legal, variables
determine who is sentenced to death. In
part, this is due to bias in jury selection,
and this problem is discussed at length.

642.   Murchison, Kenneth M. "Toward a Perspective
on the Death Penalty Cases." EMORY LAW
JOURNAL 27 (1978): 469-555.

Examines the U.S. Supreme Court's death
penalty decisions in light of the movement to
abolish capital punishment, and examines the
current status of Eighth Amendment doctrine.
Argues that both political forces and legal
doctrine must be considered to supply
consistency to the Court's decisions.

643.   Murchison, Kenneth M., and Arthur J. Schwab.
"Capital Punishment in Virginia." VIRGINIA
LAW REVIEW 58 (1972): 97-142.

Reviews the Virginia death penalty statute
(pre-Furman) and argues it should be revised.

644.   Murton, Tom. "Treatment of Condemned
Prisoners." CRIME AND DELINQUENCY 15 (1969):
94-111.

After working for one year with condemned
prisoners in Arkansas, the author argues that
they can be successfully merged with the
general prison population, and shows how this
was actually done in Arkansas.

645.   Nakell, Barry. "The Cost of the Death
Penalty." CRIMINAL LAW BULLETIN 14 (1978):
69-80.

Though lacking precise empirical data, this
paper analyzes several aspects of capital
punishment and concludes that it is much more

costly as a system than the alternative
system of life imprisonment.

646. Nakell, Barry, and Kenneth A. Hardy. THE
ARBITRARINESS OF THE DEATH PENALTY.
Philadelphia: Temple University Press, 1987.

An examination of the disposition of homicide
cases in North Carolina, 1976-77. Although
not enough death penalty cases were in the
sample for the authors to offer precise
conclusions, race of victim effects are found
at several stages of case processing. The
authors review relevant literature and
develop arbitrariness theory to attempt to
explain the patterns. Also includes lengthy
discussion of recent U.S. Supreme Court
decisions in death penalty cases, and the
views expressed by the different Justices on
the issue.

647. Nathanson, Stephen. "Does it Matter if the
Death Penalty is Arbitrarily Administered?"
PHILOSOPHY AND PUBLIC AFFAIRS 14 (1985):
149-64.

Should the death penalty be abolished because
it is arbitrarily applied? While proponents
answer negatively, Nathanson challenges this
logic. This article was responded to by van
den Haag, cited below as item 874.

648. Nathanson, Stephen. AN EYE FOR AN EYE? THE
MORALITY OF PUNISHING BY DEATH. Totowa,
N.J.: Rowman and Littlefield, 1987.

In a lengthy discussion of the moral issues
concerning the legitimacy of capital
punishment, this book evaluates the arguments
for the death penalty, such as just desert,
and rejects them all. Included is a
discussion of whether murderers "deserve to
die" and how the moral question would change
if it could be shown that the death penalty
did save lives.

649. National Council on Crime and Delinquency.
"Policy Statement on Capital Punishment."
CRIME AND DELINQUENCY 10 (1964): 105-9.

A statement condemning the death penalty and urging its abolition, accompanied by a statement of facts supporting the position.

650. National Interreligious Task Force on Criminal Justice. "CAPITAL PUNISHMENT: WHAT THE RELIGIOUS COMMUNITY SAYS." New York: NITFCJ (475 Riverside Dr., Room 1700-A, New York 10027): (no date).

Contains statements of twenty-one religious bodies opposing or urging caution in the use of the death penalty.

651. Neapolitan, Jerry. "Support for and Opposition to Capital Punishment: Some Associated Social-Psychological Factors." CRIMINAL JUSTICE AND BEHAVIOR 10 (1983): 195-208.

College students were divided into three groups: 1) those who oppose capital punishment, 2) those who support it only if it deters, and 3) those who support it even if it does not deter. The results indicate that the opponents have greater respect for human life, greater opposition to interpersonal violence, greater respect for the law, and more sympathy for the victims of homicide.

652. Neises, Michael L., and Ronald C. Dillehay. "Death Qualification and Conviction Proneness: _Witt_ and _Witherspoon_ Compared." BEHAVIORAL SCIENCES AND THE LAW 5 (1987): 479-94.

A survey was administered to 135 respondents in Fayette County, Kentucky. Twenty one and two tenths percent would have been excludable from capital service under the _Witt_ standard (including "always pro-death penalty"), but only 13.6 percent were excludable under the _Witherspoon_ standard. The jurors excludable under _Witt_ and _Witherspoon_ are compared.

653. Nesbitt, Charlotte A. "Managing Death Row." CORRECTIONS TODAY 48 (July, 1986): 90-4+.

Describes the numbers of death row inmates,

and a project being conducted by the American
Correctional Association to gather data on
how death row prisoners are being managed.

654. Nevares-Muniz, Dora. "The Eighth Amendment
      Revisited: A Model of Weighted Punishments."
      JOURNAL OF CRIMINAL LAW AND CRIMINOLOGY 75
      (1984): 272-89.

      Argues that fixed prison terms do not
      guarantee that the severity of punishment
      fits the severity of crime, and therefore
      fail the test of proportionality. While the
      death penalty is not specifically discussed,
      an offense severity scale is proposed, using
      Puerto Rician data, to rank offenses in a
      severity continuum.

655. New York State Defenders Association.
      CAPITAL LOSSES: THE PRICE OF THE DEATH
      PENALTY FOR NEW YORK STATE. Albany: New York
      State Defenders Association, 1982.

      An analysis of the expense of reintroducing
      the death penalty in New York, showing that
      such costs would be several times greater
      than the costs of a uniform system of life
      imprisonment.

656. New York State Defenders Association. "The
      Death Penalty: Invitation to a Real
      Dialogue." Published as a special issue of
      THE DEFENDER 8 (July-August, 1986).

      Includes contributions by Hugo Adam Bedau (on
      the myths concerning capital punishment),
      Watt Espy (executions of the mentally ill),
      Donna Hall (deterrence), Karen Kane (families
      of death row inmates), Michael Radelet (the
      condemnation of the innocent), Henry
      Schwarzschild (on the first decade after the
      Gregg decision), and Ronald Tabak (on the
      arbitrariness of the death penalty).

657. Nietzel, Michael T., and Ronald C. Dillehay.
      "The Effects on Variations in Voir Dire
      Procedures in Capital Murder Trials." LAW
      AND HUMAN BEHAVIOR 6 (1982): 1-13.

      Examines the voir dire in thirteen capital

trials in Kentucky, 1975-80. Four types of
voir dire are discussed: whether the
venirepersons were questioned individually or
as a group, and whether they were
sequestered. More defense challenges for
cause were sustained under conditions of
individual sequestration, and thus the
authors recommend that procedure.

658.   Nietzel, Michael T., Ronald C. Dillehay, and
Melissa J. Himelein. "Effects of Voir Dire
Variations in Capital Trials: A Replication
and Extension." BEHAVIORAL SCIENCES AND THE
LAW 5 (1987): 467-77.

Examines 18 capital trials from Kentucky,
South Carolina, and California. As in their
previous work (cited above), the authors find
that sequestered, individual voir dire
resulted in more defense removals for cause
than less extensive voir dire.

659.   Nordin, John Michael. "Criminal Procedure:
Creating Great Risk of Death to More than One
Person as an Aggravating Circumstance."
OKLAHOMA LAW REVIEW 34 (1981): 325-36.

An examination of one aggravating
circumstance in Oklahoma's statute: "The
defendant knowingly created a great risk of
death to more than one person." The author
argues that the wording of this is too
ambiguous for precise application.

660.   Normandeau, Andre. "Pioneers in Criminology:
Charles Lucas--Opponent of Capital
Punishment." JOURNAL OF CRIMINAL LAW,
CRIMINOLOGY AND POLICE SCIENCE 61 (1970):
218-28.

The author presents a brief overview of the
life of Lucas (1803-1889) and his views of
the prison system, the death penalty, and
other issues.

661.   Note. "Post-Conviction Remedies in
California Death Penalty Cases." STANFORD
LAW REVIEW 11 (1958): 94-135.

An extensive analysis of available post-conviction remedies for California death row inmates, and an investigation of the actual procedures used in 180 cases in the preceding 15 years. Gives final dispositions for the 180 California defendants sentenced to death between 1942 and 1956. Socioeconomic status is significantly correlated with sentencing outcome.

662.   Note. "Mental Suffering Under Sentence of Death: A Cruel and Unusual Punishment." IOWA LAW REVIEW 57 (1972): 814-33.

Explores the question of whether mental suffering in anticipation of death is a cruel and unusual punishment. The mental suffering of prisoners on death row is discussed at length.

663.   Note. "Constitutional Law: Death Penalty: Execution of the Insane." HARVARD LAW REVIEW 100 (1986): 100-6.

A comment on Ford v. Wainwright. Argues the Court implicitly endorsed the retributive meaning of the common law ban against executing the insane.

664.   Oberer, Walter E. "Does Disqualification of Jurors for Scruples Against Capital Punishment Constitute Denial of Fair Trial on Issue of Guilt?" TEXAS LAW REVIEW 39 (1961): 545-67.

A classic paper that argues (although without data) that death qualified juries are more likely than other juries to convict.

665.   Ogloff, James R.P. "The Juvenile Death Penalty: A Frustrated Society's Attempt for Control." BEHAVIORAL SCIENCES AND THE LAW 5 (1987): 447-55.

In a paper strongly critical of the death penalty for juveniles, the author argues that because so many are sentenced under felony-murder laws (making their intent irrelevant), executing this group is inconsistent with the theories of punishment that have been used to support the death penalty.

666. Olmstead, Judith. "The Constitutional Right
to Assistance in Addition to Counsel in a
Death Penalty Case." DUQUESNE LAW REVIEW 23
(1985): 753-72.

Must the court afford a capital defendant
assistance beyond providing an attorney?
This article argues that it is now generally
recognized that the state must provide the
defendant with a psychiatric exam if insanity
is a serious issue. Questions relating to a
right to access other experts are reviewed.
The U.S. Supreme Court's decision in Ake v.
Oklahoma was announced as this paper was in
press, and is mentioned in a footnote.

667. O'Quinn, Michael A. "Appellate Review of the
Death Sentence in Nebraska." CREIGHTON LAW
REVIEW 15 (1982): 248-62.

The author argues that the Nebraska Supreme
Court must examine all homicide cases (not
just death penalty cases) to ensure that only
the worst result in a death sentence. The
author argues that because the court reviews
only first-degree cases, it is not satisfying
the legislative requirement.

668. Oshman, Karen Appel. "An Impermissible
Punishment: The Decline of Consistency as a
Constitutional Goal in Capital Sentencing."
PACE LAW REVIEW 5 (1985): 371-402.

Examines the goals of consistency and
individualization in capital sentencing.
Consistency, the author argues, has been
reduced by the Supreme Court's decision to
allow juries to mete out death sentences
based on nonstatutory aggravating
circumstances. The author argues that
without consistency, the death penalty is
impermissible.

669. Otterbein, Keith F. THE ULTIMATE COERCIVE
SANCTION. New Haven: Human Relations Area
Files Press, 1986.

An anthropological perspective on the death

penalty. Argues, on the basis of data from
53 primitive societies, that the death
penalty is a cultural universal.

670. Palmer, Larry I. "Two Perspectives on
Structuring Discretion: Justices Stewart and
White on the Death Penalty." JOURNAL OF
CRIMINAL LAW AND CRIMINOLOGY 70 (1979):
194-213.

Justice Stewart found mandatory death
penalties unconstitutional, while Justice
White did not. While the former wants
individualized sentencing, Justice White
prefers clearly articulated standards.

671. Pannick, David. JUDICIAL REVIEW OF THE DEATH
PENALTY. White Plains, New York: Sheridan,
1982.

Compares judicial review of death sentences
in America, India, Canada, Cyprus, Japan,
Pakistan, and the Caribbean, and concludes
that problems of fairness, consistency, and
cruelty make capital punishment unacceptable.
Reviewed by Bedau in item 104 above.

672. Panton, J.H. "Personality Characteristics of
Death-Row Prison Inmates." JOURNAL OF
CLINICAL PSYCHOLOGY 32 (1976): 306-9.

The MMPI was administered to 34 death row
inmates in North Carolina and 2,551 inmates
from the general prison population. The
average I.Q. of those on death row was found
to be 90.7. Results from the MMPI revealed
resentment, hopelessness, and other signs of
stress.

673. Partington, Donald H. "The Incidence of the
Death Penalty for Rape in Virginia."
WASHINGTON AND LEE LAW REVIEW 22 (1965):
43-75.

Since 1908, 41 men, all black, have been
executed for rape in Virginia. Two whites
and ten blacks also were sentenced to death
for rape, but had their sentences commuted or
reversed. The cases are traced through the
courts. The author concludes there is no

apparent legal solution for the
discrimination absent a showing of
intentional prejudice against the defendant.

674. Pascucci, Raymond J.   "Capital Punishment in
      1984: Abandoning the Pursuit of Fairness and
      Consistency." CORNELL LAW REVIEW 69 (1984):
      1129-243.

      Reviews the emergence of the concept of
      "guided discretion" in capital cases, and
      argues that recent decisions by the Supreme
      Court have abandoned the pursuit of fairness
      and consistency in capital sentencing and
      appeals. A well-documented overview of
      current capital statutes in presented in the
      Appendix.

675. Passell, Peter.   "The Deterrent Effect of the
      Death Penalty: A Statistical Test." STANFORD
      LAW REVIEW 28 (1975): 61-80. Reprinted in
      Bedau and Pierce, 1976, in item 110 above.

      Evaluates the work on deterrence of Isaac
      Ehrlich and his critics. Using cross-section
      state level data from 1950 and 1960, the
      author finds that execution rates do not
      explain the variation in homicide rates when
      other factors are controlled.

676. Passell, Peter, and John B. Taylor.   "The
      Deterrence Controversy: A Reconsideration of
      the Time Series Evidence." Pp. 359-71 in
      Bedau and Pierce, 1976, cited above as item
      110.

      An examination of the research of Isaac
      Ehrlich, concluding that it adds little to
      the capital punishment deterrence debate.

677. Passell, Peter, and John B. Taylor.   "The
      Deterrent Effect of Capital Punishment:
      Another View." AMERICAN ECONOMIC REVIEW 67
      (1977): 445-51.

      A reexamination of the Ehrlich data, arguing
      that for many reasons, his data do not
      support his conclusions. Responded to by
      Ehrlich and Gibbons, cited above as item 295.

678. Pastroff, Sanford M.   "The Constitutional
      Rights of the Insane on Death Row."   JOURNAL
      OF CRIMINAL LAW AND CRIMINOLOGY 77 (1986):
      844-66.

      A review of the history and effects of Ford
      v. Wainwright.   Argues the ruling is
      deficient because the U.S. Supreme Court did
      not identify a test of mental fitness to be
      executed or what procedures must be used to
      deal with claims of insanity, and failed to
      outline a specific rationale for the
      exemption of the mentally ill from execution.

679. Paternoster, Raymond.   "Race of Victim and
      Location of Crime: The Decision to Seek the
      Death Penalty in South Carolina."   JOURNAL OF
      CRIMINAL LAW AND CRIMINOLOGY 74 (1983):
      754-85.

      Examines 1,686 South Carolina homicide cases,
      1977-81, using data from FBI and other
      sources; 321 of the cases were capital.   The
      dependent variable is the prosecutor's
      decision to seek the death penalty.   Finds
      this decision is correlated with the race of
      the victim and geographic region.

680. Paternoster, Raymond.   "Prosecutorial
      Discretion in Requesting the Death Penalty: A
      Case of Victim-Based Racial Discrimination."
      LAW AND SOCIETY REVIEW 18 (1984): 437-78.

      Studies 300 felony murders from South
      Carolina, and finds that after legal factors
      are controlled, the victim's race is a
      significant predictor of the decision to seek
      a death sentence.   Prosecutors were most
      likely to seek death in cases with white
      victims and black defendants.

681. Paternoster, Raymond, and Annmarie Kazyaka.
      "Racial Considerations in Capital Punishment:
      The Failure of Evenhanded Justice."   In Haas
      and Inciardi, 1988, cited above as item 413.

      An analysis of prosecutors' decisions to seek
      a death sentence in South Carolina, 1977-81,
      in which strong race-of-victim effects are
      found.

682. Patrick, Clarence H. "Capital Punishment and Life Imprisonment in North Carolina, 1946 to 1968: Implications for Abolition of the Death Penalty." WAKE FOREST INTRAMURAL LAW REVIEW 6 (1970): 417-29.

Reviews the North Carolina death penalty statute and the crimes covered under it. Data are presented on the number of executions and life sentences, 1946-68. Because a decline in the number of executions did not increase first-degree murder rates, the author advocates total abolition.

683. Pearson, Bruce L. (ed.). THE DEATH PENALTY IN SOUTH CAROLINA: OUTLOOK FOR THE 1980's. Columbia, S.C.: A.C.L.U. Press, 1981.

An overview of the death penalty in general and in South Carolina in particular, with essays supporting and opposing capital punishment, including an essay by Joseph Jacoby on deterrence and brutalization and one by Hugo Adam Bedau on social justice.

684. Peck, Jon R. "The Deterrent Effect of Capital Punishment: Ehrlich and His Critics." YALE LAW JOURNAL 85 (1976): 359-67.

Comments on the debates between Ehrlich and his critics published in earlier issues of YALE LAW JOURNAL (see items 60, 160, and 290 above). Responded to by Ehrlich in item 292 above.

685. Peterson, Ruth D., and William C. Bailey. "Murder and Capital Punishment in the Evolving Context of the post-Furman Era." SOCIAL FORCES 66 (1988): 774-807.

Examines the impact of the death penalty on state homicide rates in the post-Furman period, 1973-84, and discusses the merits of using contiguous state analysis, rather than multiple regression, in studying deterrent effects. Results indicate that, using either methodology, no deterrent effect is evident.

686. Phillips, Charles David. "Social Structure and Social Control: Modeling the Discriminatory Execution of Blacks in Georgia and North Carolina, 1925-35." SOCIAL FORCES 65 (1986): 458-75.

Examines executions in 261 counties, and finds that urbanization and minority presence explain a good deal of the variation in rates of executions for whites vs. blacks.

687. Phillips, Charles David. "Exploring Relations Among Forms of Social Control: The Lynching and Execution of Blacks in North Carolina, 1889-1918." LAW AND SOCIETY REVIEW 21 (1987): 361-74.

This examination finds that lynching and executions each complemented the other, serving similar social functions. Substitution of executions for lynchings occurred only after blacks were disenfranchised. The analysis is based on Chicago Tribune data on 48 lynchings and 104 executions.

688. Phillips, David P. "The Deterrent Effect of Capital Punishment: New Evidence on an Old Controversy." AMERICAN JOURNAL OF SOCIOLOGY 86 (1980): 139-48.

An examination of the effects of 22 highly-publicized executions in London, 1858-1921. Finds that homicides are temporarily deterred for a two-week period, but those temporarily deterred reappear after the publicized execution has faded from memory. Criticized by Zeisel (cited below as item 952), and Kobbervig et al. (cited above as item 517).

689. Phillips, David P. "Strong and Weak Research Designs for Detecting the Impact of Capital Punishment on Homicide." RUTGERS LAW REVIEW 33 (1981): 790-8.

A discussion of some common methodological shortcomings often found in deterrence research, and a suggestion of how researchers can partially overcome these flaws. Data are presented for a period before and after 19 highly-publicized executions in London, 1858-1921.

690. Phillips, David P., and John E. Hensley. "When Violence is Rewarded or Punished: The Impact of Mass Media Stories on Homicide." JOURNAL OF COMMUNICATION 34 (1984): 101-16.

Presents data that indicate the number of homicides in the U.S. increases after prizefights, but decreases after newspaper stories about murder trials and executions.

691. Phillipson, Coleman. THREE CRIMINAL LAW REFORMERS: BECCARIA, BENTHAM, ROMILLY. Montclair, N.J.: Patterson Smith, 1970.

Description of the views of Beccaria, Bentham, and Romilly, the factors that shaped their thought, and their principal achievements.

692. Pierrepoint, Albert. EXECUTIONER: PIERREPOINT. Sevenoaks, Kent: Hodder and Stoughton, 1974.

The autobiography of the British executioner, 1931-56, who followed his father and uncle in the trade and executed over 400 prisoners. Includes his reasons for shifting his opinion and becoming opposed to the death penalty.

693. Playfair, Giles, and Derrick Singleton. THE OFFENDERS: THE CASE AGAINST LEGAL VENGEANCE. New York: Simon and Schuster, 1957.

Six stories of capital crimes are presented, including the case of the Rosenbergs, and are used to illustrate the futility of capital punishment.

694. Polen, Charles A. ("Pete.") "Youth on Death Row: Waiver of Juvenile Court Jurisdiction and Imposition of the Death Penalty on Juvenile Offenders." NORTHERN KENTUCKY LAW REVIEW 13 (1987): 495-517.

Reviews the issue of the transfer of juveniles accused of capital murder to adult criminal courts. Three methods for doing so are reviewed: judicial, legislative, and prosecutorial waiver. Reviews recent state court cases dealing with juveniles who were tried as adults and condemned.

695. Polsby, Daniel D. "The Death of Capital Punishment? Furman v. Georgia." SUPREME COURT REVIEW (1972): 1-40.

An extensive examination of the Furman decision and other Eighth Amendment cases that preceded it.

696. Post, Albert. "Early Efforts to Abolish Capital Punishment in Pennsylvania." PENNSYLVANIA MAGAZINE OF HISTORY AND BIOGRAPHY 68 (1944): 38-53.

Examines the history of the death penalty in Pennsylvania and the efforts to restrict and abolish it.

697. Post, Albert. "The Anti-Gallows Movement in Ohio." THE OHIO STATE ARCHAEOLOGICAL AND HISTORICAL QUARTERLY 54 (1945): 105-12.

Examines the status of the death penalty in Ohio (mainly in the nineteenth century) and the efforts to reform and abolish it.

698. Potratz, William G. "The Prosecutor's Discretionary Power to Initiate the Death Sentencing Hearing." DEPAUL LAW REVIEW 29 (1980): 1097-117.

Discusses the Illinois Supreme Court case which overturned the decision of a circuit judge, who had declared a portion of the state's death penalty statute unconstitutional because it gave the prosecutor the sole discretion to initiate death penalty proceedings.

699. Poulos, John W. "The Supreme Court, Capital Punishment and the Substantive Criminal Law: The Rise and Fall of Mandatory Capital Punishment." ARIZONA LAW REVIEW 28 (1986): 143-257.

An examination of McGautha, Furman, and of

the legislative responses to them. The
constitutionality of the mandatory death
penalty statutes is discussed. Post-<u>Furman</u>
capital statutes are listed in an Appendix.

700.   Powers, Edwin. "The Legal History of Capital
        Punishment in Massachusetts." FEDERAL
        PROBATION 45 (Sept., 1981): 15-20.

        A brief history of death penalty statutes,
        executions, and relevant legislative debates
        in the Commonwealth of Massachusetts.

701.   Prettyman, Barrett, Jr. DEATH AND THE
        SUPREME COURT. New York: Harcourt, Brace and
        World, 1961.

        A discussion of the defendants and their
        crimes in six death penalty cases that were
        examined by the U.S. Supreme Court. Case
        histories are presented. A pioneering
        account of the arbitrariness in trial court
        and appellate practices involving the death
        penalty.

702.   Primorac, Ivan. "On Capital Punishment."
        ISRAEL LAW REVIEW 17 (1982): 133-50.

        A philosophical essay on the moral legitimacy
        of capital punishment, arguing that
        retributive arguments can justify the death
        penalty. Responded to by Sebba, cited below
        as item 784.

703.   Pugsley, Robert A. "A Retributivist Argument
        Against Capital Punishment." HOFSTRA LAW
        REVIEW 9 (1981): 1501-23.

        Discusses and rejects deterrence as a
        sufficient utilitarian justification for the
        death penalty. Outlines the classic
        retributivist position of Kant, and its
        traditional use to support capital
        punishment, but then shows that, using Kant's
        principles, a retributivist can also oppose
        the death penalty. Some of these arguments
        were expanded by Schwarzschild, cited below
        in item 778.

704.   Pulaski, Charles A., Jr. "Capital Sentencing

in Arizona: A Critical Evaluation." ARIZONA
STATE LAW JOURNAL 1984 (1984): 1-52.

Examines Arizona's death sentencing
procedures. Concludes that, on its face, the
statute appears constitutionally sound,
although future litigation will no doubt
arise challenging the statute's application.

705.   Quade, Vicki. "Cheaper to Kill? ABA Eyes the
       Death Penalty Cost." AMERICAN BAR
       ASSOCIATION JOURNAL 71 (April, 1983): 17.

       Announces a study for a special committee of
       the American Bar Association to discover if
       the death penalty is more expensive than life
       imprisonment.

706.   Quade, Vicki. "From Wall Street to Death
       Row." HUMAN RIGHTS 14 (Winter, 1987):
       18-21+.

       An interview with Ronald Tabak, a Wall Street
       attorney who does pro bono death penalty
       work. The interview probes his work and his
       feelings about the death penalty.

707.   Rabkin, Jeremy. "Justice and Judicial Hand
       Wringing: The Death Penalty Since Gregg."
       CRIMINAL JUSTICE ETHICS 4 (1985): 18-29.

       A critique, by a supporter of capital
       punishment, of the Supreme Court's "half-
       hearted" decision in Gregg, arguing that the
       Court, in this decision, abandoned many of
       the concerns expressed in the Furman ruling,
       but that the concerns in Furman were only
       "illusory" problems. The author argues the
       Court has gotten increasingly tired of death
       penalty cases since Gregg.

708.   Radelet, Michael L. "Racial Characteristics
       and the Imposition of the Death Penalty."
       AMERICAN SOCIOLOGICAL REVIEW 46 (1981):
       918-27.

       Examines 637 Florida homicide cases from 1976
       and 1977. Finds, after restricting the
       analysis to homicides against strangers, that
       those accused of murdering whites are more

likely to be condemned than those accused of
murdering blacks.

709.   Radelet, Michael L.   "Rejecting the Jury: The
        Imposition of the Death Penalty in Florida."
        UNIVERSITY OF CALIFORNIA-DAVIS LAW REVIEW 18
        (1985): 1409-31.

        Examines 326 Florida cases in which a death
        sentence was imposed since 1972, 25 percent
        of which had jury recommendations of life.
        Compares the cases by jury recommendation on
        eleven variables, and reports the frequencies
        with which each aggravating and mitigating
        circumstance are found.

710.   Radelet, Michael L.   "Sociologists as Expert
        Witnesses in Capital Cases: A Case Study."
        Pp. 119-34 in Patrick R. Anderson and L.
        Thomas Winfree, Jr. (eds.), EXPERT WITNESSES:
        CRIMINOLOGISTS IN THE COURTROOM.   Albany:
        State University of New York Press, 1987.

        Describes the author's experiences as an
        expert witness during the penalty phases of
        several capital trials, with a focus on a
        1984 Los Angeles case.

711.   Radelet, Michael L., and George W. Barnard.
        "Ethics and the Psychiatric Determination of
        Competency to be Executed."   BULLETIN OF THE
        AMERICAN ACADEMY OF PSYCHIATRY AND THE LAW 14
        (1986): 37-53.

        Reviews the issue of exempting the insane
        from execution, and the Florida procedures
        for doing so.   Argues that the Florida
        procedures are insufficient to achieve their
        goal, and reviews the ethical issues faced by
        psychiatrists who are asked to evaluate death
        row inmates for competency to be executed.

712.   Radelet, Michael L., and George W. Barnard.
        "Treating Those Found Incompetent for
        Execution: Ethical Chaos With Only One
        Solution."   BULLETIN OF THE AMERICAN ACADEMY
        OF PSYCHIATRY AND THE LAW (Forthcoming,
        1988).

        Examines the case of Gary Alvord, a Florida

death row inmate who in 1985 was found
incompetent for execution. After
interviewing mental health professionals
involved in Alvord's treatment, the authors
conclude that the ethical issues the staff
confronted are so problematic that all
persons found incompetent should have their
death sentences immediately commuted to long
imprisonment.

713. Radelet, Michael L., and Hugo Adam Bedau.
"Fallibility and Finality: Type II Errors and
Capital Punishment." In Haas and Inciardi,
1988, cited above as item 413.

A brief overview of the authors' work on
miscarriages of justice, reported more fully
in item 111 above.

714. Radelet, Michael L., and Michael Mello.
"Executing Those Who Kill Blacks: An 'Unusual
Case' Study." MERCER UNIVERSITY LAW REVIEW
37 (1986): 911-25.

Examines the case of Florida death row inmate
James Dupree Henry, who was executed in 1984
for murdering a black. Analysis of the
newspaper coverage of the case, however,
reveals that most of the coverage discussed
not the deceased victim, but rather a white
police officer who was slightly wounded while
taking Henry into custody.

715. Radelet, Michael L., and Glenn L. Pierce.
"Race and Prosecutorial Discretion in
Homicide Cases." LAW AND SOCIETY REVIEW 19
(1985): 587-621.

Examines 1,017 Florida homicides from the
1970's, gathering data from both police
reports and court records. Finds a
significant pattern of upgrading and
downgrading the severity of the homicide's
classification by victim's and defendant's
race. In cases with white victims where no
plea bargain was offered, upgrading is found
to associate significantly with the
probability of a death sentence.

716. Radelet, Michael L., and Margaret Vandiver.

"The Florida Supreme Court and Death Penalty Appeals." JOURNAL OF CRIMINAL LAW AND CRIMINOLOGY 74 (1983): 913-26.

Examines the first 145 death penalty cases decided by the Florida Supreme Court on direct appeal after 1972, 52 percent of which were affirmed. Finds that the trial jury's recommendation, number of victims, and defendants' race and victims' gender are all significantly correlated with the court's decisions.

717. Radelet, Michael L., and Margaret Vandiver. "Race and Capital Punishment: An Overview of the Issues." CRIME AND SOCIAL JUSTICE 25 (1986): 94-113.

Reviews historical records and empirical research on the relationship between death sentencing and the racial characteristics of defendants and victims.

718. Radelet, Michael L., Margaret Vandiver, and Felix Berardo. "Families, Prisons, and Men with Death Sentences: The Human Impact of Structured Uncertainty." JOURNAL OF FAMILY ISSUES 4 (1983): 593-612.

Based on extensive contact with men on death row and their families, this paper reviews the problems they encounter, particularly their isolation and chronic uncertainty.

719. Radin, Margaret Jane. "The Jurisprudence of Death: Evolving Standards for the Cruel and Unusual Punishments Clause." UNIVERSITY OF PENNSYLVANIA LAW REVIEW 126 (1978): 989-1064.

An excellent review of Eighth Amendment issues, including issues of proportionality, and an argument that the Amendment's meaning comes from evolving standards of decency.

720. Radin, Margaret Jane. "Cruel Punishment and Respect for Persons: Super Due Process for Death." SOUTHERN CALIFORNIA LAW REVIEW 53 (1980): 1143-85.

Reviews Supreme Court decisions that have

found that the process through which
defendants are selected for death can itself
be a "cruel" punishment. Links the basis for
these decisions, the uniqueness of each
individual, to the retributivist
justification for the death penalty, and
concludes that the similarities dictate that
executions should always be seen as a cruel
punishment.

721.   Radin, Margaret Jane. "Proportionality,
       Subjectivity, and Tragedy." UNIVERSITY OF
       CALIFORNIA-DAVIS LAW REVIEW 18 (1985):
       1165-75.

       Discusses the role of proportionality in
       justifications of capital punishment, and
       links the debate over proportionality to a
       larger debate over just deserts.

722.   Radzinowicz, Sir Leon. A HISTORY OF ENGLISH
       CRIMINAL LAW: VOL. I: THE MOVEMENT FOR
       REFORM, 1750-1833. New York: Macmillan,
       1948.

       A classic scholarly study of capital
       punishment in England, and the reforms which
       limited the number of offenses for which
       death could be imposed.

723.   Rahav, Giora. "Homicide and the Death
       Penalty: Cross-Sectional Time Series
       Analysis." INTERNATIONAL JOURNAL OF
       COMPARATIVE AND APPLIED CRIMINAL JUSTICE 7
       (1983): 67-71.

       A study of deterrence with pooled time-series
       analysis of data from 17 countries for
       1955-72. The results indicate the death
       penalty has a slight and inconsistent effect
       on homicide rates.

724.   Ramcharan, B.G. (ed.). THE RIGHT TO LIFE IN
       INTERNATIONAL LAW. Dordrecht, Mass.:
       Martinus Nijhoff Publisher, 1985.

       Edited by a Special Assistant in the U.N.
       Centre for Human Rights, this work is an
       overview of international human rights law.
       Included is a discussion of capital

punishment in international law.

725. Rankin, Joseph H. "Changing Attitudes Toward
      Capital Punishment." SOCIAL FORCES 58
      (1979): 194-211.

      Analyzes National Opinion Research
      Corporation (NORC) surveys (1972-76) and
      finds a strong positive correlation between
      crime rates and support for capital
      punishment.

726. Raper, Arthur F. THE TRAGEDY OF LYNCHING.
      Chapel Hill: University of North Carolina
      Press, 1933.

      Written for the Southern Commission for the
      Study of Lynching, a biracial group, this
      book analyzes the purported causes of 3,693
      lynchings that occurred from 1889-1930.
      Special care is taken to separate the alleged
      causes from the real or actual causes.

727. Reckless, Walter C. "The Use of the Death
      Penalty: A Factual Statement." CRIME AND
      DELINQUENCY 15 (1969): 43-56.

      Documents the decline in the number of
      capital crimes and the number of executions.
      The status of the death penalty
      internationally is given, as are comparisons
      of crime rates between abolitionist and
      retentionist states.

728. Reed, Carolyn Sievers. "The Evolution of
      North Carolina's Comparative Proportionality
      Review in Capital Cases." NORTH CAROLINA LAW
      REVIEW 63 (1985): 1146-62.

      Explains the process of proportionality
      review in North Carolina and how the present
      procedures have emerged.

729. Reid, Dee. "Unknowing Punishment: Mentally
      Retarded Convicts on Death Row Are Victims of
      a System They Don't Understand--And That
      Doesn't Understand Them." STUDENT LAWYER 15
      (May, 1987): 18-23.

      An overview of the status of the mentally

retarded on death row, with discussion of
some cases and the flaws in the system that
allowed the inmates to be condemned.

730.   Reid, Don, with John Gurwell. EYEWITNESS.
Houston: Cordovan Press, 1973.

An account by a journalist of the 189
executions he witnessed in Texas. Includes a
discussion of why he opposes the death
penalty.

731.   Reiman, Jeffrey H., and Sue Headlee.
"Marxism and Criminal Justice Policy." CRIME
AND DELINQUENCY 27 (1981): 24-47.

Outlines the Marxist theoretical orientation
toward criminal justice policy. Changes in
policy, such as the rejection of the goal of
rehabilitation and the resurgence of the
death penalty, are seen as responses to
economic crises and the shifting needs of the
capitalist modes of production.

732.   Reiman, Jeffrey H. "Justice, Civilization,
and the Death Penalty: Answering van den
Haag." PHILOSOPHY AND PUBLIC AFFAIRS 14
(1985): 115-48.

Argues for the abolition of capital
punishment, even though he concludes that
death is a just punishment for murder. Bases
his conclusion on the idea that abolition is
part of the civilizing mission of modern
states. Argues with the position voiced by
van den Haag; van den Haag's response is
cited below as item 874.

733.   Reiman, Jeffrey H. "The Justice of the Death
Penalty in an Unjust World." In Haas and
Inciardi, cited above as item 413.

By distinguishing the questions of the
justice of the death penalty in principle vs.
its justice in practice, Reiman argues
against the death penalty, based on its
psychological torture and discriminatory
application.

734.   Remington, Frank. "State Prisoner Access to

Postconviction Relief--A Lessening Role for Federal Courts; an Increasingly Important Role for State Courts." OHIO STATE LAW JOURNAL 44 (1983): 287-305.

Discusses the willingness of federal courts to examine death penalty cases. Reviews recent changes in procedural rules that limit access to federal courts, and argues that these limitations are likely to increase the importance of state courts in capital cases.

735. Renda, Ernest A. "The Bitter Fruit of McGautha: Eddings v. Oklahoma and the Need for Weighing Method Articulation in Capital Sentencing." AMERICAN CRIMINAL LAW REVIEW 20 (1982): 63-98.

Reviews the Supreme Court's attempt to balance consistency with individualization in capital sentencing, arguing that the Eddings decision gives inadequate resolution to how aggravating and mitigating circumstances should be weighed.

736. Reskin, Lauren Rubenstein. "Majority of Lawyers Support Capital Punishment." ABA JOURNAL 71 (April, 1985): 44.

Reports from a poll of lawyers that 68 percent support the death penalty, while 27 percent stand opposed. Support was more frequent among males (71 vs. 52 percent), and increased with age and income. Just over half oppose executions of juveniles.

737. Reynolds, Morgan O. "On Welfare Economics Aspects of Capital Punishment." AMERICAN JOURNAL OF ECONOMICS AND SOCIOLOGY 36 (1977): 105-9.

A response to an article by McKee and Sesnowitz, cited as item 610 above. McKee and Sesnowitz follow this response with a rejoinder.

738. Rhoades, Michael D. "Resurrection of Capital Punishment: The 1976 Death Penalty Cases." DICKINSON LAW REVIEW 81 (1977): 543-73.

A case note on <u>Gregg</u>, <u>Proffitt</u>, <u>Jurek</u>, <u>Woodson</u>, and <u>Roberts</u>.

739. Richards, Reed C., and Stephen C. Hoffman. "Death Among the Shifting Standards: Capital Punishment After <u>Furman</u>." SOUTH DAKOTA LAW REVIEW 26 (1981): 243-58.

An examination of the South Dakota capital statute, which the author argues has weaknesses because the U.S. Supreme Court has failed to define precise requirements for capital sentencing.

740. Richey, Linda Katherine. "Death Penalty Statutes: A post-<u>Gregg</u> <u>v</u>. <u>Georgia</u> Survey and Discussion of Eighth Amendment Safeguards." WASHBURN LAW JOURNAL 16 (1977): 497-508.

A review of <u>Gregg</u>, <u>Jurek</u>, and other 1976 death penalty decisions and a discussion of their implications for existing statutes.

741. Riedel, Marc. "Discrimination in the Imposition of the Death Penalty: A Comparison of the Characteristics of Offenders Sentenced pre-<u>Furman</u> and post-<u>Furman</u>." TEMPLE LAW QUARTERLY 49 (1976): 261-87. A revised version was published by Bedau and Pierce, 1976, item 110 above.

An examination of 407 offenders in 28 states sentenced to death between 1972 and 1976. Concludes that the statutes passed in 1972 and subsequently have been unsuccessful in reducing the discretion that leads to a disproportionate number of nonwhite offenders being sentenced to death.

742. Riedel, Marc. "The Death Penalty and Discretion: Implications of the <u>Furman</u> Decision for Criminal Justice." JOURNAL OF SOCIOLOGY AND SOCIAL WELFARE 3 (1976): 649-55.

A discussion of the <u>Furman</u> decision, particularly of what the author sees as the implications of the decision's treatment of "discretion" for non-death penalty cases.

743. Riedel, Marc, and John P. McCloskey. "The Governor's Study Commission on Capital Punishment: A Content Analysis of the Testimony by Expert Witnesses." PRISON JOURNAL 53 (1975): 19-35.

A discussion of the views presented to the Governor's Commission on Capital Punishment in Pennsylvania in 1973.

744. Rieder, Eric. "The Right of Self-Representation in the Capital Case." COLUMBIA LAW REVIEW 85 (1985): 130-54.

Examines the right of self-representation and the due process requirements in capital cases. Concludes capital defendants should be allowed to represent themselves at trial, but should have counsel for sentencing and appeals.

745. Riga, Peter J. "Capital Punishment and the Right to Life: Some Reflections on the Human Right as Absolute." UNIVERSITY OF PUGET SOUND LAW REVIEW 5 (1981): 23-46.

A philosophical-moral essay on the question of the right to life. Argues that the right to life is an absolute, and thus capital punishment cannot be justified.

746. Riley, Kathryn W. "The Death Penalty in Georgia: An Aggravating Circumstance." AMERICAN UNIVERSITY LAW REVIEW 30 (1981): 835-61.

A critical comment on the Supreme Court's decision in Godfrey v. Georgia. Concludes the Court's refusal to find that Georgia's aggravating circumstance under review was too vague will lead to further arbitrariness in death sentencing.

747. Rise, Eric Walter. RACE, RAPE, AND RADICALISM: THE MARTINSVILLE SEVEN AND COLD WAR CRIMINAL JUSTICE, 1949-1951." Masters Thesis, Department of History, University of Florida, 1987.

Examines the crimes, trial, appeals, and

executions of seven black men for rape in Virginia in 1949. Though the men were probably guilty, the case involved blatant racism and numerous due process violations, and led to involvement by the NAACP and the American Communist Party.

748. Roberts, Julian V. "Public Opinion and Capital Punishment: The Effects of Attitudes Upon Memory." CANADIAN JOURNAL OF CRIMINOLOGY 26 (1984): 283-91.

An article summarizing deterrence research on capital punishment was read by 77 people. When asked a short time later to recall what they had read, both pro-death and anti-death penalty respondents tended to remember the information that supported their original position.

749. Robin, Gerald D. "The Executioner: His Place in English Society." BRITISH JOURNAL OF SOCIOLOGY 15 (1964): 234-53.

An excellent discussion of the status of the executioner in British society. Includes a 52-item bibliography on this topic.

750. Rockefeller, Winthrop. "Executive Clemency and the Death Penalty." CATHOLIC UNIVERSITY LAW REVIEW 21 (1971): 94-102.

A statement and well-documented discussion of clemency by the former governor of Arkansas, who in 1970 commuted the sentences of all fifteen men on death row in Arkansas.

751. Rodriguez, Joseph H., Michael L. Perlin, and John M. Apicella. "Proportionality Review in New Jersey: An Indispensible Safeguard in the Capital Sentencing Process." RUTGERS LAW JOURNAL 15 (1984): 399-442.

Examines proportionality review in New Jersey, which provides greater protection under its state constitution than does the federal government. Argues that the efforts to repeal this higher standard would be unnecessary and unfair.

752. Rosen, Richard A. "The Especially Heinous
     Aggravating Circumstance in Capital Cases --
     The Standardless Standard." NORTH CAROLINA
     LAW REVIEW 64 (1986): 941-92.

     In light of the Eighth Amendment's guided
     discretion doctrine, this article examines
     state-by-state interpretations of "especially
     heinous" aggravating circumstances, finding
     that the interpretations have been too broad
     and inconsistent. Thus, the author argues
     that these vague standards do not serve to
     guide discretion, and concludes that all such
     standards should be eliminated.

753. Rosenberg, David, and Ken Levy. "Capital
     Punishment: Coming to Grips with the Dignity
     of Man." CALIFORNIA WESTERN LAW REVIEW 14
     (1978): 275-97.

     Focusing on California, this article
     describes and evaluates legislative and
     judicial actions over the previous six years
     relating to the death penalty.

754. Roy, Therese M. "Solem v. Helm: The Court's
     Continued Struggle to Define Cruel and
     Unusual Punishment." CALIFORNIA WESTERN LAW
     REVIEW 21 (1985): 590-612.

     Traces the development of Eighth Amendment
     jurisprudence. Discusses the case of Jerry
     Helm, convicted of passing a bad check in
     North Dakota, but sentenced to life without
     parole because he had previously been
     convicted of several felonies. The Supreme
     Court reversed the sentence on
     proportionality grounds.

755. Royal Commission on Capital Punishment,
     1949-53. FINAL REPORT. London: Her
     Majesty's Stationary Office, Cmd. 8932, 1953.

     The final report of the most extensive and
     in-depth formal examination of the death
     penalty that has ever been conducted under
     governmental authority.

756. Rush, Daryl P. "Constitutional Law--
     Safeguarding Eighth Amendment Rights with a

Comparative Proportionality Review in the Imposition of the Death Penalty." HOWARD LAW JOURNAL 28 (1985): 331-53.

A case note on Pulley v. Harris, summarizing its background and content. Argues the Court erred in its decision not to require comparative proportionality review.

757. Salguero, Rochelle Graff. "Medical Ethics and Competency to be Executed." YALE LAW JOURNAL 96 (1986): 167-86.

Reviews codes of medical ethics and the ethical problems faced by psychiatrists who evaluate or treat inmates for competency to be executed. Discusses the Florida cases of Gary Alvord and Alvin Ford.

758. Samuelson, Glenn W. "Why Was Capital Punishment Restored in Delaware?" JOURNAL OF CRIMINAL LAW AND CRIMINOLOGY 60 (1969): 148-51.

In 1961, capital punishment returned to Delaware after three years of abolition. The author examines homicide rates, and finds that they did not decrease after the death penalty was restored.

759. Sanson, Henri (ed.). EXECUTIONERS ALL: MEMOIRS OF THE SANSON FAMILY, FROM PRIVATE NOTES AND DOCUMENTS, 1688-1847. London: N. Spearman, 1962.

Memoirs of the family of Henri Sanson, for two centuries the family that provided executioners for France.

760. Sarat, Austin. "Deterrence and the Constitution: On the Limits of Capital Punishment." JOURNAL OF BEHAVIORAL ECONOMICS 6:311-59.

An essay on the interpretation of the Eighth Amendment by the U.S. Supreme Court, written especially in light of the research on capital punishment and deterrence.

761. Sarat, Austin, and Neil Vidmar. "Public

Opinion, the Death Penalty, and the Eighth Amendment: Testing the Marshall Hypothesis." WISCONSIN LAW REVIEW 1976 (1976): 171-206. A revised version was published in Bedau and Pierce, 1976, item 110 above.

In the Furman decision, Justice Marshall argued that "people who were fully informed as to the purposes of the penalty and its liabilities would find the penalty shocking, unjust and unacceptable." This study, with 181 subjects, found that most knew little about the death penalty or its effectiveness, but that support for capital punishment declines when people are exposed to information about it.

762.   Sargent, Douglas A.   "Treating the Condemned to Death."   HASTINGS CENTER REPORT 16 (Dec., 1986): 5-6.

Condemns the treatment by psychiatrists of prisoners found incompetent for executions, because if the prisoner recovers, he or she will be put to death.

763.   Satlow, Barry.   "Witness at an Execution." JURIS DOCTOR 2 (Nov., 1971): 13.

An account of the electrocution of Ralph Hudson in New Jersey in 1963.

764.   Satre, Thomas W.   "The Irrationality of Capital Punishment."   SOUTHWESTERN JOURNAL OF PHILOSOPHY 6 (Summer, 1975): 75-87.

The author finds that existing arguments against the death penalty are inadequate. He then outlines a philosophical approach to a theory of punishment which, he contends, provides adequate reasons for the abolition of capital punishment. His argument largely centers on the inevitability of error.

765.   Savitz, Leonard D.   "Capital Crimes as Defined in American Statutory Law."   JOURNAL OF CRIMINAL LAW, CRIMINOLOGY AND POLICE SCIENCE 46 (1955): 355-63.

A review of state laws on capital punishment,

including the minimum ages specified in the statutes and state-by-state comparisons of the types of crimes punishable by death.

766. Savitz, Leonard D. "A Study in Capital Punishment." JOURNAL OF CRIMINAL LAW, CRIMINOLOGY AND POLICE SCIENCE 49 (1958): 338-41.

Distinguishes empirical and philosophical questions in the death penalty debate. Examines four widely-publicized homicide trials in Philadelphia, all of which resulted in a death sentence. This publicity, however, had no effect on the city's homicide rates.

767. Sawyer, Darwin O. "Public Attitudes Toward Life and Death." PUBLIC OPINION QUARTERLY 46 (1982): 521-33.

Examines attitude consistency in the areas of abortion, capital punishment, euthanasia, and suicide.

768. Schedler, G. "Capital Punishment and Its Deterrent Effect." SOCIAL THEORY AND PRACTICE 4 (1976): 47-56.

A brief essay arguing that deterrence may not be relevant to the justification of the death penalty.

769. Schneck, Steven Paul. "Conviction-Prone Juries in Capital Trials." ANNUAL SURVEY OF AMERICAN LAW 2 (1986): 311-34.

Reviews the background on death-qualifying juries, analyzes the Supreme Court's decision in Lockhart v. McCree, and criticizes the Court for its interpretation of the Sixth Amendment in the case.

770. Schoenfeld, C.G. "The Desire to Abolish Capital Punishment: A Psychoanalytically Oriented Analysis." JOURNAL OF PSYCHIATRY AND LAW 11 (1983): 151-81.

Anti-death penalty arguments are analyzed and found to be seriously flawed. It is therefore posited that abolitionists have unrecognized motives to identify themselves with criminals.

771. Schornhorst, F. Thomas. "Preliminary Screening of Prosecutorial Access to Death-Qualified Juries: A Missing Constitutional Link." INDIANA LAW REVIEW 62 (1987): 295-331.

Argues that discretion by prosecutors in deciding in which homicide cases they should seek a death penalty violates the defendant's constitutional rights. Instead, a preliminary determination of death-eligibility should be made by a neutral fact-finder.

772. Schultz, Michael L. "Eighth Amendment: References to Appellate Review of Capital Sentencing Determinations." JOURNAL OF CRIMINAL LAW AND CRIMINOLOGY 76 (1985): 1051-64.

Discusses the 1985 case of Caldwell v. Mississippi, in which the U.S. Supreme Court invalidated a death sentence because the prosecutor told the jury that the ultimate responsibility for determining the appropriateness of the sentence rested not with them, but with appellate judges.

773. Schwartz, Charles Walter. "Eighth Amendment Proportionality Analysis and the Compelling Case of William Rummel." JOURNAL OF CRIMINAL LAW AND CRIMINOLOGY 71 (1979): 378-420.

Discusses the William Rummel case in Texas; the defendant was sentenced to life imprisonment after his conviction for a third felony, even though the three felonies had a total dollar value of $229.11. After an Eighth Amendment review, the author concludes the Court's logic in this case was sound.

774. Schwartz, Deborah A., and Jay Wishingrad. "The Eighth Amendment, Beccaria, and the Enlightment: An Historical Justification for the Weems v. United States Excessive Punishment Doctrine." BUFFALO LAW REVIEW 24

(1975): 783-838.

An examination of the traditional understanding of the Eighth Amendment, the Weems case, and the influence of Beccaria and the Enlightment on the Eighth Amendment.

775. Schwartz, Douglas W. "Imposing the Death Sentence for Felony Murder on a Non-Triggerman." STANFORD LAW REVIEW 37 (1985): 857-88.

A discussion of the Enmund case and the felony-murder doctrine. Criticizes the Court for careless language in the decision, and urges appellate courts to vacate death sentences in cases where the jury considered the defendant's mental status in convicting under a felony-murder theory.

776. Schwarzschild, Henry. "Homicide by Injection." NEW YORK TIMES, Dec. 23, 1982.

A strong statement against executions by lethal injections from the abolitionist viewpoint.

777. Schwarzschild, Henry. "A Social and Moral Atrocity." ABA JOURNAL 71 (April, 1985): 38-42.

A debate with Ernest van den Haag (cited below as item 875) on the death penalty.

778. Schwarzschild, Steven S. "Kantianism on the Death Penalty (And Related Social Problems)." ARSP 71 (1985): 343-72 (also available from author at the Dept. of Philosophy, Washington University, St. Louis 63130).

Outlines the views of Kant on the death penalty and the ways in which neo-Kantians have reacted to these views. Expanding on Pugsley's views (cited above as item 703), the author finds several principles in Kant's work consistent with opposition to the death penalty.

779. Schwed, Roger E. ABOLITION AND CAPITAL PUNISHMENT: THE UNITED STATES' JUDICIAL,

POLITICAL, AND MORAL BAROMETER. New York:
AMS Press, 1983.

A brief historical overview of capital
punishment, of reasons for its abolition, of
the Caryl Chessman case, and of the history
of litigation over the last fifteen years
challenging the constitutionality of the
death penalty.

780. Scofield, Giles R. "Due Process in the
United States Supreme Court and the Death of
the Texas Murder Statute." AMERICAN JOURNAL
OF CRIMINAL LAW 8 (1980): 1-42.

Argues, with reference to the Texas statute,
that the problems of administering the death
penalty accurately and reliably are so great
that any benefits gained through executions
are not worth the effort.

781. Scott, George Ryley. The HISTORY OF CAPITAL
PUNISHMENT. London: Torchstream Books, 1950.

The best history of the death penalty, its
pros and cons, psychological aspects,
techniques, and sociological aspects.
Includes a chapter on executioners.

782. Scoville, James C. "Deadly Mistakes:
Harmless Error in Capital Sentencing."
UNIVERSITY OF CHICAGO LAW REVIEW 54 (1987):
740-58.

Discusses the development of harmless error
rules. Concludes that death sentences should
be reversed when errors are found; the
harmless error doctrine does not apply to
these cases since reviewing courts can never
be certain that an error did not affect the
sentencer's decision.

783. Sebba, Leslie. "The Pardoning Power--A World
Survey." JOURNAL OF CRIMINAL LAW AND
CRIMINOLOGY 68 (1977): 83-121.

An excellent international comparison of
pardoning power. Included is a 26-page table
that compares provisions relating to
pardoning power in 100 countries.

784.   Sebba, Leslie.   "On Capital Punishment: A
        Comment."   ISRAEL LAW REVIEW 17 (1982):
        391-8.

        A comment on an article by Primorac, cited
        above as item 702. Argues that the principle
        of proportionality and the possibility of
        error should preclude the use of the death
        penalty.

785.   Sebba, Leslie, and Gad Nathan.   "Further
        Explorations in the Scaling of Penalties."
        BRITISH JOURNAL OF CRIMINOLOGY 24 (1984):
        221-49.

        Questionnaires were distributed to prisoners,
        students, and criminal justice authorities,
        and the results indicate a high consistency
        in their rankings of the severity of
        punishments; the death penalty is ranked as
        more severe than the longest imprisonment.

786.   Seguin, David G., and Irwin A. Horowitz.
        "The Effects of Death Qualification on Juror
        and Jury Decisioning: An Analysis from Three
        Perspectives."   LAW AND PSYCHOLOGY REVIEW 8
        (1984): 49-81.

        Using three theories of group decision-
        making, juror and jury behavior is examined.
        Death qualification is found to relate to
        authoritarianism, conviction proneness, and
        jury bias.

787.   Seidman, Louis M.   "The Trial and Execution
        of Bruno Richard Hauptmann: Still Another
        Case That Will Not Die."   GEORGETOWN LAW
        JOURNAL 66 (1977): 1-48.

        A legal analysis of the trial of Bruno
        Richard Hauptmann and developments in the law
        since his trial and execution. Analyzes the
        massive publicity and prosecutorial
        misconduct which occurred in the case.

788.   Sellin, Thorsten.   "Two Myths in the History
        of Capital Punishment."   JOURNAL OF CRIMINAL
        LAW, CRIMINOLOGY, AND POLICE SCIENCE 50
        (1959): 114-7.

Exposes two myths: 1) the claim that there were 72,000 hangings during the reign of Henry VIII in England (the actual number is unknown), and 2) that Benedict Carpzov sentenced 20,000 to death in the seventeenth century in Germany (the exact number is closer to 300).

789.   Sellin, Thorsten (ed.). CAPITAL PUNISHMENT. New York: Harper and Row, 1967.

A classic book of 19 essays on the death penalty. Four are descriptive essays, six concern abolition movements (including a paper on abolition in Missouri), five examine deterrence, and four deal with procedural issues (including one on executive clemency). Sellin himself wrote six of the essays; of particular interest are an examination of homicides in retentionist and abolitionist jurisdictions, and a second essay examining police safety and the death penalty. Also important are Robert Finkel's 1966 survey of the status of the death penalty in 54 jurisdictions, an essay by Giardini and Farrow on the paroling of capital offenders, and Herbert Ehrmann's classic paper, "The death penalty and the administration of justice."

790.   Sellin, Thorsten. THE PENALTY OF DEATH. Beverly Hills: Sage, 1980.

A general discussion of the death penalty, including chapters on retribution, deterrence (with empirical data), recidivism of capital murderers, and the risk of error.

791.   Seltzer, Rick, Grace M. Lopes, Marshall Dayan, and Russell F. Canan.   "The Effect of Death Qualification on the Propensity of Jurors to Convict: The Maryland Example." HOWARD LAW JOURNAL 29 (1985): 571-607.

Reviews relevant case law concerning the selection of death penalty juries and presents 1983 data on attitudes about the death penalty in Maryland. Finds that jurors who could be excluded from capital juries because of scruples about capital punishment outnumber those who would always vote for death by a ratio of 36:1, and that more blacks than whites can be excluded from capital juries because of their opinions.

792. Seneker, Carl J. "Governor Reagan and Executive Clemency." CALIFORNIA LAW REVIEW 55 (1967): 412-8.

Examines Reagan's refusal to grant clemency to Aaron Mitchell, who was executed in April, 1967. Argues that Reagan erred by refusing to attend clemency hearings, by failing to accept precedents for clemency, and in believing he should not overrule the courts.

793. Sesnowitz, Michael, and David McKee. "On the Deterrent Effect of Capital Punishment." JOURNAL OF BEHAVIORAL ECONOMICS 6 (1977): 217-24.

A critique of the work of James Yunker on capital punishment, cited below as item 945.

794. Sevilla, Charles M. "Investigating and Preparing an Ineffective Assistance of Counsel Claim." MERCER LAW REVIEW 37 (1986): 927-56.

This article is intended as a practical guide for those who pursue "ineffective assistance of counsel" claims. Although capital cases are not specifically examined, the article is an excellent resource for such litigation.

795. Sheleff, Leon Shaskolsky. ULTIMATE PENALTIES: CAPITAL PUNISHMENT, LIFE IMPRISONMENT, PHYSICAL TORTURE. Columbus: Ohio State University Press, 1987.

Discusses what penalties can be justifiably imposed on those convicted of the most serious crimes (brutal murder, terrorism, genocide) and whether prisoners should be permitted to choose between life imprisonment and execution.

796. Shelley, Marshall. "The Death Penalty: Two Sides of a Growing Issue." CHRISTIANITY

TODAY 28 (March 2, 1984): 14-7.

A brief review of the opinions of Christian abolitionists and retentionists.

797. Sherrill, Robert. "Death Row on Trial." NEW YORK TIMES MAGAZINE (November 13, 1983): 80-3+.

A general overview of the present status of the death penalty, with a focus on the death row population in Florida, its supporters, and those who are trying to speed executions.

798. Sherrill, Robert. "In Florida, Insanity is No Defense." THE NATION 239 (November 24, 1983): 539, 552-6.

An examination of several Florida cases in which the mentally ill or the mentally retarded have been sentenced to death.

799. Shin, Kilman. DEATH PENALTY AND CRIME: EMPIRICAL STUDIES. Fairfax, Vir.: George Mason University Press, 1978.

An overview of the impact of the death penalty on American and international crime rates. Several sources of data are used to examine this question, and the author concludes that the death penalty has no impact on homicide rates.

800. Showalter, C. Robert, and Richard J. Bonnie. "Psychiatrists and Capital Sentencing: Risks and Responsibilities in a Unique Legal Setting." BULLETIN OF THE AMERICAN ACADEMY OF PSYCHIATRY AND THE LAW 12 (1984): 159-67.

Discusses the increased need for psychiatric involvement in the sentencing phase of capital trials. Reviews the problems of documenting mental abnormalities as mitigating evidence and of predicting dangerousness.

801. Silberman, Charles E. CRIMINAL VIOLENCE, CRIMINAL JUSTICE. New York: Random House, 1978.

A general and excellent discussion of the crime problem in America, including its causes and problems with police and state responses to it. Although the death penalty is only briefly discussed, the book is a useful description of the problems the death penalty is intended to address.

802. Silver, Ruth Musgrave. "Constitutionality of the New Mexico Capital Statute." NEW MEXICO LAW REVIEW 11 (1981): 269-89.

Describes and examines the 1979 New Mexico capital statute, and concludes that it will pass constitutional scrutiny.

803. Silverman, Milton J. "The Burden of Proof and Procedural Fairness in Capital Cases." AMERICAN JOURNAL OF TRIAL ADVOCACY 3 (1979): 75-88.

Argues that non-capital procedural safeguards, particularly the criterion of "beyond a reasonable doubt," are not sufficient in capital cases.

804. Sinclair, Upton. BOSTON. Pasadena, Calif.: Station A, 1928.

A contemporary historical novel describing the trial, imprisonment, and execution of Sacco and Vanzetti and the worldwide efforts made in their defense. The author's account is detailed and historically accurate.

805. Sindel, Richard. "Commentary on Bullington v. Missouri." LOYOLA UNIVERSITY OF CHICAGO LAW JOURNAL 13 (1982): 841-9.

Describes the case in which Bullington, who was first sentenced to life, was later threatened with a death sentence when he won a new trial. However, the U.S. Supreme Court refused to allow the state to seek the death sentence.

806. Singh, Avtar, and C.H.S. Jayewardene. "A Research Note: Conservatism and Toughmindedness as Determinant of the Attitudes Toward Capital Punishment."

CANADIAN JOURNAL OF CRIMINOLOGY 20 (1978): 191-3.

Five hundred respondents were surveyed, and no relation between radicalism or toughmindedness and support for capital punishment was found.

807. Skene, Neil. "Review of Capital Cases: Does the Florida Supreme Court Know What It's Doing?" STETSON LAW REVIEW 15 (1986): 263-354.

An extensive review of decisions by the Florida Supreme Court in death penalty cases. Argues that the aggravating and mitigating circumstances are so broadly defined that they are applied inconsistently. Criticizes the court for discrepancies, failures to address legal issues, and inconsistent legal philosophy.

808. Sloan, Clifford. "Death Row Clerk." THE NEW REPUBLIC 196 (Feb. 16, 1987): 18-21.

The author clerked for Justice John Paul Stevens in 1985 and 1986. He discusses the hectic pace of last-minute death penalty appeals. Argues those who are sentenced to death are usually poor and/or have had incompetent attorneys.

809. Smead, Howard. BLOOD JUSTICE: THE LYNCHING OF MACK CHARLES PARKER. New York: Oxford University Press, 1986.

A detailed account of the lynching of Mack Parker in Mississippi in 1959, using newspaper accounts, court records, FBI reports, and interviews to reconstruct the events.

810. Smith, A. LaMont, and Robert M. Carter. "Count Down for Death." CRIME AND DELINQUENCY 15 (1969): 77-93.

A chilling chronology of the day-by-day life of the typical inmate in the week before his execution in California. Prison rituals and regulations are reviewed in detail.

811.   Smith, Charles E., and Richard Reid Felix.
        "Beyond Deterrence: A Study of Defenses on
        Death Row." FEDERAL PROBATION 50 (Sept.,
        1986): 55-9.

        The authors, two psychiatrists, interviewed
        34 death row inmates in North Carolina.
        Demographic and background information on all
        the inmates is given, and six psychological
        defenses (used by the inmates to deal with
        their personal stresses) are identified and
        discussed, including eight types of
        explanations of innocence.

812.   Smith, Edgar. BRIEF AGAINST DEATH. New
        York: Knopf, 1968.

        Gives the author's account of his trial for
        murder, conviction, and many years on death
        row spent contesting his guilt. The book
        also includes an introduction by William F.
        Buckley, who sought to aid Smith in his
        struggle for release. After the book's
        publication, Smith's release, and his
        subsequent arrest for other crimes, he
        admitted his guilt for the crime which
        originally sent him to death row.

813.   Smith, Gerald W. "The Value of Life--
        Arguments Against the Death Penalty: A Reply
        to Professor Lehtinen." CRIME AND
        DELINQUENCY 23 (1977): 253-9.

        A general overview of the abolitionist
        position; replies to a paper by Lehtinen, who
        takes a pro-death penalty position (cited
        above as item 550).

814.   Smith, M. Dwayne. "Patterns of
        Discrimination in Assessments of the Death
        Penalty: An Assessment of Louisiana."
        JOURNAL OF CRIMINAL JUSTICE 15 (1987):
        279-86.

        Data were collected (from FBI Supplemental
        Homicide Reports) on 504 Louisiana homicides
        eligible for capital punishment, 1976-82, 53
        of which involved a death sentence. When
        extra-legal factors were controlled, the

victim's gender and race remained
significantly correlated with the death
sentence.

815.   Smith, N.B.   "The Death Penalty as an
Unconstitutional Deprivation of Life and the
Right to Privacy."   BOSTON COLLEGE LAW REVIEW
25 (1984): 743-61.

Reviews the legal history of the right to
life, and links this analysis to the death
penalty by arguing the state does not have a
compelling interest sufficient to override
the right to life.

816.   Smith, T.W.   "A Trend Analysis of Attitudes
Toward Capital Punishment, 1936-1974."   Pp.
257-318 in J.A. Davis (ed.), STUDIES OF
SOCIAL CHANGE SINCE 1948, vol. II.   Chicago:
University of Chicago Press, 1975.

Examines public opinion on capital punishment
over a period of years, and correlates
increased support for the death penalty with
concern about crime control, level of crime,
and rate of increase in homicide.

817.   Smykla, John Ortiz.   "The Human Impact of
Capital Punishment: Interviews with Families
of Persons on Death Row."   JOURNAL OF
CRIMINAL JUSTICE 15 (1987): 331-47.

Reviews literature on the impact of the death
penalty on inmates, executioners, witnesses,
guards, jurors, and other groups.   Forty
relatives of Alabama death row inmates were
interviewed, and their responses are
described.

818.   Snellenburg, Sidney C.   "Is There a
Reasonable Alternative to the Death Penalty?"
JUDICATURE 71 (June-July, 1987): 5-6.

Opposes the death penalty because it is not
uniformly applied throughout the states.
Argues an alternative would be five years of
solitary confinement followed by life without
release in the general prison population.

819.   Snyder, Orvill C.   "Capital Punishment: The

Moral Issue." WEST VIRGINIA LAW REVIEW 63 (1961): 99-117.

A general discussion of the moral arguments for and against the death penalty.

820. Solomon, George F. "Capital Punishment as Suicide and Murder." AMERICAN JOURNAL OF ORTHOPSYCHIATRY 45 (1975): 701-11. Reprinted in Bedau and Pierce, 1976, cited above as item 110.

Examines how killing is engendered as a result of the death penalty. Develops the theme that some murderers kill with either a conscious or unconscious motive to be executed by the state.

821. Sorrell, Tom. MORAL THEORY AND CAPITAL PUNISHMENT. New York: Basil Blackwell, 1988.

An examination of various philosophical and moral theories that can be used in the capital punishment debate. Concludes that while capital punishment can be morally justifiable in certain cases, it is extremely difficult to introduce safely into general legislation.

822. Spierenburg, Pieter. THE SPECTACLE OF SUFFERING: EXECUTIONS AND THE EVOLUTION OF REPRESSION: FROM A PREINDUSTRIAL METROPOLIS TO THE EUROPEAN EXPERIENCE. New York: Cambridge University Press, 1984.

Traces the long evolution of debates about capital punishment, and the decline (after the sixteenth century) of the importance of public punishments and physical suffering. Includes extensive analysis of public executions in the Netherlands.

823. Spittler, John. "Florida Death Penalty: A Lack of Discretion?" UNIVERSITY OF MIAMI LAW REVIEW 28 (1974): 723-8.

Argues the newly-passed death penalty statute in Florida does not lack discretion -- in fact it allows too much, in part because of

vague wording of its aggravating and
mitigating circumstances.

824. Stanton, John M. "Murderers on Parole."
CRIME AND DELINQUENCY 15 (1969): 149-55.

Data were assembled for 576 murderers paroled
in New York, 1945-61, and their experiences
on parole are compared with a sample of
paroled nonmurderers. The former group had a
lower rate of violations and new convictions.
The 61 inmates who had originally been
sentenced to death did particularly well.

825. Stein, Gregory M. "Distinguishing Among
Murders when Assessing the Proportionality of
the Death Penalty." COLUMBIA LAW REVIEW 85
(1985): 1786-807.

Argues that capital crimes can be subdivided
into several different groups for
proportionality analysis, and that the
appropriateness of the death penalty for each
group must be analyzed separately.

826. Stevens, Justice John Paul. "Legal Questions
in Perspective." FLORIDA STATE UNIVERSITY
LAW REVIEW 13 (1985): 1-7.

Reviews a number of issues; labels the
provision of Florida's law allowing a judge
to override a jury's recommendation of life
imprisonment "a procedural defect."

827. Stevens, Leonard A. DEATH PENALTY: THE CASE
OF LIFE VS. DEATH IN THE UNITED STATES. New
York: Coward, McCann and Geoghegan, 1978.

A discussion of the case of William Furman,
his crime and trial, and the appeals which
brought his case to the Supreme Court.
Written for a general audience.

828. Stillman, James W. "Abolish the Death
Penalty." LEGAL REFERENCE SERVICES QUARTERLY
4 (1984): 89-95.

A general essay in opposition to capital
punishment.

829. Stolls, Michele. "Heckler v. Chaney: Judicial and Administrative Regulation of Capital Punishment by Lethal Injection." AMERICAN JOURNAL OF LAW AND MEDICINE 11 (1985): 251-77.

Reviews the case that challenged the Food and Drug Administration's refusal to regulate the drugs used in lethal injections (the Supreme Court denied the petition for certiorari). Had the Court reviewed the case, according to the author, it might have found that lethal injection can produce an unusually cruel and inhumane death.

830. Stolz, Barbara Ann. "Congress and Capital Punishment: An Exercise in Symbolic Politics." LAW AND POLICY QUARTERLY 5 (1983): 157-80.

An examination of Congressional debates over bills that would introduce a federal death penalty. Points out that although only 33 defendants have been executed under federal authority since 1930, the debates have contained important symbolic components.

831. Stout, David G. "The Lawyers of Death Row." NEW YORK TIMES MAGAZINE, Feb. 14, 1988, p. 46+.

Describes the work of several attorneys who spend most of their time defending condemned prisoners.

832. Strafer, G. Richard. "Volunteering for Execution: Competency, Voluntariness, and Propriety of Third Party Intervention." JOURNAL OF CRIMINAL LAW AND CRIMINOLOGY 74 (1983): 860-912.

Reviews the issue of defendants who waive their rights to appeal and request execution. Challenges the competency of defendants who have made this choice, as it is always made in the stressful conditions of death row. Explores the rights of third parties and condemns voluntary executions because they do not allow the state to ensure that the execution is constitutional.

833. Strauss, Frances. WHERE DID THE JUSTICE GO?: THE STORY OF THE GILES-JOHNSON CASE. Boston: Gambit, Inc., 1970.

The story of a miscarriage of justice in Maryland in 1961 that resulted in three innocent men, James and Joseph Giles and Joe Johnson, being sentenced to death.

834. Streib, Victor. "Death Penalty for Children: The American Experience with Capital Punishment for Crimes Committed While Under the Age of Eighteen." OKLAHOMA LAW REVIEW 36 (1983): 613-41.

Presents the history of the debate over executing juveniles, characteristics of executed juveniles (N=287), and an overview of contemporary debates surrounding this practice.

835. Streib, Victor. "Capital Punishment for Children in Ohio." AKRON LAW REVIEW 18 (1984): 51-102.

Examines Ohio's history of executing juveniles (19 were executed), and compares this to the overall American experience.

836. Streib, Victor. "Executions under Post-Furman Capital Punishment Statutes." RUTGERS LAW JOURNAL 15 (1984): 443-87.

Examines all eleven executions from 1977 through 1983. Information on the cases and citations to court decisions are given.

837. Streib, Victor. DEATH PENALTY FOR JUVENILES. Bloomington: Indiana University Press, 1987.

The definitive book on the history, status, future, and controversies surrounding the execution of juveniles in the United States. Included are lists of all juveniles executed in the U.S. and all juveniles currently on death row.

838. Streib, Victor L. "Imposing the Death Penalty on Children." In Haas and Inciardi,

1988, cited above as item 413.

An overview of the history and current practices of sentencing juveniles to death in the United States.

839. Styron, William. "The Death-in-Life of Benjamin Reid." ESQUIRE 57 (February, 1962): 114+, and "The Aftermath of Benjamin Reid." ESQUIRE 57 (November, 1962): 79-81+.

Describes the case of a Connecticut prisoner, on death row for murder committed at age 19. The author argues that Reed's impoverished background and low mental capacity, coupled with pretrial publicity, meant that he deserved clemency. In the latter article, Styron describes the successful clemency hearing.

840. Sullivan, J. Thomas. "The Capital Defendant's Right to Make a Personal Plea for Mercy: Common Law Allocution and Constitutional Mitigation." NEW MEXICO LAW REVIEW 15 (1985): 41-71.

Argues that defendants facing a death sentence must have an unencumbered right to make a personal plea for leniency to the jury, and that the prosecution should be prohibited from impeaching such testimony by bringing up the defendant's prior record.

841. Sullivan, Robert A. "Waiting to Die: A Prisoner's Diary from Florida's Death Row." ROLLING STONE (March 6, 1980), pp. 48-9+.

The diary of Robert Sullivan, describing his experiences during his first death warrant. Sullivan survived the first warrant, but was executed 4 1/2 years later.

842. Suni, Ellen Yankiver. "Recent Developments in Missouri: Criminal law: Homicide." UNIVERSITY OF MISSOURI-KANSAS CITY LAW REVIEW 50 (1982): 440-90.

An examination of homicide law and capital sentencing in Missouri.

843. Surfin, Ron. "'Everything is in Order, Warden': A Discussion of Death in the Gas Chamber." SUICIDE AND LIFE-THREATENING BEHAVIOR 6 (1976): 44-57.

An unusual description of California's gas chamber and what death in it is like, based on a visit to the death chamber and on an examination of accounts of death in it.

844. Sutherland, Edwin H. "Murder and the Death Penalty." JOURNAL OF CRIMINAL LAW AND CRIMINOLOGY 15 (1925): 522-36.

An early attempt by a pioneer in criminology to assess deterrence. Although no precise data on the number of homicides could be obtained, the author gives estimates and concludes the death penalty is worthless as a deterrent.

845. Tabak, Ronald J. "The Death of Fairness: The Arbitrary and Capricious Imposition of the Death Penalty in the 1980's." NYU REVIEW OF LAW AND SOCIAL CHANGE 4 (1986): 797-848.

Based on his experiences representing condemned inmates, the author argues that contemporary death sentencing procedures are unfair. He criticizes prosecutorial discretion, faulty jury selection procedures, racial discrimination, lack of appellate attorneys, and the unavailability of clemency.

846. Tao, L.S. "The Constitutional Status of Capital Punishment: An Analysis of Gregg, Jurek, Roberts, and Woodson." UNIVERSITY OF DETROIT JOURNAL OF URBAN LAW 54 (1977): 345-66.

A political scientist's examination of the 1976 U.S. Supreme Court death penalty decisions. Principles used by the Court in its decisions are identified.

847. Taylor, E.L. (Stacey) Hebden. "Retribution, Responsibility and Freedom: The Fallacy of Modern Criminal Law from a Biblical-Christian Perspective." LAW AND CONTEMPORARY PROBLEMS

44 (Spring, 1981): 51-82.

Argues that crime is a legal and moral, not a medical, issue. A conservative Christian set of criminological principles is offered in opposition to secular humanism; argues for the imposition of the death penalty upon anyone convicted of first-degree murder.

848. Teeters, Negley K. SCAFFOLD AND CHAIR: A COMPILATION OF THEIR USE IN PENNSYLVANIA, 1682-1962. Philadelphia: Pennsylvania Prison Society, 1963.

The complete history of executions in Pennsylvania, including a vignette on each person executed.

849. Teeters, Negley K. HANG BY THE NECK: THE LEGAL USE OF SCAFFOLD AND NOOSE, GIBBET, STAKE, AND FIRING SQUAD FROM COLONIAL TIMES TO THE PRESENT. Springfield, Ill.: Charles C. Thomas, 1967.

An exploration of the customs and practices of executions, using prison records, newspaper accounts, and various other sources. Numerous case descriptions are given. One of the best sources on the history of executions in America.

850. Templewood, Viscount. THE SHADOW OF THE GALLOWS. London: Victor Gollancz, 1951.

Written by a former Home Secretary and President of the Howard League, this book examines homicides and capital punishment in England, Scotland, and India. Chapters are included on clemency and on mistaken identity, the Parliamentary debates on the death penalty in 1948, and the history of the death penalty in England. The author concludes that the death penalty should be abolished.

851. Thomas, Charles W. "Eighth Amendment Challenges to the Death Penalty: The Relevance of Informed Public Opinion." VANDERBILT LAW REVIEW 30 (1977): 1005-30.

Reviews the history of Supreme Court
decisions relating to the Eighth Amendment
and the role of public opinion in those
decisions. Surveyed 3,334 residents of
Norfolk, Virginia, and finds that support for
capital punishment is rooted both in
utilitarian and retributive concerns, with
the former (defined as a belief in
deterrence) the more important.

852.   Thomas, Charles W., and Samuel C. Foster.   "A
       Sociological Perspective on Public Support
       for Capital Punishment." AMERICAN JOURNAL OF
       ORTHOPSYCHIATRY 45 (1975): 641-57. Reprinted
       in Bedau and Pierce, 1976, in item 110 above.

       A questionnaire was sent to 839 residents of
       Daytona Beach, Florida. Finds that much
       support for the death penalty stems from a
       fear of crime and that people see the death
       penalty as an effective way to fight crime.

853.   Thomas, Charles W., and Robert G. Howard.
       "Public Attitudes Toward Capital Punishment:
       A Comparative Analysis." JOURNAL OF
       BEHAVIORAL ECONOMICS 6 (1977): 189-216.

       Based on a survey of 3,334 respondents,
       factors relating to attitude toward capital
       punishment are explored. It is found that
       most supporters of the death penalty base
       their support on its alleged deterrent
       benefits.

854.   Thompson, William C., Claudia L. Cowan,
       Phoebe C. Ellsworth, and Joan C. Harrington.
       "Death Penalty Attitudes and Conviction
       Proneness: The Translation of Attitudes Into
       Verdicts." LAW AND HUMAN BEHAVIOR 8 (1984):
       95-113.

       Death qualified and excludable jurors (N=36)
       were shown a tape of testimony in a simulated
       assault trial, and the former interpreted the
       testimony as more favorable to the
       prosecution. The former also had less regret
       over the idea of convicting the innocent.

855.   Thorburn, Kim Marie.   "Physicians and the
       Death Penalty." WESTERN JOURNAL OF MEDICINE

146 (1987): 638-40.

Considers examples of the medical profession's connection with the death penalty and analyzes the ethical permissibility of involvement. Takes the position that medical involvement at any stage, from trial to execution, is not permissible by ethical standards.

856. Thornton, Tim. "Florida's Legislative and Judicial Responses to Furman v. Georgia: An Analysis and Criticism." FLORIDA STATE UNIVERSITY LAW REVIEW 2 (1974): 108-52.

A discussion of the Furman decision, the Florida statute enacted in response to it, and the Florida Supreme Court's approval of that new statute. Concludes that the new statute does not eliminate the problem of arbitrariness.

857. Thornton, Thomas Perry. "Terrorism and the Death Penalty." AMERICA 135 (Dec. 11, 1976): 410-2. Reprinted at pp. 181-5 of Bedau, 1982, cited above as item 100.

Would the death penalty deter acts of terrorism? This article explains not only why the answer is no, but also how executions might actually incite more terrorism.

858. Tifft, Larry. "Capital Punishment Research, Policy, and Ethics: Defining Murder and Placing Murderers." CRIME AND SOCIAL JUSTICE 17 (1982): 61-8.

From a radical or Marxist perspective, the author explores the relationship between state power, criminological research, and the death penalty. Argues that both capital punishment and the discourse about it reproduce the legitimacy of the state's exercise of power.

859. Townsey, Roi Dianne. STRUCTURAL FALLIBILITY: DISCRETIONARY JUSTICE AND THE DIFFERENTIAL IMPOSITION OF THE DEATH PENALTY. Ph.D. Dissertation, SUNY - Stony Brook, 1979.

Effects of discretion at each stage of
criminal justice processing are outlined and
discussed. The author concludes that extra-
legal factors are important determinants of
who is sentenced to death.

860. Triche, Charles W. THE CAPITAL PUNISHMENT
DILEMMA, 1950-1977, A SUBJECT BIBLIOGRAPHY.
Troy, New York: Whitston Publishing Company,
1979.

A 278-page bibliography of death penalty
materials, useful although it is not
annotated and many citations are from
newspapers.

861. Trogalo, Richard E. "Capital Punishment
Under the UCMJ After Furman." AIR FORCE LAW
REVIEW 16 (Winter, 1974): 86-95.

A review of capital articles in the Uniform
Code of Military Justice, positing that they
are now unconstitutional under Furman.

862. Turnbull, Colin. "Death by Decree." NATURAL
HISTORY 87 (1978): 51-66.

An anthropological approach to capital
punishment, arguing that the inhumanity of
the death penalty requires its abolition.
Discusses the effects of executions on those
who are in contact with the prisoner (e.g.,
correctional officers).

863. Tuttle, Elizabeth Orman. THE CRUSADE AGAINST
CAPITAL PUNISHMENT IN GREAT BRITAIN. London:
Stevens and Sons, 1961.

A history of the gradual decline in
executions, and the opposition to executions,
in Great Britain over the last 150 years.

864. Tyler, Tom R., and Renee Weber. "Support for
the Death Penalty: Instrumental Response to
Crime, or Symbolic Attitude?" LAW AND
SOCIETY REVIEW 17 (1982): 21-44.

Two hundred residents of Evanston, Illinois,
were interviewed. Support for capital
punishment was found most often to be based

on its value as a symbol, while the influence
of instrumental crime-related concerns was
small.

865. Tweeten, Christian D. "Montana's Death
Penalty After State v. McKenzie." MONTANA
LAW REVIEW 38 (1977): 209-20.

Examines the Montana death penalty statute
and the state Supreme Court's 1976 decision
upholding its constitutional validity.

866. Tysoe, Mayron. "And if We Hanged the Wrong
Man?" NEW SOCIETY 65 (1983): 11-3.

A brief argument against the death penalty,
with a British focus, primarily based on the
grounds of witness error and the possibility
of executing the innocent.

867. Uelmen, Gerald F. "California Death Penalty
Laws and the California Supreme Court: A Ten
Year Perspective." CRIME AND SOCIAL JUSTICE
25 (1986): 78-93.

An analysis of the first 54 death penalty
decisions handed down by the California
Supreme Court after passage of the state's
capital punishment statute in 1977.

868. Urofsky, Melvin I. "A Right to Die:
Termination of Appeal for Condemned
Prisoners." JOURNAL OF CRIMINAL LAW AND
CRIMINOLOGY 75 (1984): 553-82.

An examination of consensual executions,
arguing that there are legal and moral
justifications for permitting competent death
row inmates to choose to drop appeals and be
executed.

869. van den Haag, Ernest. "On Deterrence and the
Death Penalty." JOURNAL OF CRIMINAL LAW,
CRIMINOLOGY AND POLICE SCIENCE 60 (1969):
141-7.

A general essay in support of capital
punishment, arguing that while no precise
deterrent effect can be isolated, the
possibility of a deterrent effect is

sufficient to justify the penalty. This
paper was responded to by Bedau, cited as
item 84 above.

870. van den Haag, Ernest. PUNISHING CRIMINALS:
CONCERNING A VERY OLD AND PAINFUL QUESTION.
New York: Basic Books, 1975.

A general overview of the question of
punishment, with discussions of retribution,
justice, and utilitarian models. Different
causes of crime (poverty, racism, free will)
are discussed. The arguments against the
death penalty are reviewed and dismissed.

871. van den Haag, Ernest. "A Response to Bedau."
ARIZONA STATE LAW JOURNAL 1977 (1977):
797-802.

A response to a paper by Bedau, cited above
as item 93.

872. van den Haag, Ernest. "In Defense of the
Death Penalty: A Legal-Practical-Moral
Analysis." CRIMINAL LAW BULLETIN 14 (1978):
51-68.

Addresses the questions of whether the death
penalty is constitutional, morally
justifiable, and useful, and answers all
questions affirmatively.

873. van den Haag, Ernest. "Comment on John
Kaplan's 'Administering Capital Punishment.'"
UNIVERSITY OF FLORIDA LAW REVIEW 36 (1984):
193-9.

A comment on an article by Kaplan, cited
above as item 492. Argues that Kaplan's
piece is limited because it fails to discuss
justice, costs, and deterrence.

874. van den Haag, Ernest. "Refuting Reiman and
Nathanson." PHILOSOPHY AND PUBLIC AFFAIRS 14
(1985): 165-76.

A pro-death penalty response to two papers
opposing the death penalty, cited above as
items 647 and 732.

875. van den Haag, Ernest. "The Death Penalty Vindicates the Law." ABA JOURNAL 71 (April, 1985): 38-42.

   A debate with Henry Schwarzschild (cited above as item 777) on the death penalty.

876. van den Haag, Ernest. "The Death Penalty Once More." UNIVERSITY OF CALIFORNIA-DAVIS LAW REVIEW 18 (1985): 957-72.

   Argues the death penalty is constitutional and morally justified, even though deterrence research in inconclusive.

877. van den Haag, Ernest. "The Ultimate Punishment: A Defense." HARVARD LAW REVIEW 99 (1986): 1662-9.

   A brief critique of various abolitionist positions on the death penalty.

878. van den Haag, Ernest. "Can Any Legal Punishment of the Guilty be Unjust to Them?" WAYNE LAW REVIEW 33 (1987): 1413-21.

   Argues deterrence and retribution are the only two justifications of punishment, and that even disproportionate punishments cannot be unjust. Responded to by Bedau, cited above as item 109.

879. van den Haag, Ernest and John P. Conrad. THE DEATH PENALTY: A DEBATE. New York: Plenum, 1983.

   A chatty exchange of views on the death penalty. While points are often not well-documented, the authors do cover the major topics, and the book is useful for the lay public to learn about the principal issues surrounding capital punishment.

880. Vandiver, Margaret. RACE, CLEMENCY, AND EXECUTIONS IN FLORIDA, 1924-1966. Masters Thesis, Florida State University, 1983.

   Examines the impact of victims' and offenders' race upon grants of executive clemency in Florida. Uses descriptive and

200

statistical methods and concludes race had a
large influence.

881. Vanore, Lawrence A. "The Decency of Capital
Punishment for Minors: Contemporary
Standards and the Dignity of Juveniles."
INDIANA LAW JOURNAL 61 (1986): 757-91.

Argues the death penalty is always
inappropriate for minors. Examines the
Eighth Amendment and argues that evolving
standards of decency no longer permit the
execution of juveniles.

882. Viccica, Antoinette D. POLITICAL RECOURSE TO
CAPITAL PUNISHMENT. Ph.D. Dissertation,
Rutgers University, 1982.

The relationship between ten "politically
disturbing events" and capital sentences on a
global level is studied. The relationship is
found to exist primarily in developing
countries. Also examines efforts by the U.N.
to limit the use of the death penalty.

883. Vidmar, Neil. "Retributive and Utilitarian
Motives and Other Correlates of Canadian
Attitudes Toward the Death Penalty." CANADIAN
PSYCHOLOGIST 15 (1974): 337-56.

A survey of 144 Canadian adults, finding that
retribution is more important than deterrence
as a reason for favoring the death penalty.
Support for the death penalty also correlated
with authoritarianism, dogmatism, and
prejudice.

884. Vidmar, Neil, and Tony Dittenhoffer.
"Informed Public Opinion and Death Penalty
Attitudes." CANADIAN JOURNAL OF CRIMINOLOGY
23 (1981): 43-56.

Thirty-nine students were given information
about capital punishment, and, after reading
it, showed less support for capital
punishment. The authors conclude that if the
public were better informed on the issue,
more would oppose the death penalty.

885. Vidmar, Neil, and Phoebe C. Ellsworth.

"Public Opinion and the Death Penalty."
STANFORD LAW REVIEW 26 (1974): 1245-70.
Reprinted in Bedau and Pierce, 1976, in item
110 above.

An in-depth examination of attitudes toward
capital punishment, reviewing the types of
crimes for which people think it appropriate
and the amount of knowledge people have about
it. Various polls on this issue are reviewed
and critiqued.

886. Vidmar, Neil, and Dale T. Miller.
"Socialpsychological Processes Underlying
Attitudes Toward Legal Punishment." LAW AND
SOCIETY REVIEW 14 (1980): 565-602.

Two basic motives for punishment are
examined: behavior control and retribution.
A typology of purposes underlying punishment
is developed, based on motive and target (the
offender or others in the environment).
Propositions based on this typology are
deduced and described.

887. Waldo, Gordon P. "The 'Criminality Level' of
Incarcerated Murderers and Non-Murderers."
JOURNAL OF CRIMINAL LAW, CRIMINOLOGY AND
POLICE SCIENCE 61 (1970): 60-70.

Compares 621 incarcerated murderers with a
sample of other prisoners, and finds that the
former group had fewer previous
incarcerations, fewer escapes, and fewer
infractions.

888. Waldo, Gordon P. "The Death Penalty and
Deterrence: A Review of Recent Research."
Pp. 169-78 in Israel L. Barak-Glantz and
Ronald Huff (eds.), THE MAD, THE BAD, AND THE
DIFFERENT. Lexington, Mass.: Lexington
Books, 1981.

An excellent, though brief, overview of the
research of Isaac Ehrlich, his supporters,
and his critics.

889. Waldo, Katherine H. "The 1984 Oregon Death
Penalty Initiatives: A State Constitutional
Analysis." WILLAMETTE LAW REVIEW 22 (1986):

285-353.

An examination of the 1984 death penalty referendum in Oregon, its background and effects. Argues that a fatal flaw in Oregon's death penalty statute is its vagueness, and reviews the statute and the death penalty appellate process.

890. Wallace, Donald H. "Incompetency for Execution: The Supreme Court Challenges the Ethical Standards of the Mental Health Professions." JOURNAL OF LEGAL MEDICINE 8 (1987): 265-81.

A review of the case of Alvin Ford, and some of the issues raised by it. Discusses treating and evaluating incompetent death row inmates, and, after reviewing ethical standards of the profession, condemns participation in both.

891. Ward, Barbara A. "Competency for Execution: Problems in Law and Psychiatry." FLORIDA STATE UNIVERSITY LAW REVIEW 14 (1986): 35-107.

A review of the history and issue of exempting the mentally incompetent from execution. Includes discussion of the rationale behind the exemption and the procedures used to evaluate prisoners.

892. Warr, Mark, and Mark Stafford. "Public Goals of Punishment and Support for the Death Penalty." JOURNAL OF RESEARCH IN CRIME AND DELINQUENCY 21 (1984): 95-111.

A questionnaire was sent to 339 Seattle residents. Retribution and incapacitation were seen as the major goals of punishment. Support for retribution increases with age and decreases with education; however, retributivists constitute only a minority of those who support capital punishment.

893. Wasserstrom, Richard. "Capital Punishment as Punishment: Some Theoretical Issues and Objections." Pp. 473-502 in Peter A. French, Theodore E. Uehling, Jr., and Howard K.

Wettstein (eds.), MIDWEST STUDIES in
PHILOSOPHY, Vol. VII. Minneapolis:
University of Minnesota Press, 1982.

Outlines some conceptual and normative
requirements for an adequate theory of
punishment, and what the author finds to be
decisive objections to capital punishment
that are not generally stressed in the
abolitionist literature.

894. Weihofen, Henry. "A Question of Justice:
Trial or Execution of an Insane Defendant."
A.B.A. JOURNAL 37 (1951): 651-54+.

Reviews various theories that justify the
prohibition against executing insane
defendants, and the policy issues that this
prohibition raises.

895. Weisberg, Robert. "Deregulating Death."
SUPREME COURT REVIEW 8 (1983): 305-95.

An outstanding review of recent death penalty
decisions by the Supreme Court. Argues that
the Court has been unsystematic in its recent
attempts to regulate penalty phases of
capital trials, and most recently has
abandoned its effort to structure and
regulate the penalty phase.

896. Weisbuch, Jonathan B. "The Public Health
Effects of the Death Penalty." JOURNAL OF
PUBLIC HEALTH POLICY 5 (1984): 305-11.

Examines the impact of capital punishment
upon public health and concludes executions
increase homicides, are more expensive than
prison terms, and cause ethical conflicts for
health providers within the correctional
system.

897. Wellek, Jeffrey Alan. "Eighth Amendment--
Trial Court May Impose Death Sentence Despite
Jury's Recommendation of Life Imprisonment."
JOURNAL OF CRIMINAL LAW AND CRIMINOLOGY 75
(1984): 813-38.

A comment on the Spaziano v. Florida
decision. Criticizes the U.S. Supreme Court

for failing to adopt national standards for
the application of the death penalty.
Includes a strong discussion of the issues
raised by the jury override provision.

898.　West, Edward S.　"The Right of Confrontation
and Reliability in Capital Sentencing."
AMERICAN CRIMINAL LAW REVIEW 20 (1982):
599-615.

A review of the Eleventh Circuit's decision
in <u>Proffitt</u> <u>v</u>. <u>Wainwright</u> (1982), in which
the court ruled that capital defendants have
a Sixth Amendment right to confront
psychiatrists who submit testimony to a trial
judge during the sentencing phase.

899.　West, Louis Jolyon.　"Psychiatric Reflections
on the Death Penalty."　AMERICAN JOURNAL OF
ORTHOPSYCHIATRY 45 (1975): 689-700.
Reprinted in Bedau and Pierce, 1976, in item
110 above.

Argues that capital punishment is outdated
and immoral, and that it breeds more murder
than it deters.

900.　Whitaker, Charles.　"Should Teenagers be
Executed?"　EBONY (March, 1988): 118-25.

A discussion of the case of Indiana death row
inmate Paula Cooper, who was sentenced to
death in 1985 at age 15.

901.　White, Lawrence T.　"Juror Decision Making in
the Capital Penalty Trial: An Analysis of
Crimes and Defense Strategies."　LAW AND
HUMAN BEHAVIOR 11 (1987): 113-30.

Mock jurors were death qualified and exposed
to one of twelve mock trials.　Finds that a
conceptual argument against capital
punishment was the most effective defense,
while a mental illness was the least
effective.　Penalty decisions were influenced
by 1) juror perceptions of the defendant's
volition, 2) juror perceptions of the
defendant's future dangerousness, and 3)
juror perceptions of the competence of the
opposing attorneys.

902. White, Lawrence T. "The Mental Illness Defense in the Capital Murder Hearing." BEHAVIORAL SCIENCES AND THE LAW 5 (1987): 411-21.

Suggests that the available research indicates that a mental illness defense at a capital penalty phase will be ineffective because 1) death qualified jurors do not respond favorably to psychological explanations of criminal behavior, and 2) such a defense may mislead jurors into believing the defendant has a high probability of future dangerousness. Factors associated with successful mental illness defenses are outlined.

903. White, Walter Francis. ROPE AND FAGGOT: A BIOGRAPHY OF JUDGE LYNCH. New York: Knopf, 1929.

A classic examination of lynching, with statistics and case studies. Many aspects of the subject are considered, including religious, economic, and legal.

904. White, Welsh S. "The Constitutional Invalidity of Convictions Imposed by Death Qualified Juries." CORNELL LAW REVIEW 58 (1973): 1176-220.

Argues that convictions rendered by juries from which those opposing the death penalty have been removed are constitutionally invalid.

905. White, Welsh S. "The Role of the Social Sciences in Determining the Constitutionality of Capital Punishment." DUQUESNE LAW REVIEW 13 (1974): 279-301. Reprinted in Bedau and Pierce, 1976, in item 110 above.

Reviews the role of empirical data in the Furman decision, and discusses the probable role of the social sciences in determining the constitutionality of future death penalty statutes.

906. White, Welsh S. "Witherspoon Revisited:

Exploring the Tension Between <u>Witherspoon</u> and
<u>Furman</u>." UNIVERSITY OF CINCINNATI LAW REVIEW
45 (1976): 19-36.

Approximately 150 capital sentences were
vacated by the <u>Witherspoon</u> decision. Argues
that if <u>Witherspoon</u> were extended to
eliminate or further restrict death
qualification of juries, some of the
procedural defects noted in <u>Furman</u> might be
alleviated. This paper examines the
rationale of <u>Witherspoon</u> and its potential
effects on post-<u>Furman</u> death penalty statutes
and procedures.

907.   White, Welsh S. "Disproportionality and the
Death Penalty: Death as a Punishment for
Rape." UNIVERSITY OF PITTSBURGH LAW REVIEW
38 (1976): 145-84.

Describes the efforts to abolish the death
penalty, initiated by Justice Goldberg's 1963
dissent from a denial of certiorari in
<u>Rudolph</u> <u>v</u>. <u>Alabama</u> (in which he urged the
Court to consider whether executing rapists
was constitutional). Discusses the concept
of proportionality in sentencing, and
concludes death is a disproportionate
punishment for rape. A state-by-state
listing of rape statutes and penalties is
included.

908.   White, Welsh S. "Waiver and the Death
Penalty: The Implications of <u>Estelle</u> <u>v</u>.
<u>Smith</u>." JOURNAL OF CRIMINAL LAW AND
CRIMINOLOGY 72 (1981): 1522-49.

In the <u>Smith</u> case, the U.S. Supreme Court
ruled that psychiatrists must give <u>Miranda</u>
warnings to defendants. White argues that
the decision suggests that a valid waiver
under <u>Miranda</u> cannot occur unless 1) the
defendant knows he has been charged with a
capital offense, and 2) the defendant must
consult with an attorney before waiving Sixth
Amendment rights.

909.   White, Welsh S. "The Psychiatric Examination
and the Fifth Amendment Privilege in Capital
Cases." JOURNAL OF CRIMINAL LAW AND

CRIMINOLOGY 74 (1983): 943-90.

Discusses the conflict between the defendant's privilege against self-incrimination and the right of the state to appoint a psychiatrist to examine the defendant if sanity is an issue. Argues that further safeguards are necessary.

910. White, Welsh S. LIFE IN THE BALANCE: PROCEDURAL SAFEGUARDS IN CAPITAL CASES. Ann Arbor: University of Michigan Press, 1984.

A collection of the author's previously published essays. Included are discussions of the admissibility of confessions obtained by police trickery, the admissibility of psychiatric predictions of dangerousness, and the problems created by death qualified juries. Reviewed by Gillers in item 378 above.

911. White, Welsh S. THE DEATH PENALTY IN THE EIGHTIES: AN EXAMINATION OF THE MODERN SYSTEM OF CAPITAL PUNISHMENT. Ann Arbor: University of Michigan Press, 1987.

A detailed examination of our current system of capital punishment and recent Supreme Court rulings on it. Includes an in-depth look at plea bargaining and the death penalty, the penalty phase and what evidence the defendant and prosecutor can present, and the problems with death qualified juries. Chapters are also included on discrimination and on defendants who elect to be executed. Reviewed by Berger in item 121 above.

912. White, Welsh S. "Defendants Who Elect Execution." UNIVERSITY OF PITTSBURGH LAW REVIEW 48 (1987): 853-77.

An overview of the questions surrounding consensual executions, the dilemmas for defense attorneys, and the legal issues involved. Concludes that consensual executions should be forbidden, supporting his argument with cases of men who killed apparently because they wanted to be sentenced to death.

913. Wicker, Tom. "Defending the Indigent in
      Capital Cases." CRIMINAL JUSTICE ETHICS 3
      (1983): 2+.

      A short discussion of the problem of finding
      appropriate representation for indigent
      defendants who face a possible death
      sentence. Examples are given of condemned
      defendants who, the author believes, had
      incompetent attorneys.

914. Williams, Franklin H. "The Death Penalty and
      the Negro." THE CRISIS 67 (1960): 501-12.

      An overview of the status of the death
      penalty, deterrence, and how the penalty has
      been disproportionately used against blacks.

915. Wilson, James G. "Chaining the Leviathan:
      The Unconstitutionality of Executing Those
      Convicted of Treason." UNIVERSITY OF
      PITTSBURGH LAW REVIEW 45 (1983): 99-179.

      Argues against the death penalty for treason,
      in part because of the ambiguity of defining
      the crime. Includes a lengthy discussion of
      the history and evolution of the treason
      clause in the Constitution.

916. Wilson, James Q. THINKING ABOUT CRIME. New
      York: Basic Books, 1983.

      A general argument that crime is a rational
      behavior, and hence can be deterred.
      Includes a chapter on capital punishment, in
      which the literature on deterrence and
      discrimination is reviewed.

917. Wilson, William. "Juvenile Offenders and the
      Electric Chair: Cruel and Unusual Punishment
      or Firm Discipline for the Hopelessly
      Delinquent?" UNIVERSITY OF FLORIDA LAW
      REVIEW 35 (1983): 344-71.

      Examines whether a distinction between
      juvenile and adult offenders should be made
      in determining who should be executed.
      Argues that executing juveniles is contrary
      to society's evolving standards of decency.

918. Winick, Bruce J. "Prosecutorial Peremptory
     Challenge Practices in Capital Cases: An
     Empirical Study and a Constitutional
     Analysis." MICHIGAN LAW REVIEW 81 (1982):
     1-98.

     A study of the prosecutorial use of
     peremptory challenges to exclude jurors who
     have reservations about the death penalty,
     examining the selection process of 30 capital
     juries in Jacksonville, Florida. Argues that
     systematic exclusion of scrupled jurors
     violates constitutional protections.

919. Winick, Bruce J. "Witherspoon in Florida:
     Reflections on the Challenge for Cause of
     Jurors in Capital Cases in a State in which
     the Judge Makes the Sentencing Decision."
     UNIVERSITY OF MIAMI LAW REVIEW 37 (1983):
     825-66.

     In Florida, the jury vote on whether to
     sentence a defendant to death is advisory
     only; the trial judge is free to reject the
     jury recommendation. Because of this, the
     author argues that the removal of jurors
     opposed to the death penalty from Florida
     capital juries is unnecessary and
     unconstitutional.

920. Wirick, Richard E. "Dark Year on Death Row:
     Guiding Sentencer Discretion after Zant,
     Barclay, and Harris." UNIVERSITY OF
     CALIFORNIA-DAVIS LAW REVIEW 17 (1984):
     689-729.

     Reviews the U.S. Supreme Court's decisions in
     Zant, Barclay, and Harris. Concludes "the
     three decisions indicate a disturbing retreat
     from the Court's previous policy of strict
     sentencer guidance and appellate scrutiny for
     death sentencing statutes."

921. Wishingrad, Jay. "New Forces of Death
     Penalty Cases: Eighth Amendment 'Due
     Process.'" NATIONAL LAW JOURNAL, October 13,
     1980, at 24-5.

     A review of U.S. Supreme Court decisions over

the preceding eight years by one of the
attorneys who successfully argued <u>Beck</u> <u>v.</u>
<u>Alabama</u>. Includes a detailed discussion of
the <u>Beck</u> case.

922. Woffinden, Bob. MISCARRIAGES OF JUSTICE.
London: Hodder and Stoughton, 1987.

An in-depth examination of several post-World
War II erroneous convictions in England and
Ireland, their causes, and the barriers to
obtaining effective remedies.

923. Wold, John T., and John H. Culver. "The
Defeat of the California Justices: The
Campaign, the Electorate, and the Issue of
Judicial Accountability." JUDICATURE 70
(1987): 348-55.

An examination of the defeat of California
Supreme Court Justices Rose Bird, Cruz
Reynoso, and Joseph Grodin in their retention
elections in November, 1986. They were not
retained, largely because of their decisions
in death penalty cases.

924. Wolf, Edwin D. "Abstract of Analysis of Jury
Sentencing in Capital Cases: New Jersey:
1937-61." RUTGERS LAW REVIEW 19 (1965):
56-64.

Examines New Jersey cases in which a
defendant was convicted of a capital crime
and sentenced to death. Some support is
given to the hypothesis that blacks are more
likely to be condemned, especially for
felony-murders.

925. Wolfe, Burton H. PILEUP ON DEATH ROW. New
York: Doubleday, 1973.

An account of the legal events leading up to
the <u>Furman</u> decision, written for a general
audience. The first chapter gives a useful
summary of the case of Aaron Mitchell, the
last man to die in San Quentin's gas chamber.

926. Wolfgang, Marvin E. "Murder, the Pardon
Board, and Recommendations by Judges and
District Attorneys." JOURNAL OF CRIMINAL

LAW, CRIMINOLOGY AND POLICE SCIENCE 50
(1959): 338-46.

Examines the comments made by judges and
prosecutors to the Pennsylvania Pardon Board
in murder cases that resulted in pardon or
commutation (N=368). The judges and
prosecutors did not agree in 2/3 of the
cases, but in only 7 percent of the cases
were both their comments negative.

927. Wolfgang, Marvin E. "The Social Scientist in
Court." JOURNAL OF CRIMINAL LAW 65 (1974):
244-7.

Describes the author's testimony in Maxwell
v. Bishop, the problems he faced in court,
and his experiences in working with the NAACP
Legal Defense Fund to prepare his testimony.

928. Wolfgang, Marvin E. "Racial Discrimination
in the Death Sentence for Rape." Pp. 109-120
in Bowers, 1974, cited above as item 156.

A study of the death penalty in seven
southern states, 1945-65, drawn from the
author's testimony before Subcommittee No. 3
of the House Judiciary Committee in 1972
(item 959 below). Massive patterns of racial
discrimination against black defendants with
white victims are found.

929. Wolfgang, Marvin E. "The Death Penalty:
Social Philosophy and Social Science
Research." CRIMINAL LAW BULLETIN 14 (1978):
18-33.

Includes a useful discussion of retribution,
reflections on the author's involvement in
the Maxwell case, and ideas about the role of
social science research in the death penalty
debate.

930. Wolfgang, Marvin E., and Marc Riedel. "Race,
Judicial Discretion, and the Death Penalty."
ANNALS OF THE AMERICAN ACADEMY OF POLITICAL
AND SOCIAL SCIENCE 407 (1973): 119-33.

A pioneering overview of research on race and
the death penalty, and the principal source

for evidence that the death penalty for rape was imposed in a discriminatory manner. Based on data from over 3,000 rape cases in eleven states between 1945 and 1965. Convicted black rapists were seven times more likely to be sentenced to death than were whites.

931. Wolfgang, Marvin E., and Marc Riedel. "Rape, Race, and the Death Penalty in Georgia." AMERICAN JOURNAL OF ORTHOPSYCHIATRY 45 (1975): 658-68.

Examines 361 Georgia rape cases (1945-65), and finds, after controlling for legal factors, that blacks convicted of raping whites were disproportionately sentenced to death. Race was the single most influential variable in sentencing.

932. Wolfgang, Marvin E., and Marc Riedel. "Rape, Racial Discrimination, and the Death Penalty." Pp. 99-121 in Bedau and Pierce, 1976, cited above as item 110.

A combination of the above two papers by the authors, making this the most complete report of the research conducted by the authors on racism and death sentencing for rape.

933. Wolfgang, Marvin E., Arlene Kelly, and Hans. C. Nolde. "Comparison of the Executed and Commuted Among Admissions to Death Row." JOURNAL OF CRIMINAL LAW, CRIMINOLOGY, AND POLICE SCIENCE 53 (1962): 301-11.

Examines the case records of 439 prisoners condemned in Pennsylvania between 1914 and 1958, 341 of whom were executed. Compares those executed with those commuted on several variables, and finds type of murder, race, and type of counsel to be significantly associated with the outcome.

934. Wolfson, Wendy. "The Deterrent Effect of the Death Penalty Upon Prison Murder." Pp. 159-73 in Bedau, 1982, cited above as item 100.

An overview of homicides in prison, divided

213

into retentionist and abolitionist
jurisdictions. Concludes that the death
penalty fails to exert deterrent effects upon
this type of crime.

935. Woll, Robert. "The Death Penalty and
      Federalism: Eighth Amendment Constraints on
      the Allocation of State Decisionmaking
      Power." STANFORD LAW REVIEW 35 (1983):
      787-829.

      Argues that under the Eighth Amendment state
      death penalty statutes are subject to federal
      review, even if those statutes incorporate
      federal Eighth Amendment standards.

936. Wollan, Larry A., Jr. "The Death Penalty
      After Furman." LOYOLA UNIVERSITY OF CHICAGO
      LAW JOURNAL 4 (1973): 339-57.

      Discusses the Furman decision and its
      importance. Argues that the decision leaves
      room for both discretionary and mandatory
      death sentencing statutes.

937. Wolpin, Kenneth I. "Capital Punishment and
      Homicide in England: A Summary of Results."
      AMERICAN ECONOMIC REVIEW (Proceedings) 68
      (May, 1978): 422-7.

      A time-series analysis of homicides in
      England and Wales, 1929-68, using methods
      similar to those employed by Isaac Ehrlich.
      Finds that each execution deterred four
      potential homicides.

938. Woodward, Bob, and Scott Armstrong. THE
      BRETHREN: INSIDE THE SUPREME COURT. New
      York: Simon and Schuster, 1979.

      An unusually informative look inside the
      doors of the Supreme Court, 1969-75.
      Describes how battles are fought and
      decisions are made. Of particular interest
      is the discussion of the inside politics
      behind the Furman decision.

939. Worrell, Claudia M. "Psychiatric Prediction
      of Dangerousness in Capital Sentencing: The
      Quest for Innocent Authority." BEHAVIORAL

SCIENCES AND THE LAW 5 (1987): 433-46.

Eight states require the sentencer in a capital case to consider the issue of future dangerousness. This article argues the use of such testimony is an "elaborate subterfuge," functioning to bypass the difficult value conflicts in death penalty decisions with powerful emotional influences.

940. Wright, Ronald F., and Marc Miller. "In Your Court: State Judicial Federalism in Capital Cases." URBAN LAWYER 18 (1986): 659-705.

Examines the tension between state and federal courts when death row inmates present federal claims. The article describes appellate procedures in capital cases and suggests how state courts may be able to deal with federal claims.

941. Wyckoff, Maria. "Right to Inquire into Jurors' Racial Prejudices." JOURNAL OF CRIMINAL LAW AND CRIMINOLOGY 77 (1986): 713-42.

A comment on Turner v. Murray (1986), in which the Supreme Court invalidated the death sentence of a Virginia man because he was unable to question jurors during voir dire about their possible racial biases.

942. Yetter, John F. "The Florida Death Penalty-- Is It Unconstitutional under State Law?" FLORIDA BAR JOURNAL 52 (1978): 372-5.

Argues the Florida death penalty statute is unconstitutional because it deals with procedures, and as such must be adopted by the state Supreme Court, not the legislature.

943. Yoder, John Howard. "A Christian Perspective." Pp. 370-5 in Bedau, 1982, cited above as item 100.

This paper argues that the death penalty today is prohibited by most interpretations of Christian theology.

944. Young, Robert. "What is So Wrong with

Killing People?" PHILOSOPHY 54 (1979):
515-28.
A brief philosophical essay discussing the
morality of imposing death under various
circumstances.

945. Yunker, James A. "Is the Death Penalty a
Deterrent to Homicide? Some Time Series
Evidence." JOURNAL OF BEHAVIORAL ECONOMICS 5
(1976): 45-81 (reprinted in same journal,
Vol. 6 (1977): 361-97).

A controversial paper that examines the
relationship between executions and homicide
rates, 1930-1972. Concludes that each
execution in 1977 would deter approximately
156 murders. Critiqued by Fox in item 341
above and by Sesnowitz in item 793 above.

946. Yunker, James A. "An Old Controversy
Renewed: Introduction to the JBE Capital
Punishment Symposium." JOURNAL OF BEHAVIORAL
ECONOMICS 6 (1977): 1-32.

An introduction to a collection of essays on
capital punishment published in this volume.
Argues that increases in the crime rate have
led to increases in support of capital
punishment.

947. Yunker, James A. "Testing the Deterrent
Effect of Capital Punishment." CRIMINOLOGY
19 (1982): 626-49.

Argues that socioeconomic trends are an
insufficient explanation for the increase in
American homicides over the previous fifteen
years. Instead, the decline in the number of
executions is proposed as the best
explanation for the increase.

948. Yunker, James A. "The Relevance of the
Identification Problem to Statistical
Research on Capital Punishment." CRIME AND
DELINQUENCY 28 (1982): 96-124.

Supplements an article by McGahey, cited
above as item 606, by noting several
potential problems (such as the problem of

216

identification) with multiple regression
research.

949.   Zaller, Robert. "The Debate on Capital
Punishment During the English Revolution."
AMERICAN JOURNAL OF LEGAL HISTORY 31 (1987):
126-44.

Examines the demands for the reform of
capital sentencing laws during the
seventeenth century.

950.   Zeisel, Hans. "The Deterrent Effect of the
Death Penalty: Facts vs. Faith." Pp. 317-43
in Philip B. Kurland (ed.), THE SUPREME COURT
REVIEW. Chicago: University of Chicago
Press, 1977.

Reviews theoretical issues in the deterrence
debate, and discusses methodological issues
in studying deterrence. Criticizes the
conclusions of Isaac Ehrlich.

951.   Zeisel, Hans. "Race Bias in the
Administration of the Death Penalty: The
Florida Experience." HARVARD LAW REVIEW 95
(1981): 456-68.

One of the first articles to show race-of-
victim discrimination in death sentencing in
Florida. Compares racial characteristics of
Florida homicides (and felony-homicides) in
general with those of defendants and their
victims in death penalty cases.

952.   Zeisel, Hans. "A Comment on 'The Deterrent
Effect of Capital Punishment' by Phillips."
AMERICAN JOURNAL OF SOCIOLOGY 88 (1982):
167-9.

A critique of the research of David Phillips,
cited above as item 688. Includes a response
by Phillips.

953.   Zimmerman, Isidore. PUNISHMENT WITHOUT
CRIME. New York: Manor Books, 1973.

The autobiography of a New York man who once
came within two hours of execution, and then
spent 24 years in prison for a crime that he

did not commit. Shortly before his death in 1983, Zimmerman was awarded a $1 million indemnity for his erroneous conviction.

954. Zimring, Franklin E., and Gordon Hawkins. DETERRENCE: THE LEGAL THREAT IN CRIME CONTROL. Chicago: University of Chicago Press, 1973.

Draws together empirical and analytical work to assess our current concept of deterrence, our knowledge about it, and what directions future researchers should take.

955. Zimring, Franklin E., and Gordon Hawkins. "Capital Punishment and the Eighth Amendment: Furman and Gregg in Retrospect." UNIVERSITY OF CALIFORNIA-DAVIS LAW REVIEW 18 (1985): 927-56.

Critically examines the opinions in Furman and Gregg, arguing that in the former case the Justices failed to deal with the legitimacy of judicial abolition, and in the latter failed to put public opinion and legislative response to Furman in proper perspective.

956. Zimring, Franklin E., and Gordon Hawkins. CAPITAL PUNISHMENT AND THE AMERICAN AGENDA. New York: Cambridge University Press, 1986.

A discussion of capital punishment in the context of social, political, and moral climates of the United States in the 1980's. Also discussed are the death penalty in other western countries, the Eighth Amendment, and lethal injections.

957. Zimring, Franklin E., and Gordon Hawkins. "A Punishment in Search of a Crime: Standards for Capital Punishment in the Law of Criminal Homicide." MARYLAND LAW REVIEW 46 (1986): 115-32.

Discusses the development of standards for the death penalty in the Model Penal Code. Concludes the "efforts to provide a legal rationale for executions occurred far too late in the progress toward abolition of

capital punishment in Western society to have
any hope of success."

958.   Zimring, Franklin E., Joel Eigen, and Sheila
        O'Malley. "Punishing Homicide in
        Philadelphia: Perspectives on the Death
        Penalty." UNIVERSITY OF CHICAGO LAW REVIEW
        43 (1976): 227-52. A slightly revised
        version was published in Bedau and Pierce,
        1976, cited as item 110 above.

        Examines 204 Philadelphia homicides from
        1970, from which three defendants were
        sentenced to death. Finds widespread
        disparities in sentencing and criticizes the
        death penalty because of its over-reliance on
        prosecutorial discretion.

II. CONGRESSIONAL PUBLICATIONS

959. U.S. House of Representatives. Committee on the Judiciary, Subcommittee No. 3. HEARINGS ON H.R. 8414, H.R. 9486, H.R. 3243, H.R. 193, H.R. 11797, AND H.R. 12217 (March 9, 15, 16, 17, and May 10, 1972). Serial No. 29, 92nd Congress, Second Session (1972).

960. U.S. House of Representatives. Committee on the Judiciary, Subcommittee on Criminal Justice. HEARING ON H.R. 13360 (July 19, 1978). Serial No. 74, 95th Congress, Second Session (1978).

961. U.S. House of Representatives. Committee on the Judiciary, Subcommittee on Criminal Justice. HEARINGS ON H.R. 2837 and H.R. 343 (April 7, 1985; April 16, May 7, June 5, and July 24, 1986). Serial No. 133, 99th Congress, First and Second Sessions (1986).

962. U.S. Senate. Committee on the Judiciary, Subcommittee on Criminal Laws and Procedures. IMPOSITION OF CAPITAL PUNISHMENT. HEARING ON S.1, S.1400, AND S.1401 (Feb. 16, 1972; April 16, June 13, and July 26, 1973). 93rd Congress, First Session (1973).

963. U.S. Senate. Committee on the Judiciary, Subcommittee on Criminal Law--Procedures. TO ESTABLISH CONSTITUTIONAL PROCEDURES FOR THE IMPOSITION OF CAPITAL PUNISHMENT. HEARING ON S.1382 (May 18, 1977). 95th Congress, First Session (1977).

964. U.S. Senate. Committee on the Judiciary. TO ESTABLISH RATIONAL CRITERIA FOR THE IMPOSITION OF CAPITAL PUNISHMENT. HEARINGS ON S.1382 (April 27 and May 11, 1978). 95th Congress, Second Session (1978).

965. U.S. Senate. Committee on the Judiciary. ESTABLISHING CONSTITUTIONAL PROCEDURES FOR THE IMPOSITION OF CAPITAL PUNISHMENT. REPORT AND ADDITIONAL VIEWS ON S.114. Report No. 96-554, 96th Congress, First Session (1980).

966. U.S. Senate. Committee on the Judiciary.

HEARINGS ON S.114 (April 10, 27, and May 1, 1981). Serial No. J-97-13, 97th Congress, First Session (1981).

967. U.S. Senate. Committee on the Judiciary. ESTABLISHING CONSTITUTIONAL PROCEDURES FOR THE IMPOSITION OF CAPITAL PUNISHMENT. REPORT AND MINORITY VIEWS TO ACCOMPANY S.114. Report No. 97-143, 97th Congress, First Session (1981).

968. U.S. Senate. Committee on the Judiciary. ESTABLISHING CONSTITUTIONAL PROCEDURES FOR THE IMPOSITION OF CAPITAL PUNISHMENT. REPORT AND MINORITY VIEWS ON S.1765. Report No. 98-251, 98th Congress, First Session (1983).

969. U.S. Senate. Committee on the Judiciary, Subcommittee on Criminal Law. PRISON VIOLENCE AND CAPITAL PUNISHMENT. HEARING TO EXAMINE CAPITAL OFFENSES BY FEDERAL PRISONERS (Nov. 9, 1983). Serial No. J-98-80, 98th Congress, First Session (1984).

970. U.S. Senate. Committee on the Judiciary. DEATH PENALTY LEGISLATION. HEARING ON S.239 (Sept. 24, 1985). Serial No. J-99-53, 99th Congress, First Session (1986).

971. U.S. Senate. Committee on the Judiciary. ESTABLISHING CONSTITUTIONAL PROCEDURES FOR THE IMPOSITION OF CAPITAL PUNISHMENT. REPORT WITH MINORITY VIEWS ON S.239. Report No. 99-282, 99th Congress, Second Session (1986).

III. UNITED STATES SUPREME COURT DECISIONS

972. <u>Ake</u> <u>v</u>. <u>Oklahoma</u>, 470 U.S. 68 (1985).

When defendant makes preliminary showing that his sanity at the time of the offense is likely to be significant factor at trial, due process requires that state provide access to psychiatric assistance on this issue if defendant cannot otherwise afford it.

973. <u>Barclay</u> <u>v</u>. <u>Florida</u>, 463 U.S. 939 (1983).

Death sentence did not violate Constitution despite trial court's consideration of accused's prior record in violation of state law; nonstatutory aggravating circumstances can be used.

974. <u>Barefoot</u> <u>v</u>. <u>Estelle</u>, 463 U.S. 880 (1983).

Psychiatric testimony regarding future dangerousness admissible at sentencing hearing at capital trial; expedited procedures in consideration of appeal of denial of habeas corpus relief "tolerable."

975. <u>Batson</u> <u>v</u>. <u>Kentucky</u>, 476 U.S. 79 (1986).

The equal protection clause prevents the prosecutor from challenging jurors simply on the basis of race.

976. <u>Beck</u> <u>v</u>. <u>Alabama</u>, 447 U.S. 625 (1980).

Death sentences prohibited under an Alabama law that prohibits trial judge from giving the jury the option of convicting the defendant of a lesser included offense.

977. <u>Booth</u> <u>v</u>. <u>Maryland</u>, 107 S.Ct. 2529 (1987).

Introduction of victim impact statement at sentencing phase of capital murder trial violates Eighth Amendment.

978. <u>Bullington</u> <u>v</u>. <u>Missouri</u>, 451 U.S. 430 (1981).

Imposition of death sentence at second

capital trial of defendant sentenced to life
imprisonment at first trial held barred by
Fifth Amendment double jeopardy clause.

979. Caldwell v. Mississippi, 472 U.S. 320 (1985).

Prosecutor's comment that jury's penalty
decision not final but subject to appellate
review violates Eighth Amendment.

980. California v. Ramos, 463 U.S. 992 (1983).

California law requiring instruction as to
governor's power to commute life sentence
without possibility of parole held not to
violate Constitution.

981. Coker v. Georgia, 433 U.S. 584 (1977).

Death penalty disproportionate for rape of an
adult woman when victim is not killed.

982. Eberheart v. Georgia, 433 U.S. 917 (1977).

Death penalty disproportionate for
kidnapping.

983. Eddings v. Oklahoma, 455 U.S. 104 (1982).

Sentencing court's conclusion that it could
not consider defendant's turbulent family
history as a mitigating factor in deciding
punishment was constitutional error.

984. Enmund v. Florida, 458 U.S. 782 (1982).

Death penalty disproportionate for person who
aids and abets in commission of murder but
does not kill, attempt to kill, or intend to
kill.

985. Estelle v. Smith, 451 U.S. 454 (1981).

Testimony of psychiatrist based upon court-
ordered psychiatric examination when
defendant was not advised of constitutional
rights violates the Fifth, Sixth, and
Fourteenth Amendments.

986. Ford v. Wainwright, 106 S.Ct. 2595 (1986).

Eighth Amendment prohibits the state from
executing an insane person.

987. Furman v. Georgia, 408 U.S. 238 (1972).

Imposition of death penalty as then
administered held to be cruel and unusual
punishment in violation of Eighth and
Fourteenth Amendments

988. Gardner v. Florida, 430 U.S. 349 (1977).

Reliance on confidential presentence report
by court violated the Eighth and Fourteenth
Amendments; right to reliable procedures at
sentencing phase of a capital trial.

989. Glass v. Louisiana, 471 U.S. 1080 (1985).

Petition for certiorari denied; dissent by
Justices Marshall and Brennan gives vivid
description of cruelty of death by
electrocution.

990. Godfrey v. Georgia, 446 U.S. 420 (1980).

Death sentence invalid because of the failure
of the state court to provide a
constitutional limiting construction to the
aggravating circumstance providing for a
death penalty for a murder "outrageously or
wantonly vile, horrible or inhuman in that it
involved torture, depravity of mind or an
aggravated battery to the victim."

991. Gregg v. Georgia, 428 U.S. 153 (1976).

Georgia's guided discretion death penalty
statute, allowing imposition of death where
certain aggravating circumstances
established, upheld.

992. Heckler v. Chaney, 470 U.S. 821 (1985).

The Food and Drug Administration's decision
not to take enforcement action with respect
to drugs used in lethal injections is
unreviewable.

993. _Hitchcock_ v. _Dugger_, 107 S.Ct. 1821 (1987).

Vacated death sentence imposed before 1978 in proceedings that precluded introduction of nonstatutory mitigating circumstances.

994. _Jurek_ v. _Texas_, 428 U.S. 262 (1976).

Texas's guided discretion death penalty statute, allowing imposition of death upon determination of various factors including future dangerousness, upheld.

995. _Lockett_ v. _Ohio_, 438 U.S. 586 (1978).

Death penalty schemes must consider in mitigation "any aspect of the defendant's character or record and any of the circumstances of the offense that the defendant proffers as a basis for a sentence less than death."

996. _Lockhart_ v. _McCree_, 476 U.S. 162 (1986).

No constitutional violation found in the removal for cause of _Witherspoon_-excludable jurors from the guilt phase of a capital trial.

997. _McCleskey_ v. _Kemp_, 107 S.Ct. 1756 (1987).

Demonstration that death sentencing correlates with victim's race does not establish a constitutional claim under Eighth or Fourteenth Amendments.

998. _McGautha_ v. _California_, 402 U.S. 183 (1971).

The Due Process Clause of the Fourteenth Amendment does not require that juries be given instructions as to when the death penalty should be imposed.

999. _Proffitt_ v. _Florida_, 428 U.S. 242 (1976).

Florida's guided discretion statute, allowing imposition of death based upon weighing of aggravating and mitigating circumstances, upheld.

1000. Pulley v. Harris, 465 U.S. 37 (1984).

Comparative proportionality review not constitutionally required where not part of state's statutory scheme for imposition of the death penalty.

1001. Roberts (Harry) v. Louisiana, 431 U.S. 633 (1977).

Mandatory death penalty for killing a police officer held unconstitutional.

1002. Roberts (Stanislaus) v. Louisiana, 428 U.S. 325 (1976).

Mandatory death penalty statute held unconstitutional.

1003. Skipper v. South Carolina, 476 U.S. 1 (1986).

Defendant constitutionally entitled to introduce mitigating evidence of good conduct in jail following his arrest.

1004. Spaziano v. Florida, 468 U.S. 447 (1984).

Florida law allowing a judge to override the jury's recommendation of life imprisonment does not violate Constitution.

1005. Strickland v. Washington, 466 U.S. 668 (1984).

The benchmark for judging a claim of ineffective assistance of counsel is whether counsel's conduct so undermined the proper functioning of the adversarial process that the trial cannot be relied upon as having produced a just result.

1006. Sumner v. Schuman, 107 S.Ct. 2716 (1987).

Mandatory death sentence for murder committed while serving life sentence without possibility of parole held unconstitutional.

1007. Tison v. Arizona, 107 S.Ct. 1676 (1987).

Eighth Amendment proportionality principles
do not preclude death sentence for
accomplices in a felony-murder who did not
kill or intend to kill, if they were major
participants in felony resulting in death
and had a reckless disregard for life.

1008. Wainwright v. Witt, 469 U.S. 412 (1985).

Proper standard for determining when a
prospective juror may be excluded for cause
because of his/her views on capital
punishment is whether the juror's views
would "prevent or substantially impair the
performance of his duties as a juror in
accordance with his instructions and oath."

1009. Witherspoon v. Illinois, 391 U.S. 510
(1968).

Exclusion of anti-death penalty jurors for
cause from death penalty juries held
generally permissible.

1010. Woodson v. North Carolina, 428 U.S. 280
(1976).

Mandatory death penalty statute held
unconstitutional.

1011. Zant v. Stephens, 462 U.S. 862 (1983).

A finding of an aggravating circumstance
later ruled to be unconstitutionally vague
does not require reversal where other valid
aggravating circumstances remain.

240